'*Innovations and Challenges in Grammar* is a thoughtful and engaging discussion of a topic that evokes strong reactions from all language users and language teachers. Everyone has an opinion about grammar and its role. In this book, Professor McCarthy takes the reader on a journey that contextualizes English grammar, both historically and contextually. In addition, in an easy to read manner, Professor McCarthy wrestles with many of the thorny aspects of English grammar and the role English plays in the world.'

Randi Reppen, Northern Arizona University

'Given the passions roused by competing notions of grammar down through the ages, writing a book such as this might be seen as a massive if not impossible challenge in itself. Professor McCarthy has more than risen to the challenge and the result is a book which is authoritative in both depth and breadth, and, as we have come to expect from him throughout his impressive career, an accessible thought provoking read.'

Martin Warren, The Hong Kong Polytechnic University

INNOVATIONS AND CHALLENGES IN GRAMMAR

Innovations and Challenges in Grammar traces the history of common understandings of what grammar is and where it came from to demonstrate how 'rules' are anything but fixed and immutable. In doing so, it deconstructs the notion of 'correctness' to show how grammar changes over time thereby exposing the social and historical forces that mould and change usage. The questions that this book grapples with are:

- Can we separate grammar from the other features of the language system and get a handle on it as an independent entity?
- Why should there be strikingly different notions and models of grammar? Are they (in)compatible?
- Which one or ones fit(s) best the needs of applied linguists if we assume that applied linguists address real-world problems through the lens of language? And which one(s) could make most sense to non-specialists?
- If grammar is not a fixed entity but a set of usage norms in constant flux, how can we persuade other professionals and the general public that this is a positive observation rather than a threat to civilised behaviour?

This book draws upon both historical and modern grammars from across the globe to provide a multi-layered picture of world grammar. It will be useful to teachers and researchers of English as a first and second language, though the inclusion of examples from and occasional references to other languages (French, Spanish, Malay, Swedish, Russian, Welsh, Burmese, Japanese) is intended to broaden the appeal to teachers and researchers of other languages. It will be of use to final-year undergraduate, postgraduate and doctoral students as well as secondary and tertiary level teachers and researchers in applied linguistics, second language acquisition and grammar pedagogy.

Michael McCarthy is Emeritus Professor of Applied Linguistics, University of Nottingham, Adjunct Professor of Applied Linguistics, University of Limerick, and Visiting Professor in Applied Linguistics at Newcastle University.

INNOVATIONS AND CHALLENGES IN APPLIED LINGUISTICS

Series Editor: Ken Hyland is Professor of Applied Linguistics in Education at the University of East Anglia and Visiting Professor in the School of Foreign Language Education, Jilin University, China.

Innovations and Challenges in Applied Linguistics offers readers an understanding of some of the core areas of Applied Linguistics. Each book in the series is written by a specially commissioned expert who discusses a current and controversial issue surrounding contemporary language use. The books offer a cutting-edge focus that carries the authority of an expert in the field, blending a clearly written and accessible outline of what we know about a topic and the direction in which it should be moving.

The books in this series are essential reading for those researching, teaching, and studying in applied linguistics.

Titles in the series:

Innovations and Challenges in Applied Linguistics from the Global South
Alastair Pennycook and Sinfree Makoni

Innovations and Challenges in Language Learning Motivation
Zoltán Dörnyei

Innovations and Challenges: Women, Language and Sexism
Carmen Rosa Caldas-Coulthard

Innovations and Challenges in Grammar
Michael McCarthy

https://www.routledge.com/Innovations-and-Challenges-in-Applied-Linguistics/book-series/ICAL

INNOVATIONS AND CHALLENGES IN GRAMMAR

Michael McCarthy

LONDON AND NEW YORK

First published 2021
by Routledge
2 Park Square, Milton Park, Abingdon, Oxon OX14 4RN

and by Routledge
52 Vanderbilt Avenue, New York, NY 10017

Routledge is an imprint of the Taylor & Francis Group, an informa business

© 2021 Michael McCarthy

The right of Michael McCarthy to be identified as author of this work has been asserted by him in accordance with sections 77 and 78 of the Copyright, Designs and Patents Act 1988.

All rights reserved. No part of this book may be reprinted or reproduced or utilised in any form or by any electronic, mechanical, or other means, now known or hereafter invented, including photocopying and recording, or in any information storage or retrieval system, without permission in writing from the publishers.

Trademark notice: Product or corporate names may be trademarks or registered trademarks, and are used only for identification and explanation without intent to infringe.

British Library Cataloguing-in-Publication Data
A catalogue record for this book is available from the British Library

Library of Congress Cataloging-in-Publication Data
Names: McCarthy, Michael, 1947- author.
Title: Innovations and challenges in grammar / Michael McCarthy.
Description: 1st. | New York : Routledge, 2020. | Series: Innovations and
　　challenges in applied linguistics | Includes bibliographical references and index.
Identifiers: LCCN 2020001109 (print) | LCCN 2020001110 (ebook) | ISBN
　　9780367198350 (hardback) | ISBN 9780367198367 (paperback) | ISBN
　　9780429243561 (ebook)
Subjects: LCSH: Grammar, Comparative and general. | Language and
　　languages--Grammars. | Language and languages--Philosophy.
Classification: LCC P151 .M35 2020 (print) | LCC P151 (ebook) |
　　DDC 415--dc23
LC record available at https://lccn.loc.gov/2020001109
LC ebook record available at https://lccn.loc.gov/2020001110

ISBN: 978-0-367-19835-0 (hbk)
ISBN: 978-0-367-19836-7 (pbk)
ISBN: 978-0-429-24356-1 (ebk)

Typeset in Bembo
by Taylor & Francis Books

 Printed in the United Kingdom
by Henry Ling Limited

To the memory of Ron Carter

Friend and colleague

CONTENTS

List of illustrations   *xiii*
Preface   *xiv*
Acknowledgements   *xvii*

PART I
Where we came from   **1**

1   Introduction   3

    1.1 The first challenge: defining grammar 3
    1.2 The challenge of a historical perspective 5
    1.3 The lay perspective 5
    1.4 English grammar and the ELT perspective 6
    1.5 Innovation in grammar 8
    1.6 Corpus linguistics 9
    1.7 Varieties and variation 11
    1.8 Technologies 12

2   Grammar: Where did it all come from?   13

    2.1 Earliest origins 13
    2.2. Greek and Latin grammars 14
    2.3 Antiquity beyond Europe 18
    2.4 The Middle Ages: the Modistae *and universal grammar 19*

2.5 *English grammar: Bullokar* 19
2.6 *Universal grammar again: The* Port-Royal *grammar* 23
2.7 *Conclusion* 23

3 Eras of change and innovation: The 18th and 19th century 25

3.1 *Introduction* 25
3.2 *The 18th century: Enlightenment* 26
3.3 *The mid-18th century* 28
3.4 *Closing the century: the forgotten grammarians* 31
3.5 *The 19th century: new era, new grammars* 32
3.6 *Murray's grammar* 33
3.7 *Grammar and social class: William Cobbett* 34
3.8 *America: Goold Brown* 35
3.9 *Ending the century: Sweet and Nesfield* 36
3.10 *Culture and mindset* 37
3.11 *Conclusion* 39
3.12 *Challenges: a summary* 41

PART II
Innovations and Challenges **43**

4 Grammar and the public, grammar for ELT 45

4.1 *Introduction* 45
4.2 *Grammar and the public: usage manuals and handbooks* 46
4.3 *The outsider's perspective: reference grammars and language learning* 49
4.4 *Grammar for English language teaching* 53
4.5 *Structuralism: linguistic science meets the science of language teaching* 58
4.6 *Berlitz, James Joyce and me* 61
4.7 *New technologies, great events* 63

5 Innovation: Major new grammatical theories 66

5.1 *Noam Chomsky and his grammar* 66
5.2 *Transformations* 68
5.3 *Competence and performance* 69
5.4 *Deep and surface structure* 70
5.5 *Acquisition of grammar* 71
5.6 *The plausibility of TG* 71

5.7 Innovation in British grammar: J. R. Firth and the neo-Firthians 74
5.8 Halliday's grammar 77
5.9 The clause 79
5.10 Systems 81
5.11 Language and society 82
5.12 Halliday's enduring influence 83
5.13 Conclusion 83

6 Grammar as data: Corpus linguistics   85

6.1 Let the data speak 85
6.2 Grammar in corpora 87
6.3 Grammar and frequency 87
6.4 Concordance, pattern and meaning 90
6.5 Spoken and written grammar 94
6.6 The get-passive: pattern and context 94
6.7 Like 97
6.8 Grammaticalisation and the evidence of spoken corpora 98
6.9 Grammaticalisation: You know and I think 100
6.10 The significance of grammaticalisation 100
6.11 Emergent grammar 102
6.12 Conclusion 103

7 Grammar and discourse   107

7.1 Beyond the sentence 107
7.2 Discourse analysis and textual cohesion 108
7.3 Cohesion and speaking turns: conjunction 110
7.4 Ellipsis 113
7.5 Heads or tails? 114
7.6 Grammar in spoken and written discourse analysis 118
7.7 Special discourses, special grammars 119
7.8 Taking the turn 120
7.9 Grammar, discourse and co-construction 124
7.10 Conclusion 125

8 Grammar, language teaching and language learning   126

8.1 The canon 126
8.2 Make no mistake 130
8.3 Outside the black box: from grammar to grammaring 133

    8.4 *Staying outside the black box: Learners, grammaring and corpora* 135
    8.5 *Conclusion* 136

9   Grammar at large   137

    9.1 *Variety: standard and non-standard* 137
    9.2 *Grammatical change* 139
    9.3 *Americanisation* 142
    9.4 *Grammar and moral panic* 143
    9.5 *Conclusion: re-wilding the grammatical environment* 145

References   149
Index   167

ILLUSTRATIONS

Figures

2.1	Exercises in Greek grammar (c.300 AD)	15
2.2	Title page of Bullokar's *Pamphlet for Grammar*	21
3.1	Title page of James Harris's *Hermes* (1773 edition)	30
3.2	Front cover of *Grammar-Land; or, grammar in fun for the children of Schoolroomshire*	40
4.1	Substitution table	55
4.2	Post-modification of nouns with *to*-infinitive clauses	58
5.1	Phrase structure tree-diagram	67
5.2	Grammar rank scale	78
5.3	Systemic choices: English demonstratives	81
6.1	Extract from concordance of *moment*, Spoken BNC2014	90
6.2	Extract from concordance of *for the moment*, Spoken BNC2014	91
6.3	Random sample concordance lines for future perfect simple form, Spoken BNC2014	92
9.1	'Grammatical benchmark'	138
9.2	Use of *whom* in written documents 1900–2000	141

Tables

5.1	Levels of lexis and grammar	76
6.1	Spoken BNC2014: Negative forms of third person singular present tense *be*	88
6.2	Top-ranking frequencies in writing and speaking	95
9.1	BrE recently observed PVs (adapted from McCarthy, 2019)	142

PREFACE

This book is a story of grammatical ideas and attitudes, of grammarians, grammars and grammar teaching and how they have evolved over many centuries. It is a personal account, from two perspectives, first from my career as an English language teacher and teacher-trainer, and second as a university academic teaching courses on grammar over the past 30 years. It is not an attempt to be comprehensive; it is not an encyclopaedia of grammar. It dips in and out of theoretical streams, weaves its way through grammars and grammar-teaching questions and pauses now and then for autobiographical musings. It aims to paint a picture of great variation in thinking, of the challenges that successive generations of grammarians have confronted and innovations in thought, technologies and practice over the centuries that have kept the study of grammar firmly on the front page of language study and language teaching.

The first chapters of the book embark on a historical journey, going as far back as we have any reliable knowledge of, as regards grammar. So much of modern applied linguistics is preoccupied with the very recent past at the expense of an understanding of how much we owe to history. Well-worn metaphors of standing on the shoulders of giants and reinventing the wheel seem apt when we deal with grammatical thinking. Some of the earliest grammars are organised around categories that are still with us today. That is not to say that there is nothing new under the grammatical sun. Nonetheless, when we examine the dusty books on library shelves it is apparent that many of the ideas underpinning present-day grammatical thinking are centuries – even millennia – old, although sometimes they could just be sketched out and not fully developed by our grammarian ancestors.

Another reason for looking at the grammars of the past is the fascination of an encounter with history and the pleasure of reading through volumes whose well-thumbed pages have yellowed, which brings you into intimate dialogue with some impressive intellects. I am fortunate in having the Cambridge University Library on my doorstep, with its vast collections of old and new books and the unfailing atmosphere of scholarship in its reading room and at the quiet desks among the book stacks. There have I spent many hours chasing up references, settling into calm and unhurried reading of grammars old and new and books and articles about grammar and experiencing the joy of serendipity, discovering new sources of information and scholarship on the open shelves.

One dilemma facing me as I wrote this book was that grammar exists in all languages, but I know just a few, and only one at a native-speaker level. I do have enough French, Spanish, Swedish and Welsh and a smattering of Bahasa Malaysia to provide me with some understanding of their grammars. Nonetheless, I am trapped in an Anglocentric sphere that limits my ability to make generalisations in relation to other ways of wording the world, as well as having as my mother tongue a language that is over-supplied with scholarship. There is inevitably a whiff of linguistic hegemony in a book such as this one, written in English by an English-speaker and underpinned by English examples. The dominance of English globally has served the study of its grammar in ways unevenly advantageous to it. This is true, not least, in the area of corpus linguistics, where available software often facilitates the analysis of English while making it difficult to carry out grammatical analyses on other languages. My association with and supervision over the years of projects involving Welsh, Irish, Turkish and Burmese have led me to admire the undaunted spirits who have overcome technical obstacles when using software that breezes through English data only to stumble over the grammar of languages where phenomena such as mutations and particles play a significant role.

Another thread that I attempt to maintain in this book is the duty we have as applied linguists not to lock ourselves away in the echo-chambers of introverted academic discussion. Grammar belongs to everyone, and everyone seems to have an opinion about it. Sources of information on grammar range from complex, heavyweight academic tomes, which are largely inaccessible to the general public, through to popular usage manuals, course books and self-improvement books, as well as blogs, teaching videos and other forms of online communication. Then there are the grammatical moral panics that surface occasionally in the mass media of newspapers and broadcasting. None of these should be ignored in any applied linguistic account of grammar, and so I have tried to bring them in where appropriate and where I feel that they make a contribution to our understanding of public attitudes as opposed to what academics think about grammar. You, the reader, will judge whether this mix of ingredients amounts to a viable recipe for making sense of the world of grammar.

Every book has echoes of many voices, even though a single author's name might appear below the title. I have the luxury of more than 50 years of teaching grammar, thinking about it, reading up on it, getting research time to pursue projects and writing about it. But all this is worth little alongside the decades of discussions and exchanges with students, language teachers, colleagues and other academics and teachers in the 46 countries where I have been privileged either to live and work or to make professional visits since the mid-1960s. Recently, I have joined the circuit of speakers giving talks to local societies on issues concerning language and have the pleasure (and occasional pain) of hearing opinions on grammar from across the broad spectra of age, social class and geographical, ethnic, educational and cultural background. I try to listen to and respect people's points of view, even if I sometimes disagree with them. After all, grammar belongs to everyone.

Among the people to whom I owe a great debt as regards the long-term genesis of this book, I would like to thank Carolina Amador Moreno, Graham Burton, Paula Buttery, Andrew Caines, Angela Chambers, Brian Clancy, David and Rachel Clark, Jane Evison, Fiona Farr, Miguel Fuster, Carmen Gregori-Signes, Michael Handford, Kieran Harrington, John Hawkins, Michael Hoey, Rebecca Hughes, Almut Koester, James Lantolf, Elena Malyuga, Geraldine Mark, Jeanne McCarten, Anne O'Keeffe, Randi Reppen, Antonia Sánchez Macarro, Helen Sandiford, Nick Saville, Hongyin Tao, Scott Thornbury, Elaine Vaughan, Mary Vaughn, Steve Walsh and all the members of the Facebook ® Language Observatory Group (LOG).

Four scholars – all sadly passed away – stand out as major influences on my thinking about language, my debt to whom is immeasurable: John Sinclair, David Brazil, Amorey Gethin and my colleague and co-author of more than 30 years, Ron Carter. This book is affectionately dedicated to Ron and his enduring memory.

Cambridge, 2020

ACKNOWLEDGEMENTS

The British Library for permission to reproduce Figures 2.1, 2.2 and 3.2.
Cambridge University Library for permission to reproduce Figure 3.1.

PART I

Where we came from

1

INTRODUCTION

1.1 The first challenge: defining grammar

It is usually a good idea to consider what the general public or non-specialist understands by technical terms that enjoy currency in the non-technical world. Such applies to the word *grammar*. Not only is this a prudent starting point for a book like this one; it also helps us to keep the non-technical public in mind, for grammar belongs to them, not just to academics, and they know it. The *Oxford English Dictionary* (OED) gives its primary definition of grammar as the area of language study concerned with '… inflectional forms or other means of indicating the relations of words in the sentence, and with the rules for employing these in accordance with established usage' (OED: 2018). *Inflectional forms* – the ways that words change to show various types of meaning (e.g. a past tense ending of a verb, the number, gender and person of a pronoun) – is familiar territory occupied for centuries by accounts of grammar in reference books, textbooks and pedagogy, even though the precise terminology could have changed. The OED definition also refers to things being aligned with *established usage* – another term with which linguists, applied linguists and language educators are familiar – slippery and somewhat circular though it turns out to be. In addition, the longer OED definition of grammar refers to *syntax* – the rules for the arrangements of words to create well-formed sentences – which is another familiar domain. However, many non-specialists will go to popular websites for their understanding of technical terms and areas of study, and there they will find grammar helpfully defined as 'the study of words, how they are used in sentences, and how they change in different situations' (Wikipedia, 2019). Halliday adds a couple of twists that complicate the term *grammar*:

'the name of the phenomenon (as in the grammar of English), slides over to become the name of the study of the phenomenon (as in a grammar of English). This was already confusion enough; it was made worse by the popular use of the term to mean rules of linguistic etiquette (e.g. bad grammar)'.

(Halliday 1996: 2)

Grammar for the ancient Greek grammarians was a much broader field than the study of inflection and syntax and meant '... in its full and complete sense ... knowledge of literary compositions' (Pagani, 2011: 17). Over the many centuries since then, grammar has included the schemes of poetry, rhetoric, etymology and phonetics; indeed, Mitchell (2001: 1) refers to the 'riotous diversity' of definitions of grammar in the 17th and 18th centuries. However, our present-day conception of grammar has undergone a narrowing of purview; we no longer think of poetry and rhetoric as being essential to the teaching and learning of the grammar of a language, and for most people, the term *grammar* is associated purely with the rules and conventions of everyday language. In this book, we shall confine ourselves to this common view of *linguistic grammar*. Nonetheless, neither the confines of the area of study (i.e. whether grammar consists of more than the study of inflectional forms and the syntax of sentences) or the raw material for the study of grammar (established usage) is at all straightforward, and both areas have lacked a universal consensus since time immemorial.

What scholars think grammar is and how its objects of study are classified have evolved over the course of at least two millennia. For this reason, a historical perspective is an indispensable means of understanding the different ways we think of it today. There never has been one, straightforward definition of grammar. Dykema (1961), for example, distinguished four key meanings of the term *grammar* in contemporary understanding which still seem valid today: firstly, the complete structure of a language as learned by a child acquiring their native tongue; secondly, descriptive grammar, i.e. attempts to describe that structure; thirdly, prescriptive grammar, i.e. statements on what correct usage is, based on purist notions and often found in pedagogy; and finally, a belief in the authority of a book called *a grammar*, which will contain answers to questions and difficulties. Yet another way of approaching grammar is to seek universal principles underlying all languages regardless of their differences in forms and rules and conventions. All of these perspectives will be touched upon at various points in this book.

Applied linguists are not always good at historical perspectives. Perhaps this is a reaction to what is often seen as the stuffy academic discipline of philology (the study of the historical development of languages and the relationship between languages and language families). Present-day applied linguistics, it has been argued, lacks a historiography, so our past is a bit murky anyway. Historical research in applied linguistics is, in the words of Smith (2016), 'a pursuit without a pedigree, without an obvious mandate, and without commonly recognized or followed methodological procedures'. And, as a purely personal impression, many applied linguistics articles in journals and student dissertations, especially those concerned with language teaching, often shy away from references to any works more than 20–30 years old. This book rests unapologetically on a historical perspective to support one of its main arguments: that grammar rests and will always rest on the shifting quicksand of scientific, political, social, economic and cultural change. The quicksand affects how grammar is defined, where its boundaries lie, as well as how it evolves and is regarded by its users.

1.2 The challenge of a historical perspective

Several chapters of this book examine the historical evolution of grammar, starting with the very distant past. There have always been various distinct understandings of what grammar is, and different schools and models have vied for dominance over many centuries. Fashion and the dead hand of orthodoxy have also played their part. Thus, one of the first challenges of this book will be to trace the history of understandings of grammar, what it should include, where it comes from and on whose authority it rests, to investigate whether grammatical 'rules' are fixed and immutable and to expose some of the forces that mould and change 'established usage'.

These challenges carry within them other challenges of varying magnitude. Questions to address include: Can we separate grammar from the other features of the language system, for example, the vocabulary or is it more fruitful to acknowledge and embrace the polyphonic character of grammar and all the other elements of the system playing together like an orchestra to create discourse (Halliday, 1978: 56; Halliday, 2007: 44)? Why are there such strikingly different notions and models of grammar? Are they (in)compatible? Which one or ones fit(s) best the needs of applied linguists if we assume that applied linguists address real-world problems through the lens of language? And which one(s) might make most sense and be useful to non-specialists? If 'established usage' is not fixed but a set of norms or social conventions in constant flux, how can we persuade professionals and the general public that this is a positive observation of a natural human phenomenon rather than a threat to civilised behaviour?

1.3 The lay perspective

Grammar is a word that has wide currency both as a specialised academic term and as an everyday term used by ordinary people. As such, it is quite unusual, in that it straddles two markedly different worlds, a privileged position that not many terms within linguistics/applied linguistics have achieved. Compare, for example, terms such as *fluent, spelling* and *accent*, which, like *grammar*, have a foot in both worlds, and *phonology, collocation* and *anaphora*, which are rarely heard outside of academic contexts. Because *grammar* exists in these two separated worlds, it is, *par excellence*, an area in which applied linguists should try to build bridges, where we should speak in plain language to the public but where, at the same time, we face a significantly wide and challenging gulf to reach across. This applies also to grammar teaching: Stern (1983: 75) wisely asserts that a theory of language teaching must be founded on, among other things, 'what people in our milieu think and say about languages, language learning, and speakers of other languages'. We cannot be sure when we as professionals use the term *grammar* that we are using it in the same way that the general public does.

In my experience, the lay perception of *grammar* is based on the idea that there exists somewhere a set of rules. These rules are usually thought to be based on logic and coherent thought, the record of which is to be found in big, inaccessible books, the reliability of which is confirmed in the usage of great writers and orators, the stability of which should be sought after, and an understanding of which is generally (if you are lucky) provided by school-teachers but then frequently forgotten. I have lost count of the times that family, friends and acquaintances have reacted to my telling them I write grammar books and articles about grammar by saying, 'Oh, my grammar is terrible' or 'People's grammar nowadays is atrocious', frequently laying the blame for the latter on text-messaging and social media (for an interesting discussion on the grammar of Tweets, see Crystal, 2011: 45–48, and on grammar in text messaging, Crystal, 2008). Gentle questioning of such responses often reveals that people include in their notion of grammar spelling, irritating habits of speech and writing such as saying *less* instead of *fewer* before a plural noun, frequent use of *like* by younger speakers, media interviewees starting every answer with *so*, alongside criticism of what is perceived as poor or no teaching of grammar in schools. These types of lay perceptions simmer on social media and occasionally boil over into controversy that catches the eye of the mainstream press and broadcasting media on the lookout for a story, resulting in short-lived moral panic. Cameron (1995) looks at what was commonly perceived in the United Kingdom from the 1980s onwards as a wholesale neglect of grammar in public education, leading to such a moral panic. *Moral* could seem to be a word that has no place in the study of grammar, but in fact morality and 'goodness' are spectres that have haunted grammar over centuries and are still with us, and applied linguists ignore such perceptions and debates at their peril. We should not lock ourselves in the cosy offices and echo-chambers of seminar rooms in universities and pretend that we fully understand what grammar is and how it operates if we fail to confront and understand the place, status and perceptions of grammar in wider society.

1.4 English grammar and the ELT perspective

The English language will inevitably dominate this book. This is partly because it is my mother tongue, partly because I am not clever enough to write anything profound or original about the grammar of other languages, partly because English is a dominant, global language and partly because it has been the basis of my teaching career. However, I shall try, where possible and appropriate, to refer to my imperfect knowledge of the grammar of other languages.

In the English-language teaching and learning world, grammar has had a chequered history. When I began my career as an teacher of English as a foreign language in 1966, grammar was a taken-for-granted, core element of the syllabus, albeit my first job strapped me into the structuralist slot-and-filler oral drilling method of that time (see chapter 4). My second job, in the early 1970s, mostly involved the dissection of texts in which 'grammar points' were the material for discussion, practice and learning at a more advanced level. Thereafter, in the mid-1970s and 1980s there was a great upheaval in syllabuses and methods, with the communicative movement and notional-functional syllabuses sweeping in (Wilkins, 1976). In their strongest versions, communicative-based syllabuses pushed explicit grammar teaching to the margins, based on the observation that grammatical form and communicative function did not exist in a one-to-one relationship (see Howatt, 2004: chapter 20; Littlewood, 2011). The main tenet of the strong versions was that successful acts of communication would be a sufficient achievement and that any loose grammatical threads could be tied up as and where necessary or not, as the case may be. This was despite the fact that Wilkins – one of the prime movers of the notional-functional approach – never advocated the wholesale ditching of grammar and believed that notional and functional elements of the syllabus should be regarded as offering an extra dimension to existing grammatical frameworks (Wilkins, 1979). The idea of a more communicatively oriented pedagogical reference grammar was taken up by Leech and Svartvik, whose grammar was first published in 1975. By the time that it reached its second edition in 1994, its authors commented that the communicative approach had become 'an efficient and popular method for learning foreign languages' (Leech and Savrtvik, 1994: xi).

The communicative movement in English-language teaching turned out to be a pendulum that swung a long way away from seeing grammar at the centre of things, leaving an enduring mark, but which then swung at least some of the way back. And in many parts of the world it swung out of sync with its momentum in Europe and other first-world centres of English teaching or hardly swung at all, with older structural approaches to grammar maintaining their position in locally constrained teaching contexts in many countries, as well as reflecting an attachment to traditional educational values (e.g. Battistella, 1999; Yu, 2001; Hu, 2003; Hayes, 2009). The so-called *grammar-translation* method, where the focus was on translating written texts and their grammar and vocabulary, continued to enjoy its longevity of many centuries and remained resistant to change for a long time in the late 20th century in classrooms around the world. In the United Kingdom, a parallel debate has played out concerning the place of grammar in foreign modern languages education (Dobson, 2018). What emerges is that it cannot be taken for granted that grammar must always occupy a central place in language teaching syllabuses. I argued in the early 1980s for a resurrection of vocabulary and making it central in second-language teaching, as it too had suffered from being unfashionable (McCarthy, 1984). Grammar has to compete for attention with other possible dominant threads in the pedagogical process and has to fight for space on the all-bells-and-whistles modern course book or online programme.

Grammar has, however, enjoyed something of a privileged position in the study of second-language acquisition (SLA), where a great many studies have looked at how items of grammar are acquired and whether their acquisition follows some universal, innate principle, or whether a multitude of other factors bear upon it (Lightbown and Spada, 2006). SLA in its positivist, experimental form takes us to the heart of a core distinction between the study of language as a property of the human mind and the study of language in its external, social manifestations, reflected in the paradigm shift in English-language teaching away from cognitive-oriented structural approaches to language in favour of communicative approaches, with the already mentioned consequences for the place of grammar in the syllabus.

One persistent but largely impenetrable feature of language pedagogy is the 'grammatical canon' (Burton, 2018; 2019). The grammatical canon is an enduring compact among a variety of stakeholders, which has a core set of grammatical features considered to be indispensable in language teaching and the right ones to teach. But, as Biber et al. (1994: 171) remind us: 'Consensus does not necessarily reflect validity'. Yet the evolution of the English language teaching (ELT) canon is surprisingly resistant to historiographical analysis. Well-worn examples from English-language syllabuses are the tenses, articles, conditional sentences, reported speech, pronouns and so on, which are all deemed to be compulsory ingredients of any syllabuses, materials or grammatical assessment – ingredients best served up in progressive sequences in teaching. But if we ask the question where the consensus about such features originated and where the items that compose the consensus, their sequence of presentation and their theoretical justification are written down for all to follow, the canon becomes a phantasm detectable only in its realisations in individual course books, syllabuses, exams and piecemeal discussions of individual language features in articles in professional journals. The ELT grammatical canon, when considered against the backdrop of many centuries of pedagogy, is a relatively recent phenomenon, but it enjoys a largely untroubled and unchallenged position in the world of materials publishing and publishers' sales pitches. It has become an orthodoxy which reveals itself to be a chimera when prodded. It is a genuine grammatical challenge in the sense undertaken in this book and will be addressed more closely in chapter 8.

1.5 Innovation in grammar

There are many arguments to say that the hangover of past debates has faded and gone, and that grammar is alive and in a healthy state in various new guises which are explored in the second part of this book. Yet even in the 21st-century era of technological and scholastic advances in language pedagogy, some of the long shadows cast by previous centuries of grammar teaching and the different ideologies, orthodoxies and fashions that have surrounded it can still be traced, not least in the canon mentioned in the previous section. Nonetheless, positive developments in theory have reinvigorated its status and have successfully meshed in with parallel developments in language study, language teaching, the study of second-language acquisition and the role of technology.

With regard to how grammar is defined and where it starts and where it ends, in the past 30 years or so there have been different areas of language study incorporating grammatical considerations into their academic purview, and vice-versa. For example, discourse analysis – the relationship between language and its contexts of use – or, equally, the study of language 'beyond/above the sentence', seems now largely to be comfortable working with labels such as *the grammar of discourse, discourse grammar* or *grammar in discourse*. Language 'above/beyond the sentence' is based on the premise that the reach of grammar runs out once the sentence is described, and such matters as paragraphs or essays in writing, conversations, story-telling events or turn-taking conventions in speaking can be tackled only at the level of discourse. Indeed, it is possible to devise models for larger language events, such as lessons in a classroom, with little or no mention of the conventional terminology of grammar – an achievement of the seminal work on discourse by Sinclair and Coulthard (1975), where smaller structural elements (e.g. pupils' responses) fit together to form larger units such as teacher–pupil exchanges, strings of which may form teaching sequences, and on up to the whole lesson. All this structure-building can be accounted for and described without recourse to conventional grammatical terminology. However, much recent work has probed the role of grammar in the creation of key features of discourse such as textual organisation and the sequence of conversational utterances. At the same time, grammar has been explored in relation to its role in pragmatics, the study of meanings in context (such as how politeness is achieved, how one delivers an appropriate apology or what speakers mean by words such as *here* and *we*). And in the field of interactional linguistics, grammar occupies an important space in explicating the unfolding of interaction. These interdisciplinary connections mean that grammar no longer remains in a black box wherein are locked inflection and syntax, with the only key that will unlock it having a large 'S' on its fob, meaning 'sentence'. Grammar of a different sort gains visibility in areas where the idea of the well-formed written sentence cannot adequately describe the grammatical phenomena in the data, as we shall see in chapters 6 and 7.

1.6 Corpus linguistics

Foremost among the developments that have revived applied linguistic interest in grammar since the 1990s was the advent of corpus linguistics. Although corpus research initially affected language pedagogy via dictionaries (e.g. COBUILD, 1987), it was not long before it also began to work its way into grammar reference (e.g. COBUILD, 1990) and, ultimately, into teaching materials. Corpora had a four-fold effect on perceptions and understandings of grammar that have influenced the English-language teaching context. In the first place, they showed that corpus analysis of large collections of texts could provide evidence to back up or challenge conventional grammatical descriptions and the pedagogical grammatical canon. Secondly, they unearthed significant differences between the grammar of speaking and writing and suggested the need for new ways of describing and labelling grammatical phenomena. Thirdly, more recently, smaller, targeted corpora have enabled fine-grained descriptions of grammar and pragmatics in special domains such as academic and business language. Finally, corpora enabled texts produced by learners to be analysed and described from the point of view of grammatical knowledge and development at different levels of proficiency.

Corpora have had a direct effect on innovation in grammar description. Not least has been the development of software which can tag (i.e. label words in data according to their word-class) and parse (i.e. label elements in the data in terms of their functions in clauses and sentences, such as subject or object). Such tools are constantly evolving and being refined, thus enabling the automatic grammatical labelling of vast amounts of data to a high degree of accuracy, especially in written corpora. Much remains to be done in enabling the automatic tagging and parsing of spoken data, but here developments go hand in hand with the ever-increasing volumes of corpus-based research into speaking, from various perspectives, together with more sophisticated machine-training and the evolution of automatic speech recognition and artificial intelligence. Once the data are tagged, corpus software can typically search not only for single grammatical items such as nouns or prepositions but complex strings of words and their inflections. Results from complex searches have shown just how regularly patterned the grammar is, such that the term *pattern grammar* has gained traction in description and pedagogy (Hunston and Francis, 2000).

At the same time, corpus searches of complex strings have challenged the traditional distinction between grammar and lexis, as choices of lexical items seem to entail recurring configurations of grammar and vice-versa, leading to the widespread adoption of the term *lexicogrammar*. The term was originally coined by Michael Halliday (see chapter 5) and is used throughout his works to refer to the 'wording' of grammar in its broadest sense, but its adoption by the wider community of applied linguists reflects the statement of Halliday and Matthiessen (2004: 7), that 'grammar and vocabulary are not two separate components of a language - they are just the two ends of a single continuum'. At the same time, the notion of *collocation* (Firth, 1951/1957; McIntosh, 1961) – the likelihood of co-occurrence of words – has grown in importance as corpus analyses have given statistical underpinning to its omnipresence in data. Collocability disrupts the belief that lexical items can simply be dropped into grammatical slots to produce well-formed sentences. Many combinations of words that work syntactically fail to make sense lexically or else generate weird collocations. Overall, evidence-based views of the interdependence of grammar and the lexicon have had consequences for the traditional compartmentalising of the syllabus in language teaching.

Publicly available corpora, online searchability and more user-friendly analytical software suites have also facilitated direct access to corpus data for teachers and learners, giving rise to *data-driven learning*, where the acquisition of grammatical principles and conventions are based on inductive approaches; learners arrive at the underlying conventions via the cumulative observation of many individual examples of a grammatical pattern brought to the surface by the software (Johns, 1991). Data-driven learning, in its most effective manifestations, allows the bypassing of the reference grammar and 'established usage', taking teachers and learners directly into the world of raw data from which they can draw their own conclusions as to the nature of usage.

1.7 Varieties and variation

Differences between the grammar of speaking and the grammar of writing, explored in chapter 6, have led description and pedagogy away from the more homogenous world of writing to the more diverse world of speaking where, in the past, the status of 'inner circle' (Kachru, 1985) varieties of English (e.g. British, North American) overshadowed varieties spoken in non-inner circle countries (e.g. Asian and African varieties). Voices from non-inner circle varieties and their accompanying grammar can now be explored from the point of view of their grammar in the spoken corpora that capture and archive them (e.g. the ICE corpus project; see Greenbaum, 1996). Closer to home for the present author, recent work on the grammar of spoken Irish English (Filppula, 1999; Farr and O'Keeffe, 2004; Clancy, 2010; Vaughan and Clancy, 2011) has noticeably altered the status of that variety from one historically overshadowed by British English to one offering the opportunity of a homespun grammar pedagogy. More profoundly, corpus-based explorations of varieties of English and of other languages have raised the potential for independent grammatical modelling not necessarily dependent on the characteristics and categories of major, dominant languages such as English. This is especially relevant to the description and pedagogy of less widely spoken languages and minority- and lesser-studied languages, as exemplified in the National Corpus of Contemporary Welsh project (www.corcencc.org). The Welsh, Scottish and Irish Gaelic languages have morphosyntactic characteristics not found in English, such as mutations (changes in the sounds and spellings of words in different syntactic environments) that demand different approaches to corpus data annotation as compared with English.

The assumption, in the case of corpora, that bigger was always better was certainly borne out in the compilation of dictionaries, where huge amounts of data were required in order to yield enough occurrences of low-frequency words and idiomatic expressions for robust, empirically-grounded generalisations to be made concerning meaning, and similar criteria for data size underpinned the creation of large reference grammars such as those of Biber et al. (1999) and Carter and McCarthy (2006). Soon, however, researchers in more specific and more circumscribed areas of language study such as business language or academic language began to see the value of smaller, targeted corpora and were able to observe connections between grammatical features and characteristic pragmatic functions of those special contexts: for example, the use of certain types of modality for hedging and indirectness. Conrad (2000) saw the move towards more specific grammar pedagogy as a direct consequence of corpus studies. Chapter 7 briefly looks at corpus-based grammatical insights in specialised uses of language.

Innovation also extends to our understanding of and approaches to the grammar that learners know and use at different proficiency levels. Analysis of large amounts of text written (mostly) and spoken (less so but increasingly) by learners has given empirical substance to benchmarking systems such as the Common European Framework of Reference (CEFR) (Council of Europe, 2001) and has led to the construction of databases freely accessible to teachers and other educators, which offer a window into how learners around the world from different language backgrounds characteristically use the grammar of English as they attain the several lock steps of the English version of the CEFR (O'Keeffe and Mark, 2017). Chapter 8 of this book looks at innovation in this area and in addition considers the implications of corpus-based grammatical research of learner data in relation to the study of second-language acquisition and to the viability of the English grammatical canon.

1.8 Technologies

Telegrams were a significant way of transmitting urgent or important messages that reigned for a century or more. But you had to pay per word. What this led to was 'telegraphic grammar', whereby senders would omit unnecessary words. Nobody ever puzzled over what 'MEET ME STATION. ARRIVING 2.30.' meant. People often forget such examples of grammatical adaptability when they react with irritation against the grammar of text-messaging and its economy of spelling and grammar. Innovation in language often results directly from technological innovation. Corpora represent a major technological innovation that has influenced the modelling, description and teaching of grammar. Equally, social media present both a challenge and an opportunity for the investigation of grammar. The internet in general now provides massive amounts of data for research into the grammar of electronic communication. Most striking of all the effects of e-communication has been the breaking-down of boundaries between speaking and writing; social media postings and text-messaging are 'written' in the sense that they are typed into a machine (phone, tablet, computer), but bear all the hallmarks of spoken conversations. These include short and rapid back-and-forth turns between sender and receiver often in real time, reduced, 'elliptical' grammar, phrases in preference to well-formed sentences, a high degree of assumed shared context and knowledge, and so on, just as face-to-face social conversation does. Grammar is not and cannot be immune to these circumstances of utterance, and new, highly creative and innovative uses of grammar have emerged. Just as we thought we had begun to unlock the differences between the grammar of speaking and the grammar of writing, the quicksand has shifted again, and the ground beneath our feet seems a little uncertain, with a future that might hold just about anything. I nervously pressed 'send' on my first email a mere 25 years ago, but in that short time, grammar seems to have undergone a bewilderingly fast evolution, which challenges the idea that although vocabulary changes rapidly, grammar always seemed to change at a slower pace. The innovations of e-grammar could be something that books like this one will find it hard to keep up with.

This book deals with challenges and innovations in grammar. In a way, all challenges offer opportunities for innovation. Innovation rarely comes out of the blue, but is most likely to be a response to a challenge of some kind and to build on what is already there, as is borne out by the historical development of applied linguistics over the decades (Weideman, 1999; Harris: 2001–02). Innovations always present new challenges. Thus, although this book is divided into two sections, I hope that the relationship between the challenges and the innovations will be seen to exist in something akin to a dialectical one. As Mitchell (2001: 1) puts it, 'Grammar is a natural battlefield for the intellect'.

2

GRAMMAR

Where did it all come from?

2.1 Earliest origins

This chapter dwells on the far-distant past, not for the sake of tedious erudition but to trace our professional ancestry, as we might trace our personal family history, to understand more clearly who we are and to forge an identity for ourselves. And if the chapter dwells excessively on Europe and on the trajectory of English grammar in particular, it is because, however we may judge it, the English language, the study of its grammar and its dominant role in world education have played a disproportionate part in the history of our present-day profession of applied linguists. English is also the language that I have been involved with the teaching of and about for more than five decades. In this chapter, I will sample the works of grammarians who, I believe, left a significant heritage that subsequent centuries and our own have benefited from, however invisibly. The survey that follows is not comprehensive and cannot be in such a short work as this, and some will find omissions and inclusions that are not to their liking; I am happy to take the blame for both.

We cannot be certain as to who the very first grammarian was or where and when the first concepts of grammar were formulated in people's minds and written down, or how long before anything was written down that there may have been oral transmission of grammatical notions and descriptions. Oral transmission was certainly common at the time, when what we believe to be the first written grammars emerge, about 2,400–2,500 years ago (Goody, 1987: 116), and oral transmission and written texts existed alongside and complemented each other. The earliest origins of written grammatical description must probably be consigned to the mists of impenetrable history, albeit scholars have argued that complex oral texts for memorisation and recitation could hardly have been created without some basis in written form (Goody, ibid.). Whatever the case, our best evidence for early grammar must be found in what fragments of written texts have survived the ups and downs of history, and for those that have perished, we seek evidence in what others have said about them whose lives were nearer to them in time than ours are.

The ideas expressed in one grammar that has survived from that ancient past of about two-and-a-half millennia ago influenced grammarians of the 19th and 20th centuries, and the work is still regarded by many scholars as significant. This accolade belongs to the grammar of Pāṇini, a Hindu scholar of the Sanskrit language believed to have lived around 400 BC. The modern cornerstones of linguistic analysis, phonology (the study of units of sound and their organisation), morphology (the study of the smallest units of meaning and their combinations in words) and syntax (the study of arrangements and sequences of words and phrases in sentences) can all be traced back to Pāṇini's era and can be seen to have influenced linguists of the 19th and 20th centuries. Familiar grammatical features such as word-formation (e.g. derivations and compounds) and inflection were central concerns of Pāṇini. Kiparsky (2009: 33), in laying out the 'architecture' (his term) of Pāṇini's grammar, acknowledges 'the completeness of its descriptive coverage of the spoken standard language (bhāṣā)', meaning the spoken language of the educated class of that time. Pāṇini's grammar and other ancient Sanskrit works are said to have influenced major figures of the modern era of linguistics directly or indirectly, including, among others, Franz Bopp (Whitney, 1893: 196), Ferdinand de Saussure (see his work on Sanskrit: de Saussure, 1881), Roman Jakobson and Leonard Bloomfield (Rogers, 1987), with a range of linguists from both structural and generative traditions finding things in it to bolster their grammatical philosophies. Noam Chomsky, in the preface to *Aspects of the Theory of Syntax* cites Pāṇini in support of his argument for a generative grammar (Chomsky, 1965: v). More recently, Kiparsky (2009: 1) asked the question 'Why do linguists who don't approve of each other nevertheless agree in extolling Pāṇini?' The history of grammar and grammatical authority can have a very long and broad reach indeed, and we should not think that our sophisticated understandings and refinements of the subject were invented only yesterday, or that current authorities can rest their case solely on their own scholarship. There is little that is new under the sun.

2.2. Greek and Latin grammars

The ancient world saw the emergence of Greek and Latin grammars which also exercised an enduring influence in Europe. Significant among these was the grammar of the Greek Dionysius Thrax, who was writing around 100 BC. The first of his translators, Davidson (1874: 3), refers to the grammar as: 'This famous little pamphlet, the first attempt at a systematic grammar made in the Western World, and for many generations a text-book in the schools of the Roman Empire'. Thrax's grammar came to the attention of modern-day linguists in the 19th century through re-publication and translation. Davidson's 1874 translation gives us a window into its philosophy and structure and its basis in 'the usages of language as generally current among poets and prose writers' (Davidson 1874: 3). Thrax laid out eight parts of speech all familiar to us today: 'Noun, Verb, Participle, Article, Pronoun, Preposition, Adverb, and Conjunction' (p. 8), although adjectives are a sub-heading of nouns. Much of the detailed description of each word class (with some exceptions) would be familiar to present-day readers, for example the definition of a noun: 'A Noun is a declinable part of speech, signifying something either concrete or abstract (concrete, as stone; abstract, as education); common or proper (common, as man, horse; proper, as Socrates, Plato)' (p. 8). Thrax's grammar can be admired for its analytic detail, its descriptive lucidity and the power of its generalisations. It is not overtly prescriptive in the sense of saying what usage should be like; it simply describes the Greek language as evidenced in the great texts of its time. One significant detail of his grammar is its Greek title, *tékhnē grammatikē*, where *tékhnē* roughly equates to 'science'; Thrax saw grammar as a science, not just a question of observation (Langendoen, 1966). Robins notes that Thrax's work became 'the model for the description of virtually all subsequent grammars of European languages' (Robins, 1996: 3). Thrax's influence persisted through the two millennia that succeeded him, whether continuously or whether leapfrogging over time, landing occasionally, rising in significance in subsequent centuries, especially in the mid- to late 19th century. This was the time when philologists turned to Sanskrit and Graeco-Roman classical texts in support of their investigations of the origins, nature and family memberships of Indo-European languages.

As well as the existence of Greek grammars, we also have evidence that people engaged in practical exercises to learn Greek. Figure 2.1 shows exercises in Greek grammar on a wooden tablet, for use in a Greek school in Egypt in about 300 AD.

Thrax influenced the Latin grammarians who followed him. One of these was Varro, who lived during the first century BC and who translated Thrax's definition of grammar quoted above into Latin, such that Thrax's philosophy 'remained a pervasive part of the study of grammar' (McNelis, 2010: 286). Varro, in those parts of his monumental work *De Lingua Latina* (*On the Latin Language*) that survive, presents a

FIGURE 2.1 Exercises in Greek grammar (c.300 AD)
British Library Add. 37516 © The British Library Board, 10 November 2019. Reproduced with permission

detailed etymology of a huge catalogue of words and their derivations (Varro, 1938). He believed that etymology was fundamental to the understanding of language and that the job of the etymologist was to find the true origins of words as a support to achieving correct speech (von Fritz, 1949). Varro went further than just describing Latin. He saw processes such as derivation (the formation of new words from existing ones) as a 'universal generative principle' (Langendoen, 1966: 35). We see here an attempt to understand the underlying nature of grammar and human language in general – another persistent theme that crops up over time. Robins (1996: 6) comments that a particular section of *De Lingua Latina* 'reads very much like the prescriptive techniques of the modern field worker', on the principle of describing as many regularities as possible in the grammar and leaving the residue of irregularities to the lexicon. The idea of the field worker who looks for regular patterns in a language will re-emerge in chapter 4 when we consider 20th-century structuralism. Although Varro is little known now, Taylor (1996) comments about how his reputation as a major scholar lasted well into the Medieval period and beyond.

When referring to *speech* in the works of the grammarians of antiquity, we should not forget that grammar was linked with oratory and rhetoric – the art of informing and persuading through good and effective speaking. This led to notions such as correctness and purity in expression, with correct and pure examples of language found most readily in the works of great poets and philosophers, certainly not in the common parlance of the ordinary people. As Atherton puts it:

> 'Ordinary usage was itself typically regarded as sub-standard, as shot through with irregularities and inconsistencies. The primary focus of grammarians' efforts and expertise was the literary canon, its textual correction, exposition, and assessment, at all levels of sophistication and originality'.
>
> *(Atherton, 1996: 240)*

Correctness and purity in language was something that could – and had to be – trained into an individual (Atherton, ibid.). Training in rhetoric included acquiring a knowledge of literature, philosophy, logic and grammar, and it was 'the door to the professions' (Stewart 1979: 104). The Latin writer on rhetoric and education, Quintilian, in his *Institutes of Oratory*, which dates from about the end of the first century AD, set out his vision of the perfect orator, but also had a lot to say about the role of the grammarian in the process. He states in Book I, Chapter V:

> 'Since all language has three kinds of excellence, to be correct, perspicuous, and elegant, ... and the same number of faults, which are the opposites of the excellences just mentioned, let the grammarian consider well the rules for correctness which constitute the first part of grammar'.
>
> *(Quintilian, 1910: 1, V)*

The influence of Quintilian's work and the continuation of the rhetorical tradition in the pre-Medieval and Medieval era underwent changes and revision in ways of thinking during the European Renaissance, but persisted nonetheless (Ward, 1995; Knappe, 1999). Grammar, logic and rhetoric were seen as the three pillars of a good education. And, as we shall see in chapter 9, the equation of grammar with correct, good expression and the building of character is far from dead in the 21st century.

Two further grammarians of antiquity must be mentioned here because of their lasting influence in Europe. The first, Aelius Donatus, lived in the fourth century AD. His grammar, *Ars grammatica*, contained a description of eight parts of speech and was popular as a teaching text until the Medieval era. It also benefited from the advent of printing and became even more popular as a result. It contains categories that have survived in accepted descriptions of present-day English, for example the positive-comparative-superlative distinction, although such a tripartite distinction was by no means universally accepted by grammarians (Michael, 1970: 108–10). Secondly, in the late Roman era, around 500 AD, the grammarian Priscian published a massive grammar of Latin (about 1,000 pages in a modern edition) that was to have a long-lasting influence into the European Medieval era in the study and, significantly for later generations, the teaching of Latin. Priscian's grammar, *Institutiones Grammaticae* (*The Institutes of Grammar*), in 18 books, takes inspiration and material from Varro and Donatus (see above), follows the pattern of moving from phonology to morphology and word-classes to syntax and extensively quotes the great Latin writers. It also continues the strong emphasis on etymology which we saw in Varro. As Amsler puts it in reference to Priscian's thinking:

> 'To determine a word's proper meaning, the grammarian must determine not only the word's function in the grammatical system but also its origin and derivation, including its derivation within the grammatical system and its relation to Greek or earlier Latin forms'.
>
> *(Amsler, 1989: 80)*

Robins singles out Priscian's and Donatus's works as being significant in the development of European descriptive linguistics and also notes that their heritage 'became the basis of language teaching and of much linguistic theorizing in European education and scholarship' (Robins, 1966: 3). Maat, in discussing grammatical, logical and rhetorical theories current in the 17th century sees a clear line that can be traced back to antiquity: 'Priscian and Donatus for grammar, Aristotle for logic, and Cicero and again Aristotle for rhetoric' (Maat, 2010: 285). C. C. Fries, in discussing the (for him, negative) legacy of 19th-century school grammars, refers to Priscian's and Donatus' grammars as the 'type and source of the Latin and Greek grammars of Medieval and Modern Europe' as well as being the models for the first grammars of the European vernaculars in the 16th century (Fries, 1927: 227). The historical reach of these ancient grammarians is spectacularly long.

2.3 Antiquity beyond Europe

It is all too easy from a Euro-centric perspective to discuss ancient Greek and Roman grammatical scholarship at the expense of scholarship in other parts of the world. We should not forget that scholars and philosophers in China were interested in the role of language in human society from the Christian era onwards, albeit this sometimes took the form of imports from India (Itkonen, 1991: 89). Itkonen's survey of ancient linguistics notes that the Chinese philosopher and ethical thinker whom we know as Confucius commented on good speaking as part of the good gentleman's moral repertoire (Op. cit.: 90–91), a little like the value attached to rhetoric in the Greek and Latin world. However, scholars seem to agree that there is not the same thread of grammatical description of the kind we have inherited from Greece and Rome. Indeed, Mair (1997) states that the earliest grammars of Chinese were written by Westerners, and that it was only at the end of the 19th century that the Chinese began to write their own grammars.

Itkonen's (1991) survey also takes in Arabia and, more specifically, the Islamic tradition (with important work emanating from Persia), which flourished some 1,200 years ago and which, although possibly influenced by the Greek tradition, developed a robust and independent line of linguistic enquiry. One major figure of that era, Sībawayh, wrote the oldest surviving grammar of classical Arabic, which was influential for a long time. As with others that we have mentioned, good and proper grammar was linked with morality and ethics. But Sībawayh was also innovative; indeed, some have argued that Sībawayh's grammatical theory had a discourse perspective, with speakers and hearers and context being considered relevant to the grammatical description (Itkonen, 1991: 150ff), further evidence that there is little that is new under the sun.

Much more could be said about non-European grammarians of antiquity, but, inevitably, we have focused here more on the Graeco-Latin tradition, which, together with the Indian linguistics represented by Pāṇini, were held by Robins (1966) to be the two most important predecessors of modern Western linguistics. It is the Graeco-Latin tradition – and the role of Latin especially – that has been handed down to us today and whose extensive reach still influences the description and teaching of European languages, with English and English language pedagogy seeing a greater global spread than any other European language.

This and the previous section have dealt with just a couple of examples of how ancient grammarians shared many of the preoccupations of today's scholars, for the purposes of underlining the importance of examining the origins of our ways of thinking and for continually stressing the value and challenges of a historical approach. It is only by looking at history that we can observe the unbroken continuity of grammar and at the same time become aware of the relative nature of grammatical thinking in terms of the different social contexts in which it has arisen. In a society where rhetoric enjoys a high status, grammar is closely linked with rhetorical goals and principles. In societies where other matters dominate (e.g. the spread of popular education and aspiration), grammar will be seen through a different lens. The story of the ancient Greek and Latin grammarians does not end here; suffice it to say here that their influence in the Western world stretched over many centuries.

2.4 The Middle Ages: the *Modistae* and universal grammar

One powerful concept in modern thinking is that of universal grammar: the idea that underlying the surface forms of different languages lie processes of the human mind that are the same for all languages – a theory to which we return below and in later chapters. Yet the idea of universal grammar is not a new one. Thomas (2004: 24–5) sees its origins in ancient Greek philosophy: for example, in the Aristotelian notion of the universality of concepts, and we have already mentioned Varro in this context. The 13th-century English philosopher and scientist, Roger Bacon, has been much quoted for his statement 'Grammar is one and the same in all languages, substantially, though it may vary, accidentally, in each of them' (Murphy, 1976: 154).

The medieval (13th- and 14th-century) philosopher-grammarians known as the *Modistae* (*Modists*, thus called because of their philosophy of modes of signifying) continued the long-established tradition of studying word-classes but also believed in the importance of relating language to the human mind and to the world and the nature of reality (Bursill-Hall, 1966), which in several ways presages the framework of Chomskyan linguistics, with its emphasis on the relation between language and mind. Itkonen (1991: 229) sums up their position by saying that it was clear to the *Modistae* that 'every language contains the same principles which, taken together, constitute the universal grammar'. The *Modistae* were seeking 'the universals by which all languages were generated from one's understanding of the world' (Kelly, 2002: 9–10). Grammar is a science. 'There is only one grammar, just as there is only one physics' (Formigari, 2004: 75). These ideas pose the challenge of finding an underlying, universal cognitive structure to grammar that is independent of the forms it takes on the surface in different languages. Thus, grammar becomes as much the study of the human mind as the study of forms displayed by words on the page or in speech.

2.5 English grammar: Bullokar

We now leapfrog over time to an important stage when Latin and vernacular languages stood side by side in Europe. During the late 15th and early 16th century, Latin texts still dominated the spread of knowledge. However, in its native country, English was attracting growing attention, owing partly to the invention and spread of printing, partly because of a decline in the use of Latin and a demand for translations of learned and scientific texts and partly because of a general increase in esteem and respect for the vernacular. But when grammars of English began to appear, the influence of Latin grammar was overbearing. 'Even the style of the English used in many formal texts was apparently praised according to how close it came to Latin models' (Gwosdek, 2013: 123). At the same time, in explaining Latin rules, teachers and scholars began to give more thought to the rules of English; this was the period when Latin grammars written in English 'also encompass the beginnings of the teaching of English' (Gwosdek, 2013: 127).

The first grammar of English is widely attributed to William Bullokar, whose *Pamphlet for Grammar* from 1586 gives us a picture of English during the 16th century. Bullokar's grammar had a pre-existing model in William Lily's Latin grammar (written in English), which was published in 1534. Lily was an important figure of his age, after King Henry VIII ordained that Lily's grammar should be the only authorised textbook for the teaching of Latin. One of Bullokar's modern editors has commented that Bullokar's grammar simply uses Lily's system and is an attempt to force English to comply with the rules of Latin (Turner, 1980). The interesting features of Lily's Latin grammar go beyond its influence on English grammars; he also had a lot to say about grammar teaching. He commented that, although the sanctioning of just one grammar text by the king was a good thing, how the grammar was taught should be varied and diverse, and that grammar teaching should not be a rushed affair but should proceed at an appropriate pace (Lily, 1534/1680: 3). Dissemination through printing and the idea of a standard textbook were to have an influence on thinking in both grammatical description and pedagogy that has extended to our present time, with items such as structured national syllabuses and approved course books made possible by the widespread use of officially sanctioned books.

Bullokar's title page (Figure 2.2) includes the following, in modernised spelling:

> 'Sufficient for the speedy learning how to parse English speech for the perfecter writing thereof, and using of the best phrases therein, and the easier entrance into the secrets of grammar for other languages'.

Bullokar's grammar follows the normal practice of introducing the word classes, exploring their forms and functions and then commenting (in a shorter section on syntax) on how they combine to create sentences. The eight classes he describes are noun, pronoun, verb, declined participle, adverb, conjunction, preposition and interjection (Bullokar, 1586: 13), most of which we are familiar with today (*declined participle* refers to present and past participles). He subdivides nouns into substantive nouns (what we recognise as nouns today) and adjective nouns (i.e. adjectives). Latin is mentioned frequently, for example in the advice on how to parse English sentences 'in many points agreeing with Latin' (Bullokar, 1586: 68).[1] His grammar also gives us an insight into how he viewed English in relation to other languages. He saw his grammar not only as a description of English but as a support to anyone learning a foreign language, in relation to which, comparing the relative simplicity of the English inflexional system to the complexities of Latin, he says: 'English has short rule (therefore soon learned) yet having sufficient rules therein to make the way much easier for the learning of any other language unknown before to the learner' (p. 1; *short* here means 'limited' or 'contracted'), and, in an early reference to our modern profession of English as a foreign language, 'very aidful to the stranger to

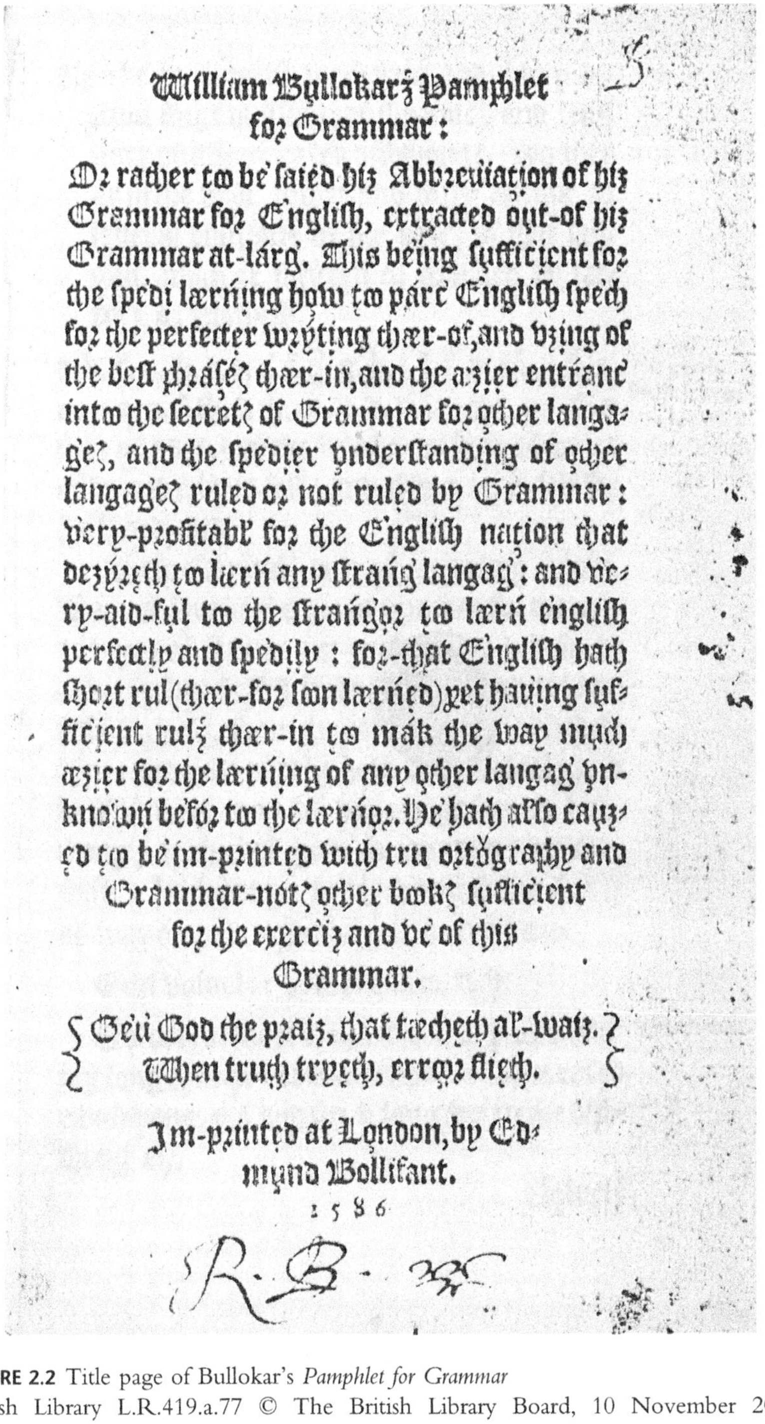

William Bullokarz Pamphlet
for Grammar :

Or rather too be saied hiz Abbreuiation of hiz
Grammar for English, extracted out-of hiz
Grammar at-larg. This being sufficient for
the spedi lærning how too parc English spech
for the perfecter wryting thær-of, and vzing of
the best phrasez thær-in, and the æzier entranc
intoo the secretz of Grammar for other langagez, and the spedier vnderstanding of other
langagez ruled or not ruled by Grammar :
very-profitabl' for the English nation that
dezyreth too lærn any strang langag' : and ve-
ry-aid-ful too the strangor too lærn english
perfectly and spedily : for-that English hath
short rul (thær-for soon lærned) yet hauing sufficient rulz thær-in too mak the way much
æzier for the lærning of any other langag vn-
known befor too the lærnor. He hath also cauz-
ed too be im-printed with tru ortography and
Grammar-notz other bookz sufficient
for the exerciz and vc of this
Grammar.

{ Geu God the praiz, that tæcheth al-waiz. }
{ When truth tryeth, error flieth. }

Im-printed at London, by Edmund Bollifant.
1586

FIGURE 2.2 Title page of Bullokar's *Pamphlet for Grammar*
British Library L.R.419.a.77 © The British Library Board, 10 November 2019.
Reproduced with permission

learn English perfectly and speedily' (*aidful* means 'helpful'; *stranger* means 'foreigner'). Spelling and punctuation were very different and varied greatly in Bullokar's time (the previous quote, for instance, appears as 'very-aidful too the strangor too læm English perfectly and spedily' in the original) but were in the process of reform and becoming more standardised.

Gwosdek (2013: 131) sees significance in Bullokar's use of the term *grammar* to describe his work, as *grammar* had previously been applied only to books for the study of Latin. Nowadays we take for granted the twin-pronged, uncountable and countable uses of the word: *grammar* is a subject of study, and you can have *a grammar* or several *grammars* of English on your bookshelf (recall the discussion in chapter 1). Bullokar's grammar was undoubtedly influenced by Lily's Latin grammar, yet it shows a respect for the English language and its ability to stand on its own two feet. Although he gave a lowly status outside of the word classes to articles (*a/the*), which did not exist in Latin, he also noted interesting non-Latin English features, such as the use of the present tense with future meaning (p. 38).

Bullokar gives us a glimpse not only of how grammarians conceptualised and constructed their scholarship at that time, and how the grammar of his time compares with that of present-day English, but also how the prescriptions of grammarians could be at odds with contemporary usage – a dilemma that has probably always existed. For example, in the abridged version of his grammar, on the subject of comparison, Bullokar states the conventional rule of then and of today, that comparatives are for comparing two entities, but acknowledges that: 'we English use the superlative also when we compare but two things together'. He could have been describing the usage of large swathes of the present-day English-speaking population. Clearly, if you base your grammatical descriptions and prescriptions on an external model such as the grammar of Latin, you are likely to be out of kilter at various points with the everyday usage of the population whose language you are attempting to describe or prescribe. Most grammar books, including present-day volumes, will in one way or another be out of date as soon as they are published.

Bullokar's grammar marks a shift to describing English grammar in English. His work was followed by other grammars of English written in English or in Latin in the 17th century, an excellent survey of which may be found in Dons (2004). One of these, by the dramatist Ben Jonson, is transitional, in that it treats the English language as independent and comparable with other languages but also includes, side by side with the grammatical account of the English language in English, copious quotations in Latin from ancient authorities, including Varro, Quintilian and Priscian (see chapter 1), and quotations from great English authors such as Geoffrey Chaucer and Thomas More. Like Bullokar, Jonson sees his grammar as useful for foreigners to learn English (occasionally comparing English grammar with other language such as French, Dutch and German), but adding to the traditional eight word-classes, he designates the articles *a* and *the* as a ninth word-class (Jonson, 1640/1909: 78). Jonson's attachment to the ancient classical languages as the greatest authorities for the grammarian is a reflection of the scholastic ambience of his time.

2.6 Universal grammar again: The *Port-Royal* grammar

The seventeenth century saw the publication of a grammar generally referred to as the *Port-Royal* grammar (named after a monastery in France where its authors resided). The Port-Royal grammarians were interested in the relationship between language and logic and sought the underlying, universal principles of mental processes. Words realise thoughts, with most word-classes signifying the objects of our thoughts; verbs and conjunctions signify 'manners of thoughts' (Itkonen, 1991: 262). Such logical processes underlie all languages and all human beings possess the capacity to engage in them and to realise them in speech. The Port-Royal grammarians valued the speech of living languages rather than the great literary texts studied by earlier grammarians. Their grammar was hailed in the twentieth century as an important precursor of modern linguistic theory, including by Chomsky (1966). However, Itkonen (1991: 262–5) dismisses claims that the Port-Royal grammar was revolutionary and original and sees nothing in it that cannot be found in the writings of Aristotle and Plato, as well as in the ideas of medieval philosopher-linguists. Even more trenchantly, Arsleff (1970) attacks Chomsky's account of the Port-Royal grammar as completely misguided and as granting undue significance to it (see also Hall: 1977). Whoever is right, the notion of a universal grammar has persisted over the millennia until our present time and has influenced not only grammatical thinking but investigations into language acquisition too.

2.7 Conclusion

The story of the 17th century is not all concerned with grammatical theory. The spread of the printing press offered huge potential to the creation and spread of textbooks for learning languages; at the same time, the Czech philosopher-grammarian and educator, Comenius, was advocating universal education and writing textbooks for schoolchildren. He had no time for the drumming of classical Latin into the minds of the young via textbooks full of rules, irregularities and exceptions and believed that progressive learning, from the child's mother tongue to a new language, could be achieved through good pedagogy, which included the use of pictures as an aid to learning (Sadler, 1970, 2014; Besse, 2001).

This chapter has sampled the evolution of grammar over the course of more than two thousand years, and it is no more than a series of brief glances at grammatical works. Much more could be said, many more works could have been surveyed, and the leapfrogging over centuries could have been avoided, but that would have been a different book. Although many texts are lost to us today or have faded into obscurity, we do, I hope, learn much from the past. We learn that what constitutes grammar in the minds of scholars is not fixed and absolute for all time, and that grammar has been conceived as inseparable from other aspects of human expression, such as rhetoric, poetry, good thinking and moral education. Grammars have been designed for and used in pedagogy from the earliest times, and the influence of some ancient works has displayed remarkable longevity. The models on which grammarians based their descriptions were overwhelmingly the speech and writing of the literate, educated classes, and that, for western Europe at least, ancient Greece and Rome were viewed as the fount of linguistic understanding. Yet one important change in the European landscape did have a long-lasting effect: the rise of the vernacular languages in the late Medieval period and respect for and pride in them, which meant that Latin and Greek were no longer the only pathway to a knowledge and an understanding of grammar. We saw, too, an example of how the invention of printing enabled those in power to spread the authority of chosen grammatical texts. The next chapter takes us nearer to our own times, but also explores the stubborn persistence of old ways as new approaches to the grammar of English and its pedagogy emerged to reflect historical forces at work in the 18th and 19th centuries.

Note

1 Quotes from Bullokar are given here in modernised spelling and orthography.

3

ERAS OF CHANGE AND INNOVATION

The 18th and 19th century

3.1 Introduction

If we allow ourselves to leap over time here and there in this chapter, 'turning the accomplishment of many years into an hour-glass', as Shakespeare said,[1] it is because this book is not an encyclopaedia of grammar and grammarians. The reason for delving into history is to remind us that modern grammars do not appear out of thin air, and that what was written even two thousand years ago can be traced in many of the debates of later centuries right up until the present day. This represents a challenge to applied linguists, as few people outside of narrow academic circles will have the time, energy or inclination to ponder where attitudes to grammar have sprung from and to question why the occasional splenetic debate in the mainstream media and online over some grammatical issue verges on moral panic which considers educational and cultural standards to be on a downward spiral. We may not be able to solve our present-day grammatical dilemmas by acquainting ourselves with the history of grammar, but we can go a long way towards understanding how and why they arise, through a greater awareness of how grammatical description and theorising have evolved over many centuries. This is the first step in confronting the challenges that public controversies present to us now.

Seventeenth and 18th-century grammarians used the word *grammar* to cover a wider and more distinct range of objects of study than it does today; to the grammarians of 300 years ago, grammar 'could mean anything from parts of speech to spelling and punctuation' (Mitchell, 2001: 1). The whole subject was in flux. Movement towards creating some sort of standard or agreed norms for the vernacular languages of Europe was gaining momentum and, in the case of English, the 17th century had seen a marked increase in the number of grammars published (Tiken-Boon van Ostade, 2008), but how the grammatical landscape was to be carved up remained open to debate.

The 18th and 19th centuries were enriched by new grammars for English and marked by further moves towards codification and standardisation. In this regard, the building blocks of grammar were always a mix of the fine, elevated speech of the educated classes and orators and/or the great writers of antiquity. The masses did not get a look in. The rhetorical tradition was concerned with good speaking, providing an ethical and moral backdrop to the notion of correctness in grammar and the avoidance of barbarisms. The target audience for grammar consisted overwhelmingly of scholars and rich young men. Equally significant was the continued dominance of Latin as a model, even after the time when the European vernaculars began to stand on their own two feet in terms of educated and scientific use and codification in grammars such as Bullokar's.

3.2 The 18th century: Enlightenment

The beginning and middle of the European 18th century are often referred to as the Age of Enlightenment – an era when reason and radical thinking dominated, and when great political change was fermented. The period witnessed a broadening of the audience for grammar, towards a wider range of readers and, among grammarians, a growing interest in matters of correct and incorrect usage and in grammars written for a younger population of learners (Tiken-Boon van Ostade, 2008). For the first time in relation to English, there seems to emerge a 'community of practice' of grammarians with a shared repertoire of concerns (see the discussion in Watts, 2008). Against this background, we find a steady growth towards the end of the century in the desire for standardisation and the number of what are generally referred to as prescriptive grammars, which are concerned with laying out what were considered good and correct ways of speaking and writing.

A significant feature of English grammars published at the beginning of the 18th century is a collective desire to describe and teach English on its own terms and not through Latin (Buschmann-Göbels, 2008). Equally, the early 18th-century grammars avoided overt prescriptions to the reader. *The Grammar of the English Tongue* (1711), here quoted in the eighth edition (1759), the title page of which attributes the authorship to John Brightland (although scholars attribute it instead to Charles Gildon), rails against grammars that 'force our Tongue in every Thing to the Method and Form of the Latin and Greek' (Brightland, 1759: v).[2] This was one battle in what has been referred to as the 'Grammar War': the struggle was partly between those advocating the supremacy of Latin and those advocating the English vernacular, and partly between those wishing to preserve the language unchanged (prescriptive grammarians) and descriptive grammarians, who recognised that language changes according to the habits of users (Mitchell, 2001: 17). The Brightland/Gildon grammar clearly states its purpose: 'to convey a Grammatical Knowledge of the Language we now speak' (p. viii), rejecting as irrelevant where words might anciently have derived from, but still quite clearly based on the language of the learned and educated classes. The grammar works its way through letters, sounds and words to how words combine in sentences. but also has lengthy sections on the arts of poetry, rhetoric and logic, showing the enduring link between grammar and the arts of good speaking and writing.

In 1737 James Greenwood published *The Royal English Grammar*, whose lengthy subtitle was 'Containing what is Necessary to the Knowledge of the English Tongue Laid down in a Plain and Familiar Way'. It was an abridged version of an earlier grammar by the same author, and it went into a number of editions. Greenwood says in his preface that the aim of the book is: 'that they who never learnt any Latin, may attain to a good knowledge of the Nature and Genius of their Mother Tongue' (Greenwood, 1737: vi). He goes on to say that grammar is a useful art and that, although young gentlemen and ladies may be able to get away with things in speech without much grammatical knowledge, he cannot see how they could write anything 'with a tolerable correctness' without some knowledge of grammar. Correctness is essential; that is what a grammar is for. However, Greenwood finds fault in grammars which force English into the Latin mould, which results in 'many useless precepts' about cases and genders and declensions.

As a reminder of the pedagogical purpose of these grammars, each description in Greenwood's grammar is followed by what we would nowadays call Q & A sections, for example, *Q: What do you learn grammar for? A: To learn to speak and write truly and properly. Q: What do you mean by speaking and writing truly and properly? A: Speaking and writing after the custom of the best speakers and writers.* (p. 3). He divides grammar into four parts: orthography, etymology, syntax and prosody (prosody deals with what we would generally call word-stress and rhythm). Concerning orthography, there are lengthy sections on the vowels, diphthongs and consonants and their relation to the letters of the English alphabet. Etymology deals with the traditional eight parts of speech – the same ones that we saw in Bullokar's grammar (i.e. with adjectives subsumed under nouns, and articles seen as a kind of adjective) and with derivation. Greenwood comments on Latin cases, but affirms that English only has a separate genitive (possessive) case from the base form of a noun, with other Latin case-functions being realised by prepositional phrases, 'whereby we are freed from a great deal of trouble and difficulty that is found in other languages' (p. 35).

Greenwood is in many ways enlightened in his rejection of forcing English into a Latin mould. He is, for example, clear that English has only two tenses – the present and past – with all other expressions of time being realised through 'helping verbs' (p. 59). This is a principle that has often broken down in the wording of many present-day English language materials, which will frequently have recourse for pedagogical convenience to terms such as 'the past perfect tense' or 'the future tense' (see the discussion in Blyth 1997 and chapter 8). His sections on syntax contain detailed information on word-order and phenomena such as ellipsis (the non-use of elements normally considered obligatory in a construction). Greenwood's grammar is remarkable in its descriptive breadth and its faithfulness to attempting to describe English on its own terms, but he is nonetheless quite prescriptive as to what is good English and what is not, and, as before, the models of good usage are the best writers and speakers, for which read the educated classes and the great names of English literature. In fairness to our ancestors, in an age where the masses mostly could not read or write and audio technology did not exist, what reasonable option was there for grammarians other than to plunder the texts of great authors? In the United Kingdom, newspapers, pamphlets and broadsheets were in circulation in the 18th century, but it would be a long time before they were regarded as respectable sources of evidence for the writing of grammars.

3.3 The mid-18th century

Although not primarily a grammar, Samuel Johnson's *A Dictionary of the English Language*, published in 1755, has interesting things to say about the state of the English language at that time, which seemed to adhere to no standard, including in grammar. In his *Preface*, he says:

> 'When I took the first survey of my undertaking, I found our speech copious without order, and energetick [sic.] without rules: wherever I turned my view, there was perplexity to be disentangled, and confusion to be regulated; choice was to be made out of boundless variety, without any established principle of selection; …'

(p. 2)

Johnson divides grammar into the same four parts as Greenwood: orthography, etymology, syntax and prosody. He devotes only the briefest section (less than a quarter of a page) to syntax, justified by the fact that English 'has so little inflection, or variety of terminations, that its construction neither requires nor admits many rules' (p. 49). What rules he does quote (those of subject–verb agreement and government) are stated in Latin terms: prepositions and transitive verbs take an 'oblique case' (i.e. are followed by object pronouns) and a noun with possessive 's is described as 'the genitive' – terms familiar to anyone with a classical language background.

One major, influential work of the mid-18th century was Bishop Robert Lowth's (1762) *A Short Introduction to English Grammar* (here cited in the 1799 edition). Lowth is remembered principally for his overtly prescriptive approach, and some of his prescriptions remain relevant to this day. However, it would be an over-simplification to view Lowth as the arch-prescriptivist, as Tieken-Boon van Ostade (2010a) clearly shows: he was part of that scholarly tradition that looked to standardise English and to present a model for those aspiring to good, standard usage.

The *Preface* to Lowth's grammar is a fascinating document appraising the English language as simple in terms of rules of inflection; it is not the fault of the language that grammar is in a woeful state, rather it is the neglect of its users, who take it for granted because of that very simplicity (Lowth, 1762/1799: vi) – another complaint that echoes down the centuries (see chapter 9). Lowth is clear that English can be subjected to systematic description for the purposes of presenting the reader with rules for correct usage and even criticises some of the great writers for not being the best models for accuracy and for committing 'gross mistakes' (p. vii); 'propriety and accuracy' (p. vii) of expression should be the goals of the user. All this is important, for it means that good speaking and writing is not just an aspiration in the sense of exercising best practice based on the respected authorities; it is now a question of avoiding error and sticking to the rules as put down by the grammarian. Indeed, Lowth is confident that his grammar is exceptional in teaching 'what is right, by showing what is wrong' (p. viii).

Lowth's prescriptions are many: he condemns as improper double comparatives and double superlatives (p. 27), the use of *either* instead of *each* when the meaning is 'both' (p. 90) and confusion of *who* and *whom* (p. 95), but he readily admits that some of the forms that he condemns as 'improper' are nonetheless common and indeed, some of what he considers errors come from Shakespeare (see chapter 9). Most famously, and with a probable sense of self-irony, Lowth states, concerning what are often referred to as stranded prepositions (prepositions separated from the relative pronouns that they govern): 'This is an idiom, which our language is strongly inclined to' (p. 95). He accepts that such usage might be acceptable in common conversation or familiar written style, but he concludes that placing the preposition before the relative pronoun is more appropriate to 'the solemn and elevated style' (p. 96). For a full discussion of Lowth's and other grammarians' views on preposition stranding, see Yáñez-Bouza (2008). Some of Lowth's prescriptions can still be heard put forward today by members of the general public, which, by any standards, is an achievement, given that more than 250 years have passed since their publication. I have long since ceased to be surprised when I get questions about stranded prepositions and *who* versus *whom* posed in obvious irritation at falling standards by members of the general public in lectures that I give on grammar and dialects to local clubs and societies.

In his grammar, Lowth praises a previous publication, James Harris's *Hermes, or a Philosophical Inquiry Concerning Universal Grammar* (published in 1751, here cited in the edition of 1773). Lowth calls Hermes 'the most beautiful and perfect example of analysis, that has been exhibited since the days of Aristotle' (Lowth, 1762/1799: x). Harris's preface to *Hermes* is a document of the Enlightenment, referring as it does to mathematics and logic and the advancement of science. Harris was interested in the interplay between language, mind and meaning and their relationship to a theory of science and learning, and he believed that the same universal, underlying reason and truth had always existed (Probyn, 1978). Behind everything lay a universal set of psychological principles that enabled sentences to be constructed. Yet Harris was not popular with his contemporaries because of his devotion to the philosophers and grammarians of antiquity during an age when empirical science was on the rise (Subbiondo, 1976). Harris's text is full of quotations in Greek and Latin, as well as numerous quotes from Shakespeare and John Milton.

The theme of universal grammar was mentioned in chapter 2; Harris's *Hermes* has been called 'the first clear example of a work on the subject in English' (Emsley, 1933). Universal grammar is at the heart not only of logic, but of rhetoric and poetry as well (Harris, 1751/1773: 6). Harris defines universal grammar as that which ignores the idiomatic aspects of individual languages and pays attention to 'those principles that are essential to them all' (p. 11; modernised orthography). Although *Hermes* is philosophical and complex, modern readers will occasionally find in the work familiar devices for the description of grammar, such as using lines

HERMES

OR Aa 9 30

A PHILOSOPHICAL INQVIRY

CONCERNING

VNIVERSAL GRAMMAR

BY IAMES HARRIS ESQ.

ΕΠΕΙΔΗ ΣΑΡΡΟΝΤΑΙ ΕΙΝΑΙ ΓΑΡ ΚΑΙ ΕΝΤΑΥΘΑ ΘΕΟΙΣ.

THE FIFTH EDITION.

LONDON:

Printed for F. WINGRAVE, Succeſſor to
Mr. NOURSE, in the Strand.

M.DCC.XCIV.

FIGURE 3.1 Title page of James Harris's *Hermes* (1773 edition)
Reproduced by kind permission of the Syndics of Cambridge University Library

and geometrical analogies to represent time and tenses (pp. 103, 115), and his examples of the unknown and known entities realised in the indefinite and definite articles (p.215–6) are as clear and helpful as anything presented in a modern English language course book. Harris's work was followed by another 18th-century philosophical treatise, that of Beattie (1783: 105), who set out to demonstrate that behind the differences in languages lay a 'universal or philosophical grammar'. He cites as an example expression of comparison, which, although different in various languages, in one way or another must be needed in all languages (Beattie 1788: 182).

3.4 Closing the century: the forgotten grammarians

It will not have escaped the reader's attention that so far in this book every grammarian reviewed has been male. In societies where men dominate public life, women are often ignored, even if they have made notable contributions to public discourse, and grammar in former times was no exception. In an excellent doctoral thesis, Cajka (2003) surveys nine female grammarians of the 18th century whose works have largely been ignored, dismissed or overshadowed (owing partly to the feminist preoccupation with women's creative literature). The neglect of female writers was in no small way due to the fact that a classical education (which gave access to much grammatical scholarship) was something for boys and men and that women were typically advised by men in matters of correct usage, not vice-versa (Tieken-Boon van Ostade, 2010b). The female grammarians reacted against the dull, obscure grammars of their time and sought to make grammar more interesting for teachers and students alike, especially female ones (Cajka, 2003: 5–6). These grammars were a sign of a changing social climate: women were slowly taking greater charge of their affairs, as well as finding themselves often in the position of mother-and-teacher to their children (Percy, 2010). The authors' names are probably known only to a few scholars even today: Ellin Devis, Dorothea DuBois, Mrs M. C. Edwards, Mrs Eves, Ellenor Fenn, Ann Fisher, Jane Gardiner, Blanche Mercy and Mrs Taylor. The grammars written by these women were by no means marginal in terms of publishing success, with editions continuing into the 19th century.

Ellin Devis's book, *Miscellaneous Lessons Designed for the Use of Young Ladies. On a New Plan* (Devis, 1782) gives us a window into the place of grammar towards the end of the century. Under the heading of *Grammar* (p. 88), she quotes Bishop Lowth in support of its importance – an indication of his influence at that time – and grammar is one of the 'Accomplishments' for a young lady, together with reading, cyphering (mathematics and counting), dancing, needlework, drawing, music, French, Italian, history, geography and natural history. Grammar is a thread in the delicate moral and social tapestry of the well-rounded young lady. Devis's *The Accidence; or First rudiments of English grammar. Designed for the use of young ladies* opens with the statement that:

'A Grammatical Study of our own Language is at present thought so essential a Part of Education, that it is presumed, very little Apology can be requisite for attempting to render that Study less difficult to Children'.
(Devis, 1797: iii). [capitalisation as in the original]

Watts (2008) sees four key ideologies in play as the 18th century drew to a close: the idea of the standard language, notions of politeness, the idea of an educated language and the ideology of success and social improvement. These ideologies were the backdrop to the evolution of attitudes towards grammar, how it should be described and prescribed and who the audience for grammar was to consist of.

3.5 The 19th century: new era, new grammars

At the end of the 18th century there was a great rise in the number of grammars produced for English on both sides of the Atlantic (e.g. in the USA, Alexander, 1795), but it was the 19th century that really witnessed an explosion in the numbers of publications. The century was also marked by a move away from prescriptive grammars, which focused on correct ways of speaking and writing, towards descriptive grammars, whose goal was to describe the language as found. At the same time, technological changes such as the easier and wider dissemination of information (for example, advances in printing and the spread of railways), the growth of an educated middle class and, not least, changes in usage, all contributed to a new era of grammatical description and pedagogy. As before, we shall simply pick out a few names to give a flavour of what was, for grammar, a very crowded century. Busse et al. (2018) provide a useful list of some 40 19th-century grammars and, using corpus-linguistic methods, show a dense network of cross-referencing from one grammarian to another, suggesting a genuine community of scholars and tracking the shift from prescriptive approaches to descriptive.

One of the first significant grammars of English in the 19th century was written by the Danish linguist Rasmus Rask and published in 1832. We shall see in the next chapter how a tradition of northern European and Scandinavian grammarians has contributed to ever greater refinement of the description of English, challenging the notion that native speakers are the best suited to write grammars of their own language. Rask was interested in comparing the various Indo-European languages and tracing them back to their origins, which was a major development in the linguistics of the 19th century. He also published (in Danish) grammars for Spanish and Italian in 1824 and 1827 and *A Grammar of the Danish language for the use of Englishmen* in 1830. Pāṇini's grammar (see chapter 2) had been translated into English in 1809. Rask had worked on Sanskrit (Basbøll and Jensen, 2015), and it was against this background that diachronic and comparative linguistics came to the fore. Rask's English grammar takes the familiar path through letters and sounds, to word-stress, spelling, word-classes, auxiliary verbs, tense and aspect forms; although written in Danish, it gives translations of grammatical terms in English in parenthesis (Rask, 1832).

Michael (1991) tells us that anywhere up to a thousand English grammars for school use were published in Britain during the 19th century, peaking in the period 1840 to 1890, and some of these went into many editions. The market grew, owing to the importance given to grammar in the schools and in the mind of the general public. Despite, or perhaps because of, their great number, Michael describes most of them as 'dull' because they 'impose on the language a stifling form of analysis' (1991: 11). However, Tibbetts (1966) argues that the grammar, rhetoric and composition textbooks of the 19th century were not really prescriptive but rather were concerned with practical questions, such as clarity of expression.

3.6 Murray's grammar

A principle name to consider is Lindley Murray. Although his grammar was first published in 1795 and thus belongs, in the strictest terms, to the 18th century, its life and influence belong to the 19th century (and indeed beyond). By 1822 no fewer than 35 editions had been published, and it is the 1822 edition that we cite here, reprinted in 1996 (Murray, 1822/1996). Reibel, in his introduction to the 1996 reprint, notes that Murray's grammar 'very early on virtually eliminated all competition in Britain', while in the United States, his book was often pirated or cloned (pp. x–xi). Reibel also notes the significance of both Lowth and Murray in contributing to the fixing of norms and standardisation of English, specifically the English of the 'gentlemanly classes', to which a rising middle class aspired (pp. xiv–xvii). By this time, too, the names of word-classes had become fixed in a way that we recognise today – for example nouns and adjectives are now separated and articles are given full treatment.

Murray continually revised and abridged the grammar and produced exercises for it. It was, in all senses, a pedagogical grammar, which was first produced for the education of young women in the Quaker religious community in York, northern England. The grammar was closely modelled on that of Lowth, but Murray also added to the traditional four sections an appendix entitled *Rules and Observations for Promoting Perspicuity and Accuracy in Writing*. In the Appendix, which is a manual of style, he contrasts 'best usage' with 'low expressions' (p. 275).

The book was intended for ease of reading and clarity; the most important rules are given a larger typeface. Forms that are improper are presented and corrected. For example, Murray notes that many people in conversation use *them* instead of *these* or *those*, as in 'Give me them books' (Murray, 1822/1996: 150) – a form that is alive and well in the local dialect of the place where I write this book. He also comments on the use of *there is* with a plural complement instead of *there are* (p. 139) – a usage that is widespread among educated speakers of English to this day. In the section on participles, there are warnings to be careful not to confuse the past tense with the past participle, as in 'He begun' instead of 'He began' (p. 186) – once again something often heard in the present day in many English dialects in different parts of the English-speaking world. In fairness to Murray, he is most concerned with establishing norms for good writing, and his prescriptions are regularly expressed as things to be careful of rather than things which are forbidden. Nonetheless, it is illuminating to see how grammatical forms that he considered unsuitable were, and still are, alive and well in the usage of the people. One reason for the popularity of Murray's grammar (and similar ones of the time) was that it was straightforward to teach, with clear rules which made the task of a non-specialised and inadequately trained teaching profession that much easier (Michael, 1991).

However, change did occur in the 19th century, both in what 'grammar' was considered to include and the pedagogy that accompanied it. The old notion of prosody, for example, as one of the pillars of the discipline began to have less importance. At the same time, a gradual move towards teaching the language as it was at that time, rather than what it was in its origins and historical past, came about. Michael (1991) notes the trend in the last part of the century towards more analytical approaches, encouraging analysis of sentences and clauses and considering notions such as word-classes in contexts of use. A similar trend towards analytical approaches was seen in the United States (Downey, 1991).

3.7 Grammar and social class: William Cobbett

One of the most interesting figures of the 19th century in England was William Cobbett. He was a radical political thinker who believed that the working classes were oppressed by a wicked system. However, he was at the same time reactionary in the sense that his vision yearned back to a pre-industrial state where workers reaped the benefits of their toil instead of the system that exploited them in the new industrial society (Osborne, 1964). Cobbett was particularly scornful of people who had crammed a knowledge of Latin and Greek but had little else to offer and 'frequently allowed himself the pleasure of criticizing the style and punctuation of government dispatches and was particularly fond of analyzing the syntax of the king's annual speech from the throne' (Osborne, 1964: 11). He in no way equated wisdom with high birth. His 1818 *A Grammar of the English Language*, which is cited in the 1831 edition (Cobbett, 1818/1831), is written in the form of letters addressed to his 14-year-old son, but its title-page dedicates it to a wider audience of 'Young Persons in General; but More Especially for the Use of Soldiers, Sailors, Apprentices, and Plough-Boys', no longer just the young gentlemen and ladies of the higher social classes. The grammar is listed as 'among the best-selling books of the nineteenth century' (Aarts, 1994), and it went into many editions, selling some 100,000 copies by the mid-1830s (Mugglestone, 1997). The grammar stressed the importance of the written language as a powerful instrument for those pressing their cause in public life, for example in the writing of political petitions.

Cobbett deals with the parts of speech (the traditional division of *etymology*) and syntax and has very little to say on the traditional headings of orthography and prosody, retained merely through convention. Of pronunciation (prosody), he asserts that children learn it 'as birds learn to chirp and sing', and he is respectful of regional pronunciations, as the message is more important than one's accent

(Cobbett, 1818/1831: Letter II). The word-classes are by now fully recognisable to the present-day reader: articles, nouns, pronouns, adjectives, verbs, adverbs, prepositions, conjunctions and interjections (Letter III). The reader of the letters is taken step by step through the word-classes and thence to syntax. The grammar is prescriptive, and the advice is given in terms of taking care to observe the principles and avoiding carelessness. Some of his advice on subject-verb agreement rings true to concerns lay friends and acquaintances express to me these days, typically the query as to whether one should say 'a team of scientists *is*? / *are*? working on the problem' (see Letter XIX). Cobbett was prescriptive, but he recognised that common usage could and should, where necessary, trump ancient rules (Letter VI, paragraph 57). The final part of the book takes to pieces speeches and dispatches of the great and the good (royalty, parliamentarians and officials), pointing out their bad writing and 'false grammar'.

3.8 America: Goold Brown

On the other side of the Atlantic, Goold Brown's *The Institutes of English Grammar* (1823, here cited in the edition of 1856) was enormously influential in American schools. Brown wanted his grammar to be practical, recognising that the language was 'the common property of all who use it' (Brown, 1823/1856: viii). Nonetheless, he is clear as to where the standard lies: 'It is not the business of the grammarian to *give law* to language, but *to teach it*, agreeably to the best usage. The ultimate principle by which he must be governed, and with which his instructions must always accord, is that species of custom which critics denominate GOOD USE; that is, present, reputable, general use'. (p. iii – italics and capitals as in the original). The grammar is traditional and prescriptive. Brown retains the four-fold division of orthography, etymology, syntax and prosody, and each chapter is divided into numbered rules, and advice is worded in what 'should' and 'should not' be used. Brown's established position in the United States did not go unchallenged. Advocates of a more inductive approach came to the fore, and the old, four-fold division of grammar was rejected in favour of a greater interest in words in relation to syntax and sentence-building. Downey (1991) provides a good survey of American grammars of this period.

The earlier 19th century was a hangover from the 18th century, and, indeed, C. C. Fries saw the negative influence of 18th- and 19th-century prescriptivism alive and well, and 'deeply rooted in popular prejudice' a century or more later (1927: 223). The latter part of the 19th century was marked by a shift towards practical English grammars and texts that took a more analytical approach based on the components of clauses (subject, predicate, etc.) and which offered exercises (Michael, 1991). The era was one of a burgeoning of mass education and great demand for self-improvement. At the same time, linguistics in general was becoming more scientific (the term *linguistics* seems to be established by the mid-19th century) and more especially interested in phonology, thus prompting a move towards the study of speech. Some important developments in this regard were made at the end of the century.

3.9 Ending the century: Sweet and Nesfield

One of the most significant works that marked the end of the century was Henry Sweet's *A New English Grammar: Logical and Historical,* published in two parts (Sweet, 1892 and 1898). It is notable that in his *Preface* to Part I, Sweet labels the contemporary situation in the study of grammar as still 'unsettled', with considerable and sometimes contradictory variation in definitions among grammarians (1892: v-vi). Part I of the grammar has major sections on words, word-formation and the familiar list of word-classes. Only one word-class might strike the present-day reader as unfamiliar, that of *Verbals* (basically, nominal forms of verbs), which cover the infinitive form and the *supine* (a Latin-grammar term; nowadays we call it the *to*-infinitive), participles and gerunds. This kind of terminology is illustrative of Sweet's intention to retain traditional labels where they are deemed useful and lacking proper alternatives; for example, he shuns the 'misleading' term *possessive case* and prefers *the genitive*, while *noun* is preferred to the traditional *substantive* simply because it is shorter (p. vii). The grammar is both historical and 'logical', and phonetics underlies the historical aspect, which is indicative of the growing interest in speech and dialect variation. *Phonology* (the sound system) and *Accidence* (inflexions and morphology) form two major sections of Part I, after the basic elements of words, word-classes, sentences and the history of English have been dealt with. *Accidence* is dealt with historically, with each word-class in turn getting a section on Old English, Middle English and Modern English. The second volume of the grammar deals with syntax.

Sweet says: 'The first business of grammar, as of every other science, is to observe the facts and phenomena with which it has to deal, and to classify and state them methodically' (p. 2). His aim is descriptive, not prescriptive:

> 'In considering the use of grammar as a corrective of what are called "ungrammatical" expressions, it must be borne in mind that the rules of grammar have no value except as statements of facts: whatever is in general use in a language is for that very reason grammatically correct.'
>
> *(p. 3)*

Sweet was an applied linguist in the late 20th-century sense of a practical linguist committed to the science of philology and phonetics, but his was a living philology, and he rejected the subordination of living languages to dead ones. The title of his 1899 work *The Practical Study of Languages: A Guide for Teachers and Learners* is testimony to his desire to apply the scientific study of languages to the practical problems of teaching and learning them (Sweet, 1899). He believed in the phased learning of a foreign language, based first on phonetics and pronunciation, followed by a grammatical stage based on graded authentic texts containing target grammatical structures that illustrate the rules. Only then would the student be ready to study a grammar. For a full discussion of Sweet's methodological approach, see Véronique (1992).

Another trend towards the end of the century, which may be observed in the output of J. C. Nesfield, a popular author of grammars, was to bring to the fore the sentence and the clause and their component parts in preference to the old habit of giving primacy to word-classes (the traditional division of *etymology*) at the beginning of one's grammar, and to deliver advice on good writing and composition beyond the sentence. Nesfield's *Manual of English Grammar and Composition* (Nesfield, 1898; the 1908 reprint is cited here) is a massive, detailed manual that takes the user from sentences and clauses, through the word-classes and syntax (with a thorough treatment of word-order and variations of word order for emphasis, etc.), to a section entitled *Composition: Force and Propriety of Diction*, followed by sections on rhetorical devices (e.g. similes, metaphor) and the old division of prosody (prose and poetry in this case). Only then, at the end of the book, does Nesfield deal with the history of the language. He sees the goal of his grammar as expounding purity and proper usage – a goal that can be achieved by avoiding extraneous matter, what he calls 'the dross of language' (p. 151). This includes shunning vulgarisms such as *that angry* instead of *so angry*, as well as various types of vocabulary, for example colloquialisms (which should be used only sparingly or not at all) and provincialisms (regional dialect forms). On questions of grammatical propriety, he has a lot to say about the use of the possessive apostrophe, infelicitous pluralisation of abstract nouns (e.g. *stupidities*), using *them* instead of *those* (p. 157) and many other prescriptions that are still debated in the present day.

3.10 Culture and mindset

Nesfield was a colonial official of the British Empire in India, where his books were much used. The British Empire was reaching its zenith – the empire upon which the sun never set – and with the spread of its global political power came the spread of English education and the English language. Nesfield's books were widely used in India, and their influence spread beyond the Empire to include China, where his books were used in schools and where his work influenced Chinese grammarians – an achievement that Sweet's grammar could also claim (Peverelli, 2015: 35, 89, 179 *et passim*).

One of the more subliminal aspects of grammars that we have not yet touched upon is the content of example sentences. The examples that grammarians choose to illustrate their descriptions and prescriptions are inevitably influenced by the mindset of the author and the cultural milieu in which the book is produced. This is no less true for the present day, and we should hesitate to see ourselves as somehow superior or possessed of greater objectivity than our scholastic forebears; least of all should we mock or sneer at example sentences and texts that at best appear quaint and old-fashioned or at worst seem culturally insensitive. No doubt, our own age will be judged by future ages as culturally naïve, prejudiced and blinkered in ways that we cannot begin to perceive at present.

Nesfield's *Manual of English Grammar and Composition* contains no fewer than 28 references to India. Many of them are neutral, geographical references; some strike us as images of Empire. In a sentence illustrating the present perfect, users are reminded that the 'British Empire in India *has succeeded* to the Mogul Empire' (p. 51, italics in original), while another example, on verb ellipsis, notes 'My regiment is bound for India; yours for Gibraltar' (p. 119). The user is also reminded that the English language has spread beyond its native homeland to North America, Australia, New Zealand, India, Burma and South Africa, 'and is beginning to be spoken by the natives in Egypt and in several parts of China and Japan' (p. 304). What we should take from these examples is a picture of the increasingly important role of English in a vast empire and in the world as a whole – a paternalistic enterprise that would lead to particular forms of language experience and approaches to grammar spreading across the globe to become entrenched for a long time. The influence of this mindset in India in particular is discussed by Singh (1987), who traces the changes in cultural perspectives vis-à-vis grammar teaching through pre- and post-independence India.

Interpreting the cultural milieu of the colonial period, especially the role of colonial education, is vital in our quest to understand the evolution of grammar in the English language context, although we should not forget that Spanish, French and Portuguese spread across their respective empires too. For a general discussion of colonialism and language, see Ostler (2005: Part III); for an interesting discussion on European colonisers' attitudes to the local languages they encountered, see Errington (2001).

In relation to the spread of English, Sweeting and Vickers (2007) note that British colonial education is under-researched – a situation they graphically label as 'the dark continent of imperial historiography' (p. 1). Charges of linguistic imperialism, especially laid upon the 19th century but by no means confined to that period, have been made not entirely without justification, including by Pennycook (1996, 1998), and in many respects, the spread of English-medium education, promoting a standard version of the language, can be seen as a global spread of the local process of standardisation that evolved in Britain in the 18th and 19th centuries. The fact that the dominant model for the standard derived from the politically and economically powerful South East of England itself brought with it a dominance of middle-class values in education – values that still dominate the teaching of English as a foreign language. However, in their trenchant critique of Pennycook's analysis of English linguistic imperialism, Sweeting and Vickers (2007) give a much more nuanced and empirically founded historical portrayal of the role of English in the educational, social and economic development of Hong Kong from the 19th century onwards. The picture emerges as complex, and one in which colonial rule is seen as more collaborative and pragmatic, with English language education being more correctly understood when viewed from bottom up rather than as a top-down, overarching ideological imposition.

Whichever side one takes, the challenge to this book is never to divorce grammar from its historical, social, economic and political environments. Grammar can seem on the face of it to be something abstract, unchanging, rule-bound in a universal, logical sense, but it is not. It is only 'logical' if seen through the lens of an era where logic is elevated to a central component of public discourse; it is only 'universal' if it is believed that a core of universal facts and truths underlie human existence. It is diverse and pluralistic in societies that value those qualities. It is only unchanging if we see grammar as a set of timeless laws corrupted by its users in different ages. Pennycook (2012) rightly warns against viewing languages as objects divorced from their ideological contexts, yet these contexts are necessarily extremely complex and ought never to be reduced to over-simplified praise or condemnation. The primary sources that we deal with here (old grammars and their authors' prefaces) reveal attitudes of their ages and cultural milieux, but also the individual mindsets of authors, who rarely entirely fit the stereotypes of 'prescriptivists' or 'conservatives'.

3.11 Conclusion

The 19th century was an era of rapid change: industrialisation, technological developments in transport and communication (including greater dissemination of printed material), urbanisation and imperialism all played their role in transforming the philosophical, social, political, cultural and educational environments. These forces moulded the evolution of grammar, how it was understood, its voices of authority, its modes of transmission and its exploitation in the hands of its end users. As the century drew to a close, the study of grammar was ever more standing on its own two feet. Woods (1986), in an excellent survey of 19th-century grammar manuals that pays particular attention to their evolution in North America, notes in the grammars of the end of the century:

> '... their desire to simplify, to avoid the "technical" or "theoretical" parts of grammar. They offer a "practical, functional" series of lessons, each quite short, unified (with no loose ends or doubtful ambiguities), and shored up by appropriate oral and written exercises'.
>
> *(p. 17)*

Compared with the grammars of early centuries, laden with Greek and Latin terms and quotations, founded on categories often obscure and divorced from the realities of contemporary English, grammars were now becoming practical, aimed more at analytical and inductive approaches to understanding instead of rule-giving and blunt prescriptions, and even promoting grammar-learning as enjoyable for the young (Figure 3.3). That is not to say that large, learned grammars were no longer produced, as we shall see in the next chapter when we enter the 20th century – a century that, once again, saw major upheavals in the theory and practice of what constitutes 'grammar' and innovations in pedagogy.

A review in *The Guardian*, a British newspaper, of *Grammar-Land* described it thus:

> 'It is a courtroom drama: the hero, Judge Grammar, is a likeable old cove, given to snoozing in his robes and eating pages of the dictionary for lunch; flanked by assistants Brother Parsing and Dr Syntax, he interrogates all the Parts of Speech one by one'.
>
> *(Poole, 2010)*

FIGURE 3.2 Front cover of *Grammar-Land; or, grammar in fun for the children of Schoolroomshire*. By M. L. Nesbitt. Fourth edition (London, 1889)
British Library 12981.bb.46. Reproduced with permission © The British Library Board, 10 November 2019

As before, I have merely sampled the two centuries with which this chapter is concerned; I have not mentioned a number of grammars whose approach and content might colour even further the picture presented here. My choice gives what I believe to be a taster of the two periods, and I have referred to works that are readily accessible rather than obscure, and which are available in original, facsimile or online editions in libraries and through relevant websites. Nothing beats an unrushed and open-minded study of these primary sources. We cannot fully understand the innovations that we proudly parade without confronting the challenges that have washed down to us on the tide of centuries.

3.12 Challenges: a summary

So far, this book has traced the evolution of grammar from its earliest beginnings to an era where English had learnt to stand on its own two feet and, largely speaking, although not entirely, shaken off the Latin straitjacket as the only worthy model. In this chapter we have seen how social and cultural developments in the 19th century broadened the scope of grammar beyond the traditional domain of privileged education. Grammar and grammar pedagogy have always been subject to a series of innovations, but innovations that, in their wake, always leave unresolved challenges which, in turn, lead to further innovations, and so on through time. What kinds of innovations in thinking, in practices and in technology have sought to address these questions will be the framework of the second part of this book.

Notes

1 Prologue to *Henry V*.
2 Capitalisation of nouns was normal at the time.

PART II
Innovations and Challenges

4

GRAMMAR AND THE PUBLIC, GRAMMAR FOR ELT

4.1 Introduction

In the previous two chapters, the emphasis was on the evolution of grammar from its earliest surviving documents up to the end of the 19th century. In this chapter, the emphasis will be on the different approaches to grammar and the writing of grammars and grammar teaching that dominated the 20th century, which are still with us in their distinct and often competing forms and which have left their mark on the present. We look at a type of grammar aimed at a broad, educated readership, at the first wave of popular language courses and their grammar content and also look at the emergence of the new profession of the English as a foreign language (EFL) applied linguist.

Over the centuries, some ideas about grammar have come and gone and come back again, revived in different and renovated forms, an example being the notion of universal grammar, which has received differing degrees of intellectual prominence over time (see below). Things do not always travel in a straight line. However, if we adopt the century-by-century approach taken so far, we should remember that the clock striking midnight at the start of a new century never means a sudden paradigm shift in anything; the 20th century at its outset was still drifting on the ebb tide of the 19th. Firth (1930/1964: 195) noted, for example, that the idea of 'educated' English, although traceable back to the 17th century, was given a major boost by the British Education Act of 1870, which had the effect of stigmatising uneducated speech, the effects of which lasted for several decades into the 20th century. Nonetheless, century boundaries do give us a series of time markers to organise our observations of evolution; as Halliday (1991: 40) rather humorously put it in relation to the end of the 20th century and its thinking, we were 'packing up for the move into the twenty-first century'.

Major wars tarnished the 20th century. On the one hand, the First World War disrupted scholarship and pedagogy in a number of ways, but on the other hand, the Second World War and subsequent conflicts and the needs of the armed forces prompted significant innovations in the study and teaching of foreign languages and how grammar was dealt with. In the decades following the First World War, the field of grammar expanded into new territory, owing to the explosion of research in universities and other professional contexts, the writing of 'big' grammars in pedagogical contexts and the proliferation of journals devoted to the study of language in all its forms. Existing prestigious journals in linguistics and applied linguistics such as the *Transactions of the Philological Society* (1854), *PMLA* (1884), *American Speech* (1925), *Language* (1925), *Word* (1945) and *English Language Teaching Journal* (1946) were supplemented in the second half of the century by titles such as *Linguistics* (1963), *TESOL Quarterly* (1967), *Language in Society* (1972), *Studies in Language* (1977), *Studies in Second Language Acquisition* (1977) and *Applied Linguistics* (1980), which bear witness to the great expansion in research and professional activity (see also Harris, 2001–02). In addition, those titles have, in the past 30 or 40 years, been supplemented by a number of journals devoted to areas such as pragmatics, discourse analysis, corpus linguistics and cognitive linguistics, all of which, at some point or another, turn their attention to the role played by grammar in their respective disciplinary sub-fields. These journals arose out of shifts in theories and applications of linguistics and applied linguistics, and the way they treat grammar reflects those shifts.

4.2 Grammar and the public: usage manuals and handbooks

From an academic's viewpoint, we tend to think of grammars as large scholastic tomes, so accustomed have we become to the weighty volumes that have graced library shelves from the 19th century to those that do so now (e.g. Quirk et al., 1985; Huddleston and Pullum, 2002). Alternatively, we might remember a more modest grammar book or course manual that we used at school or university in the learning of our own or of a foreign language. In this section we consider the innovative role played by popular grammar and usage manuals before looking at large reference grammars, for it is manuals aimed at schools and a wider, non-specialist public that influenced, and still influence, attitudes to grammar outside of the rarefied atmosphere of the universities. To ignore what may seem, academically, to be the poor relations of the major scholarly works on grammar would be to abdicate our role as applied linguists whose concern is with the role of language in wider society and the perspectives and attitudes of the non-expert population. Once again, we cannot possibly cover all the countless manuals and school-texts published during the period under examination, but we shall look at some that achieved great popularity and that stood the test of time.

Undoubtedly, the most popular and influential manuals of English usage of the first part of the 20th century were written by the Fowler brothers, Henry and Francis. However, before we look at their works, we note that Burchfield (1991) mentions two important late 19th-century British and American precursors, Henry Alford and Richard White, respectively. Similarly, Macht (1991) shows a progression in the evolution of English grammar manuals published in Germany from the late 19th century and into the 20th century by Karl and Max Deutschbein.

Alford's (1864) manual goes by the title *The Queen's English: Stray Notes on Speaking and Spelling*. The phrase *Queen's/King's English* goes back to the mid-16th century and is generally understood to be a metaphor for correct British standard usage, rather than the way that any king or queen uses the language; as Alford himself puts it, English is 'open to all of common right, and the general property of our country' (1864: 1–2). The 'stray notes' reference in the title is due to the fact that the book's 257 pages are filled with, on the face of it, unconnected entries concerning words, phrases and grammatical headings such as *Nouns made into verbs, Elliptical sentences* and *Present, past and perfect tense*. Alford tackles thorny grammatical issues, some of which are to this day still fretted over by purists, but with a gentle touch and carefully worded explanations that show understanding of the complexities of context, for example, on *different to* versus *different from* (p. 176) and on preposition-stranding (pp. 147–50).

White's (1871) manual (here referred to in the fifth edition of 1882) is unlike Alford's in that it has fewer headings and is a set of essays rather than a reference book, but it is significant as an expression of its era. White sees the principle of reason as being what correctness should be based on, and he does not defer to the authority of great writers (p. v). He clearly states that the book is not aimed at scholars and philologists, nor at 'the unintelligent and entirely uninstructed', but rather to 'intelligent, thoughtful, educated persons, who are interested in the study of the English language, and the protection of it against pedants on the one side and coarse libertines in language on the other' (p. 7). What one notices most in White's arguments is the rejection of a Latin-based description of English, seen in his dismissal of terms such as *auxiliary verb* or *passive voice*, and in his conclusion that English has just one voice, two tenses and one variant noun-case (p. 317), albeit his counterarguments are at times tortuous.

These two earlier works have things in common that set a framework for the works of the Fowler brothers. Both books are aimed at an educated, professional but non-academic public, are written in accessible styles; Alford and White's work can be seen as representing modern approaches to grammar and rejecting many of the strictures of earlier grammarians. Both refer to correspondence received from outsiders who have informed their texts. The two works arose from, and were suited to, societies that had become more democratised, where education in general and an interest in and need for a knowledge of grammar were reaching ever-wider audiences. The Fowler brothers issued their books in that same cultural context.

The King's English (1906, referred to here in the second edition of 1922) was jointly authored by the Fowler brothers. We note again the phrase *King's/Queen's English*, which was still in widespread use, and which cloaks a particular view of usage with an invisible authority, unassailable and unifying, like the monarchy itself. The Fowlers offer their manual as bypassing the daunting comprehensiveness of big reference grammars; their book will not dwell on rules that are 'seldom or never broken' but will focus on 'all blunders that observation shows to be common' (p. iii). Blunders include examples of errors of case-marking in pronouns, owing, in their opinion, to the very fact that English has lost most of its case-endings! *Between you and I* (as opposed to *between you and me*) is considered 'a bad blunder'. They are less condemnatory of forms such as *It is me* (rather than *It is I*) and *Who do you mean?* (instead of *Whom do you mean?*) but only tolerate them in conversation, not formal writing. Other major sources of error include lack of concord between compound subjects and their verbs, comparatives and superlatives, split infinitives and the punctuation of defining and non-defining relative clauses – all matters that continue to exercise the public, as I know from my experience of Q & A sessions in the talks that I give on grammar and usage to lay audiences of native and expert users of English.

The King's English was followed by the monumental *A Dictionary of Modern English Usage* (1926), authored by Henry Fowler alone (but dedicated to his brother, who passed away before it was finally written). Here I refer to my own, prized copy of the first edition. The first edition of the dictionary remained in print until 1965, and as recently as 2015, Oxford University Press published a fourth edition (Butterfield, 2015), which is a testimony to its staggering popularity. The dictionary bears that rare distinction of being commonly referred to by the surname of its author, so questions such as 'What does Fowler say on the subject?' or 'Fowler agrees' are a mark of its deep rootedness in the popular consciousness. Yet we should not be carried away: although a wider public had become engaged with grammar at the time that the Fowler brothers wrote their work, the use of theirs and similar manuals was, and still is, largely a middle- and upper-class occupation. Nonetheless, the appeal of Fowler remains: it is alphabetical, gets to the heart of the very questions that its readers are interested in, as opposed to trying to describe the whole language, and it gives advice on how and whether or not to use features of English, especially those aspects of grammar likely to cause insecurity in its users. What is more, Butterfield (2015: ix) states that it is wrong to think of Fowler as an ardent prescriptivist who laid down 'cast-iron rules to be adhered to absolutely'.

The notion of 'usage', as in Fowler's dictionary title, encompasses vocabulary and pronunciation as well as grammar. The grammars of centuries before Fowler had also indirectly embraced vocabulary (centring as they did on the word) and, as we have seen in the previous chapters, covered wider topics such as poetry and rhetoric. It is only relatively recently that 'grammar' narrowed down its focus to matters of syntax and morphology, and, for many members of the public, grammar still has that wider meaning which includes word-choice, spelling, punctuation and pronunciation. In the manuals of which Fowler is the epitome, 'usage' is the term that covers all those popular anxieties about how to express oneself correctly. In among the thousands of individual word entries in Fowler we find plentiful advice on grammatical appropriacy. The lengthy six-page entry on *that* as a relative pronoun alongside *who* and *which* (where Fowler distinguishes sensibly between written and spoken usage) is a good example of his acceptance of the lack of morphological neatness: *who* has two possessive forms – *whose* and *of whom*, while *which* has only one – *of which*, and relative *that* has none. Such matters, for Fowler, deserve detailed discussion. And no manual of usage would be complete without tackling the perennial question of 'stranded' prepositions. Fowler devotes a lengthy section of nearly two whole densely printed pages to the debate. He refers to the common belief that English prepositions must come before the word that they govern as a 'cherished superstition' (p. 457) and correctly lays the blame for it at the door of 'Latinism' (p. 458). Here and in other matters of grammatical debate, Fowler gives numerous examples from the great names of English writing where authors have apparently broken some oft-quoted 'rule'. All in all, Fowler's approach to grammar is evidence-based, but carrying on the tradition of using the texts of great writers to back up his statements.

Grammar and usage manuals stand in contrast to the big comprehensive 'scientific' reference grammars that were put out from the time of Henry Sweet, whose work we discussed in the previous chapter. The two types of books represent two worlds: one the concerned, educated public, eager to speak and write correctly according to the standards laid out by authors like the Fowlers, the other representing the academic world, speaking to the academic community of professors and their students and basing their architecture on historical and scientific knowledge. This latter type is interesting not only from the point of view of their content but also who wrote them.

4.3 The outsider's perspective: reference grammars and language learning

In reflecting on major English grammars published around that time, a reviewer identified only as A. G. K. wrote in 1928:

> 'It is somewhat humiliating to have to admit that most of these great grammatical collections of English have been made by foreign scholars working in the special field of English'.
>
> *(A. G. K. 1928: 335)*

With the more cosmopolitan attitudes towards the ownership of English in the present day, we might be inclined to feel delighted rather than humiliated that non-native expert users of English should devote their energies to its description. And English is not alone in receiving the generous attention of expert non-native users. When I studied Spanish at university in the late 1960s, our indispensable manual of grammar was one by Lewis Charles Harmer and Frederick John Norton, two decidedly non-Spanish names (Harmer and Norton, 1935). This is not a minor point: the perspective of the 'outsider', together with careful evidence-based analysis, will match and often trump the introspection of the native user. We have already mentioned Rask in chapter 3; in this section we explore further our immense debt to non-native expert-user grammarians.

While grammar manuals of the type described in the previous section were enjoying popularity among non-specialist users, the trend towards greater scientific and historically based grammars epitomised by that of Sweet continued. In earlier centuries, a historical approach typically meant citing the great Latin and Greek writers of antiquity in support of the establishment of rules for a language such as English. However, in the last part of the 19th century and the first part of the 20th century, the new, scientific approach was concerned with the evolution of languages and, in the case of English, a desire to explain its character not just in terms of classical influences but in its evolution from Old English through to the present day.

It is in this context that we see European non-native expert users of English making major contributions to the study of English grammar. Foremost among them was the Danish linguist Otto Jespersen (1860–1943). Jespersen is best known for his monumental English grammar published in seven meticulously detailed volumes (Jespersen, 1909–40). One of his other works, *Growth and Structure of the English Language* (Jespersen, 1905) gives us a good summary of his views on English and the writing of grammar in its preface, where he says that his book is an attempt 'to write at once popularly and so as to be of some profit to the expert philologist' (p. iii), although 'popularly' here is somewhat stretching the scope of the word. Jespersen argues that it is wrong 'to expect usage to be guided always by strictly logical principles' (p. 12). He emphasises the flexibility of English, reflected in the ability of a collective noun such as *family* to take a singular or plural verb, depending on how the speaker sees it (p. 14) and in the proclivity of words to hop around different grammatical classes (p. 15), citing examples such as 'his then residence' (adverb used as adjective) and 'a stay-at-home man' (clause used as an adjective). Jespersen discusses widely the Scandinavian influences on English, for example, the freedom to place prepositions clause-finally and to omit relative *that* (p. 81–2). These points are reinforced by a long list of great English writers who have demonstrated such freedom and flexibility and who have defied Latin logic in their usage.

Jespersen (1905: 205) also tracks the emergence over time of various grammatical forms in English: the progressive (continuous) verb aspect forms were not fully developed even at the time of William Shakespeare (1564–1616), and as the range of aspect forms increased, so the use of moods (e.g. the subjunctive) decreased, while the use of auxiliary *do* in negative and interrogative verb phrases was not fully established in the modern way until the 18th century. These are not minor details. They remind us that features of present-day grammar that we as applied linguists and language teachers might consider to be absolutely basic and fundamental were at one time not in existence and could, one day, be gone with the wind. The historical evidence of the fluidity of grammar poses a challenge not only for lay perceptions that grammar must, in some sense be permanent, logical and encoded in a set of unchanging rules, but also for the notion of a static grammar, loaded *a priori* with its features, which we shall see came under criticism from those who espouse an 'emergent' view of grammar (see chapter 6). Fluidity also has implications for a grammatical canon in language pedagogy – the consensus that authors, publishers, curriculum designers and other stakeholders adhere to with regard to what should be in the grammar syllabus and how it should be described. The stability and reliability or otherwise of the English language teaching canon is a question to which we return in chapter 8.

Another important work by Jespersen is his book *The Philosophy of Grammar* (Jespersen, 1924). In it he asserts the primary status of the spoken language, stating that 'writing is only a substitute for speaking' (p. 17). He also makes a distinction between *formulas* and *free expressions* (pp. 18–24) – a precursor of the present-day distinction to which many of us adhere between what Sinclair (1991) called the *idiom principle* versus the *open choice principle*, wherein the central role of unanalysable chunks in communication is demonstrated with numerous examples from corpora. Jespersen also discusses at some length the idea of universal grammar (pp. 46–52), which is a theme that has waxed and waned in grammatical thinking over many centuries. In short, Jespersen's grammar was a true precursor to our present-day approaches.

Another non-native expert user, the Dutch linguist Hendrik Poutsma (1856–1937), although not a university academic, produced a massive four-volume grammar of English (Poutsma, 1904–26), the subtitle of which designated it 'For the Use of Continental, Especially Dutch, Students'. It is an example of a tradition of continental European grammars of English for use in tertiary-level educational contexts which continued throughout the 20th century. Poutsma breaks from the traditional format of dealing with words and their inflexions (accidence) before going on to syntax and instead goes straight into sentences, starting with the sentence elements and their meanings. In his preface to the first volume (here referred to in the second, much revised edition of 1928), he makes a distinction found in many other grammarians' works: 'It has been my constant endeavour to distinguish carefully between different forms of diction: i.e. between those occurring in literary, poetic, ordinary, colloquial, and vulgar language' (1928: vi). His sources of evidence included not only literary and scientific works but also newspapers and periodicals. We should not underestimate the immense and time-consuming work with which the great grammarians of the past marshalled their evidence to support their descriptions and prescriptions in an era before ours, where we enjoy the luxury of computerised corpora, the searchable internet and the global digital environment. Unlike Jespersen's historical narrative that takes its reader back to Old English, Poutsma focuses on the evidence of the era just prior to his own and claims to have 'shaken off the trammels of Latin grammar' (p. ix). He also tells us that he has, in the second edition, withdrawn the statement that the book is aimed at continental European and Dutch students because students as far afield as Japan and the USA would seem to have benefitted from his work. We glimpse here an emerging English language teaching (ELT) context that has grown into the worldwide teaching and textbook industry that many readers of this book have been, are or will one day be involved in.

Poutsma's descriptions resonate with present-day approaches in that he focuses on meaning and function as well as form. On the verbs *seem* and *appear*, for example, he argues that they are more like modals than copular verbs, as they express the speaker's attitude towards an event or state (p. 4) – a view of modality that re-emerged in the latter part of the 20th century with the advent of language corpora (Holmes 1983; Stubbs 1986). As regards sentence structure, we travel through familiar territory of declarative, interrogative and imperative types. Poutsma's language has a friendly tone; witness his description of the function of end-weighting in the clause: 'The best way of throwing any element of the sentence into particular relief is to give it end-position', and on fronting: 'Another way of giving prominence to whatever is uppermost in our minds is to mention it the first thing in the sentence' (p. 377). We have come a long way from the learned grammars of the 18th and 19th centuries.

Yet another Dutch linguist, Etsko Kruisinga (1875–1944), provided an external observer's enduring description of English grammar. The second volume of his four-volume 1909–19 *Handbook*, dealing with inflexions and syntax (Kruisinga, 1911, here referred to in the fifth edition of 1931) is once again strikingly familiar to us as present-day readers. As with Poutsma, we have an approach that does not go into historical origins and which quotes sentences from newspapers and spoken utterances of native speakers jotted down by the author. This underscores at once the admixture of novelty and familiarity of Kruisinga's book for 21st-century students of grammar. Kruisinga announces his grammar as being one of 'standard British English', which he modifies in the face of obvious variations within that term to 'common English' (1931: ix). This common English accommodates spoken forms and colloquialisms, but Kruisinga devotes a separate and special section to literary constructions. The second volume of the *Handbook* in the edition which I refer to here is devoted to the verb, which Kruisinga sees as being at the very heart of English grammar (1931: 505). Apart from terms such as *preterite* (which for Kruisinga has two functions – expressing past time and as a modal meaning), *stem* (base form of the verb) and *oblique case* (objective), which have fallen out of use in much present-day language pedagogy, and for which Kruisinga provides very clear definitions and examples, we are presented with familiar headings. These include the -*ing* and -*ed* forms, present tense, prepositional object, aspect, auxiliaries (which includes detailed discussions of modal verbs such as *can, may, must* extending over many pages), progressive, and so on. In Kruisinga's work, as in Poutsma's, we are in the presence of a modern grammar based on a broad range of written and spoken evidence, and one that can be of great assistance to learners of English as a foreign language.

These non-native expert users' insights into English grammar certainly did not end in the middle of the 20th century. In the 1940s Zandvoort's *A Handbook of English Grammar* was published (Zandvoort, 1945). It ran to 15 editions and was used widely in universities in its Dutch homeland and abroad right up to about 1970. Aarts (1987) describes it as a traditional and conventional grammar and lists some of its shortcomings, but nonetheless it can be singled out for its convenience of use, running to a mere 350 pages compared with the gigantic works discussed above, and its accessibility, which has been put down to its conservative approach (Dobbie, 1949). Zandvoort lists the works he is indebted to in his handbook; these include books by Jespersen, Kruisinga, Poutsma, C. C. Fries, Harold Palmer and

Sweet, revealing a continuity of thought and shared perspectives through to his own time. Zandvoort starts straight off with the verb, describing the various forms (infinitive, gerund, etc.), the tenses, mood and modality. After nouns, pronouns, adjectives and adverbs, he then goes into sentence structure and word order. Just over a decade after its publication, Quirk (1958: 448) noted that Zandvoort's grammar: 'has become thoroughly established far beyond Holland, and it is probably the most important grammar of English as a foreign language for university use in north-west Europe'.

Non-native grammarians have made and continue to make huge contributions to the description and pedagogy of English grammar. It is by no means defensible to assert that native users are best placed to observe the grammar of their own language. And when we enter the era of corpus linguistics towards the end of the 20th century, we find non-native expert users still at the forefront, with linguists such as the Scandinavians Jan Svartvik and Stig Johansson playing a part in the authorship of major reference and pedagogical grammars of English.

4.4 Grammar for English language teaching

English grammars had, for centuries, been a mix of works of scholarship for the educated public and practical manuals for use in schools and universities. We have also seen, in previous chapters, how the dominance of Latin as a model for English was challenged, with a growing belief that the living language should be described on its own terms and not through the lens of another, dead language. Equally, we have seen the tensions between prescriptivism and descriptivism play themselves out, with description ultimately winning the day among scholars, although prescriptivism survives in full health to this day among the wider public. Another parallel long-term debate relates to the status of the *evidence* for grammatical description or prescription, with the works of the great literary writers ceding more and more space to the evidence of newspapers and other non-literary documents, together with evidence from the spoken language. All these tensions are thoroughly explored in Mitchell (2001) under the amusing title of *Grammar Wars*. These tensions existed alongside social changes, with the rise of an enterprising middle-class intent on success and self-improvement who were to become the wider audience for grammar beyond that of the privileged grammar schools and universities. But it was not just in its native home that the teaching and learning of English grammar was on the move.

The centuries-long ebb and flow of thought and activity in grammar laid the foundations for the emergence of a profession (and ultimately a global industry) of English language teaching to speakers of other languages. Sweet had already built robust bridges between the scientific study of philology and grammar and the practicalities of language teaching, as we saw in chapter 3. The grammars of Jespersen, Poutsma and Kruisinga showed how firmly established the study and learning of English grammar was in continental Europe. Meanwhile, the spread of English had already taken place across the British Empire, as we saw in the discussion of Nesfield's grammar in chapter 3. Nonetheless, Howatt and Widdowson (2004: 235) argue that much English teaching in the British colonies was conducted as if English were the pupils' first language – quite different from the burgeoning English as a foreign language pedagogy.

Beyond Europe and the British colonial territories, Japan was one example of a thriving environment for English teaching, and it was there that Harold E. Palmer (1877–1949) carried out research into English language teaching which was greatly influential and which ushered in new approaches to the teaching of grammar. Palmer is often held to be the father of modern British applied linguistics (Stern, 1983: 100). His career, briefly interrupted by the start of the First World War, took him from being a language-school teacher and proprietor to secondary school teacher, then through more academic and professional pathways which contributed to the crystallisation of his ideas about the science of language and the science of language teaching.

One of Palmer's earliest works consisted of a manual of what we would now call slot-and-filler substitution tables, based on the notion that substituting semantically meaningful items of the same word-class for any sentence slot (e.g. the subject, the verb, an adverb, etc.) would yield a large number of correct sentences which would function as wholes (Palmer, 1916). The tables were intended to be used alongside a grammar book. But what is of equal interest is the attention given to pronouncing the sentences correctly and fluently, to which end, all the tables are given first in phonetic script. Orthography and correct spelling might only come later, says Palmer in his introduction (p. xiii). The emphasis on phonetics shows a direct line of influence from and reflects his collaboration with Sweet. It also reveals Palmer's firm belief in the primacy of the spoken language which informed all of his work. Figure 4.1 shows a typical substitution table with the first column consisting of a range of possible subjects with auxiliary *do*, the second column with adverbs and the third with verbs and objects or adverb complements. Thus, the first line (*he doesn't always do it*) can be substituted by *he doesn't really know it, she doesn't usually put it here, my friend doesn't always stay here* and more than 700 other mathematical permutations of the pattern.

The same substitution table is then presented in the orthographic section of the book (p. 60). The notion of substitution drills as a way of instilling grammar survived into the beginning of my own career as an EFL teacher in the late 1960s, when I taught with the Berlitz method; indeed, the method survived well beyond that time. Reading aloud verbatim from our Berlitz book, starting with *Is the yellow pencil long?* we would substitute *Is the black pencil long?* then *Is the long pencil yellow?* and *Is the black pencil short?* all followed by appropriate affirmative and negative answers – a challenge to maintain interest for teacher and students, although thankfully not through the medium of phonetic script (Berlitz, 1966: 10). My clear memory is that, somehow or another, the method worked, and students were soon able to create novel sentences to express their personal experiences based on the structures that they had drilled with mind-numbing dedication.

8

Table 15.
27 simple and 720 compound permutations.

	I.	II.	III.
1	hi·'dʌznt	'ɔːlweiz	'duːit.
2	ʃi·'dʌznt	'ɔːfn	'teikit.
3	dəzi·	'dʒenrəli	'siːit.
4	'dʌznti·	'juːʒuəli	'nouit.
5	'dʌzntʃi·	'riəli	ʌndə'stændit.
6	əf'kɔːsi·'dʌznt		'kiːpit.
7	'waidəzi·		bi'ginit.
8	'haudəzi·		'finiʃit.
9	mai'frend'dʌznt		fə'getit.
10	dəzjɔː'frend		ri'membərit.
11	dəzjɔː'fɑːðəʳ		'stei'hiə.
12	'waidʌzntjɔː'frend		'putit'hiə.

FIGURE 4.1 Substitution table
(Palmer, 1916: 8)

We find out more about Palmer's views on this and other aspects of grammar teaching in his book *The Scientific Study and Teaching of Languages* (Palmer, 1917). Palmer acknowledges his debt to Sweet and Jespersen, and he tells us that when he left continental Europe with the onset of the First World War, he found in England 'abundant signs of a new spirit in the language teaching world' and a movement towards 'scientific' and 'organized' methods (p. 7). The notion of teaching being scientifically informed and organised is at the heart of Palmer's approach to grammatical description and teaching methodology, and it is a theme that found an echo on the other side of the Atlantic too. As regards the scientific study of language, Palmer refers to the contribution of philology in revealing the evolution of languages, including the insight that Latin, instead of being a 'god-given speech' was simply 'the daughter of some unknown mother' (p. 31). This is not just a humorous dig at the reverence with which Latin was regarded by many, but a challenge to its authority and relevance to a living language such as English. In a complex diagram representing his entire perspective on language teaching and learning, Palmer stresses the skill of 'catenizing' – the ability to reproduce 'with fluency and without conscious calculation the longer units of speech (e.g. phrases and sentences)' (p. 74). Such fluency is fostered and supported by spoken practice with the kinds of substitution tables that we have seen in Figure 4.1, which also enrich the learner's vocabulary, but the understanding of rapid, fluent speech, according to Palmer, is independent of any type of grammatical drill (p. 135).

To suggest that Palmer's 1916 and 1917 books adequately summarise his scholarship would be to short-change his extraordinary output. One of Palmer's basic tenets was the central role of listening and speaking in language learning, which should precede reading and writing. This influenced his view of grammar and how it should be described and taught. Around that time, the Swiss linguist Ferdinand de Saussure had introduced the notion of structuralism – that the elements of language should be understood in relation to one another in a system. De Saussure famously made a distinction between *langue* – very roughly speaking the systematic code – and *parole* – the actual realisation of language when it is used by the individual (Saussure 1916/1971: 28–40). Palmer took this idea and made it a central tenet of his approach to teaching the *use* of language rather than teaching *about* language (Smith, 2011). In his 1922 book on the oral method of teaching languages, he points out that demand for spoken English classes is growing around the world, in contrast with formal, traditional grammar, translation and reading – the usual pedagogical approaches. The oral method discouraged writing at the early stage of learning and stressed listening and speaking. It also discouraged deductive grammar (going from rules to examples) and fostered memorising and habit-forming (Palmer, 1922: 11). There was a preference for using the immediate physical environment and objects as a context for teaching grammatical structure (p. 79–81), which was also true of the Berlitz method mentioned above, and an inductive (examples before rules) approach to grammar (p. 124–5). The oral method also emphasised the importance of word-groups as opposed to focusing on single words (Lemieux, 1964). In this respect, Palmer's approach is a precursor of the importance given to chunking phenomena in the recent era of corpus linguistics. For Palmer, words formed grammatical and idiomatic groups, which were the key to efficient memorising and to fluent and natural production.

Palmer's most distinctive work is his *Grammar of Spoken English* (Palmer, 1924) – a product of his time in Tokyo. The introduction first addresses the question of distinguishing between *full words* and *form-words* (following Sweet's terminology), which would be more familiar to readers nowadays as lexical words versus grammatical or function words. English is dominated by function words rather than inflexions (of which it has few) in the expression of grammatical meanings, groups of words catenated by function words are a challenge for any learner, and a grammar for foreign learners of English is different from one for English-speaking children in English schools (p. xxviii). The formation of novel sentences is done by analogy with existing, memorised sentences, by substituting words of the right grammatical class in each of the 'slots' (subject, object, adverb, etc.), and this process of substitution must be an important one for non-native speaking learners, as we saw in Figure 4.1, above.

It is important to remember that Palmer defines his use of 'spoken English' in the title of his grammar as referring to the everyday usage of educated people (especially speakers in the south of England) in ordinary conversation or in informal, intimate letters to friends (p. xxxi). Palmer's words here pre-date the present era of emails, text messages and online postings, but we note his view that certain types of writing are more like conversation. Conversely, his definition of written English includes not only books and newspapers but 'the language of public speakers and orators, or possibly in formal conversation (more especially between strangers)' (p. xxxi). This hybrid view of speech and writing has significant implications for what might be included in a grammar for learners – a debate that I and my late friend and colleague Ron Carter became embroiled in in the 1990s. But more of that later.

Palmer (1924) divides his grammar somewhat unconventionally. Instead of a two-fold division of what was traditionally (see previous chapters) referred to as etymology (the grammar of words) and syntax (the grammar of sentences), he starts with phonetics, then the parts of speech, then parts of sentences, then what he calls logical categories – things that do not fit into the other sections, such as indirect questions, echo questions, various ways of expressing future time, reported speech and so on. Of interest is Palmer's division of conditional sentences with *if*. He distinguishes six types expressing varying degrees of condition or supposition; compare the present-day canon of the three types that seem obligatory in any ELT coursebook. However, many of Palmer's categories survive in the present-day grammatical canon subscribed to with little or no questioning by textbook authors, publishers and syllabus designers. What does not survive is the most distinctive feature of the 1924 grammar: all the examples are in phonetic script, together with intonational marking. This makes the grammar extremely difficult for anyone not fluent in reading phonetics and at the same time restricts the pronunciation of the examples to the southern English variety that Palmer takes as his model. This in some ways is a pity, as it has relegated to a secondary place in history a work that contains so many acute observations of everyday speaking, hardly surpassed until the advent of corpora began to provide statistical evidence for just such observations.

Grammar in Palmer (1924) is seen as dialogic, with descriptions not only of what speakers say but how listeners answer, for example, listener tags as in *A: I'm tired B: Are you?*, with B's response having the option of rising or falling intonation and their different meanings (p.265); in other words, it is a discourse grammar as well as being a sentence grammar. One feels that Palmer would have loved to be let loose on a large corpus of spoken English (or French, in which he was fluent); his grammar would have probably far outstripped the achievements of corpus grammarians nowadays. Palmer's grammar was detailed and thorough, but it did depend on the user being able to read phonetic script. It is hard to imagine any but the most academically oriented language learner (or teacher) nowadays rising to the challenge of reading about noun post-modification with *to*-infinitive clauses in the way shown in Figure 4.2.

In case you are not familiar with phonetic script, the first line reads 'I haven't found a place to go to', with falling intonation on *go*. The last line reads 'You surely don't think he's such a fool as to agree to that!', with a fall on *surely* and a *rise* on that.

Grammars with all the examples in phonetic script never caught on, and Palmer's work remains somewhat obscured by the history of more popular pedagogical grammars. Moreover, phonetics has generally become confined to the role of a pronunciation aid in dictionaries nowadays and often does not feature at all on language teacher training programmes. With the advent of free, online dictionaries where pronunciation can be accessed in audio form at the click of a mouse, phonetics could well retreat further beyond the mental horizons of material writers and

162   GRAMMAR OF SPOKEN ENGLISH

Group III. *Various.*
ai hævn̩t faund ə pleis tə ˈgou tuˑ.
ðæt s ə ˉdifik|t saund tə prəˈnauns.
ai v gɔt ə ˉlɔt əv ˈletəz tə rait.
hiər ə səm ˈbuks (fɔˑ juˑ) tə riːd.
hiˑ faund ˉplenti əv ˈwəːk tə duː.
juˑ ˈʃɔˑəli dount θiŋk hiˑ z sətʃ ə fuːl əz tuˑ əgriː tə ˌðæt!

FIGURE 4.2 Post-modification of nouns with *to*-infinitive clauses
(Palmer, 1924: 162)

curriculum designers for second language and foreign language learning purposes. All this is not to say that Palmer is completely forgotten; articles on his life and work have appeared in more recent times (Tickoo, 1982; Smith, 2011), and the significance of his work has been acknowledged by those working in the field of spoken grammar and debates on the canon (e.g. Carter and McCarthy, 2017; O'Keeffe and Mark, 2018; Burton, 2019). I could not dream of writing this book without paying homage to such an independent-minded pioneer.

4.5 Structuralism: linguistic science meets the science of language teaching

We have mentioned the work of Ferdinand de Saussure and the notion that language was systematically structured. The interrelated parts of a language, from its phonemes right up to its syntactic configurations and sentences were, for the structuralists, accessible through observation of actual utterances and the activity of classifying them. This was the basic premise behind Palmer's grammar. The idea was to describe a language synchronically, i.e. as it is at the time of observation, so the historical approach to grammar was seen as largely irrelevant. In the broader field of linguistics, structuralism became predominant in Europe and the USA and had a lasting influence on grammatical description, remaining generally unchallenged in theoretical linguistics until Noam Chomsky's works heralded a reaction to it. In grammar pedagogy, the structural approach lasted well into the 1970s, when the communicative approach to language teaching rose to prominence and became a largely unquestioned orthodoxy.

One of the key concepts of structuralism was the notion of paradigmatic and syntagmatic relations among language elements (whether phonemes, morphemes, words), such that the initial phonemes in *sit, bit* and *hit* in English distinguish three words in a phonological set. In lexis, *red, blue, yellow, green*, etc. distinguish items in the lexical set 'colours'. These are paradigmatic choices. But we also string together items in sets according to rules and conventions, such that *I have a new car* is permissible in English but not **I have a car new*. These are syntagmatic choices. This notion of continuous choice within the language systems is the basis of systemic functional linguistics, whose foremost advocate was Michael Halliday (Halliday 1978, 1985, 2007; Halliday and Mathiessen, 2004) and which we examine in greater detail in chapter 5.

In the USA, Leonard Bloomfield was a major figure in the development of structuralism. He was influenced in the formation of his ideas by the grammar of the ancient Hindu scholar of the Sanskrit language, Pāṇini (e.g. Bloomfield, 1927), whose work we reviewed in chapter 2, where we noted the extraordinary reach of Pāṇini's influence over more than two millennia. Bloomfield and others advocated – and carried out – extensive fieldwork into lesser-studied and unstudied languages which did not enjoy the privileged codification in grammars and dictionaries that the major world languages did. This, added to the lack of written evidence for many of the languages under investigation, meant that a historical approach was usually impossible (Koerner, 1970).

In both the USA and the United Kingdom, grammar teaching based on structuralist notions was common practice. Indeed, structuralism could be said to represent the coming of age of the relationship between thinking about language and thinking about language teaching that had begun with figures such as Sweet and Palmer. In the USA, a programme was initiated to cope with the urgent language demands of the armed forces during the Second World War. This took the form of intensive, structure-based courses, with an emphasis on speaking and for the learning of foreign languages spoken in the various theatres of war, and this was one of the reasons why structuralism took such a firm hold in foreign language teaching (Richards and Rodgers, 2014: 58–9).

Alongside the military programmes, Charles Carpenter Fries at the University of Michigan published two important works that demonstrated the twin preoccupations of the applied structuralists: best practice in teaching the language and how to adequately describe it for that purpose (Fries 1945, 1952). Marckwardt (1968: 205) notes that Fries began his work at a time when 'school textbooks, generation after generation, had simply parroted a series of rules which were strongly suspect as far as any basis in fact was concerned'. In the preface to his book *Teaching and Learning English as a Foreign Language* (Fries, 1945), we find a statement of his purpose: 'to interpret, in a practical way for teaching, the principles of modern linguistic science and to use the results of scientific linguistic research' (para. 1). He cites Bloomfield in support of the claim that schoolteachers know nothing of the results of linguistic research (para. 2). He goes on to say that the principles of teaching English as a foreign language expounded in his book can be applied to the teaching of any foreign language, and just as EFL teachers need to be aware of the different first languages of their students, so the English teacher teaching English as a native language needs to know about English; the ability to speak it is not enough (para. 8). Fries takes the classic structuralist path of dealing with phonetics and pronunciation first, then moving to grammatical structure. His 1945 book includes sample English conversations for practice of pronunciation and intonation, with a two-column layout, a left-hand column in phonetic script and the same sentences in a right-hand column in ordinary orthography. The students cover the right-hand column while they listen to and imitate the teacher (Fries, 1945: 79). The principle is one of habit-forming and is applied to grammatical patterns too, which Fries elaborates as 'making automatic the use of the devices of arrangement and form' (1945: chapter III), which is the approach advocated by Palmer.

Fries's 1952 work is also significant in the evolution of grammar in foreign and second language pedagogy. Fries recorded 50 hours of telephone conversations involving some 300 speakers and totalling about 250,000 words to provide evidence for his account of the structure of English: an example of corpus linguistics *avant la lettre*. Once again, the evidence is on grammatical patterns, recurring structures or 'sames' as he calls them (Fries, 1952: viii). His purpose is to provide a scientific basis for grammar teaching for those who have rejected traditional grammar but who have nothing to replace it with. He stresses that his description of English is a description of how his native-speaking informants really use the language, not how authorities think they should (p. 3). He does, however, introduce the caveat that the study of vulgar English, although a matter of scientific importance, should not be taken to mean that it should be substituted for the grammar of standard English (p. 5). The status of the grammar of the ordinary people continued to have low or no priority in the minds of grammarians, and at this point in history it seems that the language of the uneducated masses still does not get a look in, just as in classical antiquity.

Nonetheless, *The Structure of English* is a remarkable work. By basing his work on spoken evidence, Fries understands that the 'sentence' is a difficult concept to apply. He prefers instead the term 'utterance unit' (1952: 23) to describe a stretch of speech bounded by pauses: they are 'chunks of talk that are marked off by a shift of speaker' (ibid.). The marking of utterances on transcripts of conversations instead of sentence boundaries yields evidence about the types of expressions that can stand alone – minimal free utterances that can constitute an utterance unit in themselves or expansions and combinations of free utterances (p. 37). Such utterance units include listener responses: for example, minimal response tokens such as *yes* and *no*, single words and short phrases, as well as things that look more sentence-like in the traditional sense (pp. 45–53). This is revolutionary grammar in terms of the pedagogical domain – as radical and innovative as that of Palmer; both grammarians offer us what we would now call a grammar of discourse. It is, therefore, not a complete picture of applied structuralism to suggest that it was just concerned with habit-forming and drilling of surface patterns at the expense of context or meaning.

Structuralism dominated grammar teaching for a long time. In my first job as an English language teacher in Spain in the mid-1960s I taught using structuralism's methodology and materials, although at the time I had no idea that I was doing so. Most of us in the profession had come through the Modern Languages route at universities or had qualifications in English literature. It was the era before training programmes for EFL teachers, and all that was required of me was to be a native speaker of English, to deliver the carefully graded drills in the textbook, to correct mistakes, to smile and to present a generally respectable and pleasing image to my students and to pick up my pay packet at the end of each month.

4.6 Berlitz, James Joyce and me

In 1966 I became a grammar teacher. I did not think of that as my principle role when I started as a full-time teacher of English at a Berlitz school in Spain. However, I soon realised that much of the time spent in teaching the carefully controlled material in the coursebook was devoted to getting my students to repeat grammatical patterns flawlessly, substituting different items of the strictly controlled vocabulary into the same grammar slots over and over again and correcting some of the weird and incorrect utterances that they occasionally produced. I had behind me a secondary-school education in traditional formal grammar taught to me by an excellent schoolmaster, but I rarely if ever needed to resort to the terminology of predicates, inflexions and moods. And probably thanks to the combination of my youthful enthusiasm and the materials that demanded nothing of me other than to deliver them, my students learnt to express themselves quite adequately in reasonably correct and intelligible spoken English.

The founder of the Berlitz schools, Maximilian Berlitz (1852–1921), set in motion a massive enterprise for the teaching of foreign languages based on the structural-oral method, where listening and speaking preceded reading and writing and where exclusive use of the target language in the classroom was paramount. The Berlitz approach was to shun formal grammar and its terminology, most especially in the initial stages of language learning, and to instil grammatical patterns through the direct, oral method, utilising the immediate environment and objects to hand to demonstrate meaning, and a controlled, graded vocabulary. Translation was strictly forbidden. Grammar was discussed only when sufficiently automated use of such things as inflexions and verb conjugations had already been thoroughly drilled. Reading passages were included in the manuals and were there for extensive reading, with no overt new matter for the student to learn. By the 1950s there were Berlitz language schools in 22 countries in Europe and beyond, and the Berlitz course books had been translated into 42 different languages (Stieglitz 1955). The Berlitz organisation represents one of the first examples of the international, private language school industry through which millions have learnt and continue to learn English and other foreign languages. Thus, its methods and achievements cannot be shunted off to the margins of our professional history, despite the fact that its approach and philosophy were never fully expounded in the same academic way that Sweet, Palmer and Fries elaborated theirs.

The great Irish writer James Joyce was a Berlitz teacher for a time during his sojourn in several European countries in the first two decades of the 20th century (Bowker, 2011). I have little else in common with Joyce, except that we both found the Berlitz method rather restrictive and mind-numbing in its adherence to systematic delivery from the teacher, with no licence to expand creatively or spontaneously, especially at the elementary levels. Joyce was known to depart from the rigid script in his classes (Gottfried, 1979), as did I, but I always did it with a feeling of trepidation and spoke in a lowered voice, lest my boss would pass by the room and hear me chatting with the students. And just by the way, the Berlitz method and his teaching experience of it has been seen by Joycean scholars as subtly influencing his great literary work *Ulysses* (Switaj, 2013).

Howatt (2004: 226) makes the point that the most important Berlitz customers were evening-class students who came from a range of backgrounds. My own experience bears that out. It was another step in the democratisation of grammar. My students were not the university students who would doggedly work their way through the extensive, learned European grammars of Poutsma, Kruisinga and Zandvoort; they were professionals, members of the public desirous of travel and encountering new cultures and language-hobbyists. Maximilian Berlitz was an innovator in that his schools epitomised the new global industry of private language establishments which still serves us well today and in which countless EFL teachers have cut their teeth. The simplicity of his method and the immediate teachability of his materials enabled non-specialists (like me) to teach foreign languages to a non-academic public that did not have to wrestle with the arcane world of gerunds and subjunctives.

We conclude this section with two extracts from the constant companion of my first teaching job, the *Berlitz English First Book*. The first extract is a presentation that illustrates the pattern practice that was at the heart of Berlitz grammar, this time for a set of three prepositions of location, with sentences that could easily be enacted in the immediate classroom environment, with the teacher announcing the statements and asking the questions, and the students answering:

> On, under, in
>
> The brown box is *on* the table, the red book is *under* the table, the yellow card is *in* the box.
>
> Is the brown box on the table? Is the red book under the table? Is the yellow card in the box?
>
> Is the pencil on the chair. No, it is not. Is it on the blackboard? No, it is not. Where is the pencil? It is in the book. Where is the box? Where is the book? etc......
>
> (Berlitz, 1966: 12. Italics as in the original)

The second extract is from a typical reading passage, which the students would read for further practice in the vocabulary and structures that they had already drilled in systematic fashion in the previous lessons. The subject matter here is shopping for an umbrella in a department store in London. Note the final instruction to the student to repeat their part in the conversation.

When you arrive at the umbrella counter you say: I should like to see some umbrellas, please. I should like a silk umbrella. Is this a good one? Is the other one better? Is this silk a good quality? What is the price of this one? How much is this one? How much does that one cost? I'll take this one.' (Repeat what you may have to say when you buy an umbrella).

(Berlitz, 1966: 124)

We react to this nowadays as quaint and pedagogically dull at the same time and from a world long past, when elegant silk umbrellas were desirable, and tacky, plastic, retractable ones had not been invented. However, we should not sneer at previous generations' attempts at recreating what were then perceived as useful situations for students to practice their grammar and speaking. Despite its now outdated methodology and (to us) quirky content, the Berlitz system worked. Future generations will undoubtedly look upon our present-day materials with equal bemusement and wonder how anyone ever survived them and learnt any grammar at all.

4.7 New technologies, great events

During the course of this book we have seen how technologies have influenced the evolution of grammar and grammar pedagogy. Not least, the invention of writing systems in ancient societies meant that ideas could be recorded with a degree of permanence, whether on stone, wood, papyrus, parchment or paper (recall the wooden tablet for practising Greek grammar on p. xx). The later invention of printing meant not only that ideas could be disseminated to a wide audience, but also that those in power could mandate the use of particular books for the study of grammar, with a consequential push towards standardisation. By the end of the 19th century, a growing market for school and university grammars and manuals of usage had created an ever-expanding industry of grammar publishing.

The development of audio and audiovisual technology prompted the next significant revolution in grammar pedagogy. Three related innovations stand out: sound recording on gramophone records and magnetic tape, the advent of radio and television broadcasting and advances in photography and film. When I went back to university to train as a language teacher and studied phonetics in the mid-1970s, we listened to the phonetician Daniel Jones reciting the cardinal vowels on scratchy old 78rpm records and repeated the sounds until we had learnt to articulate them properly. That was a technology that was at the time already well out of date but one that, when it first became available, was a boon to language teaching. Harold Palmer, for instance, saw the value in using gramophone records in his aural/oral method of teaching spoken language (Smith, 1999: 131). Meanwhile, the advent of film, radio and television broadcasting had a unifying and levelling effect across countries where many local varieties existed and gave another nudge towards standardisation. And events had their effect on what people were exposed to. During the First World War, men speaking different varieties of English were thrown together in the horrors of the trenches; during the Second World War in the United Kingdom, the contrasts among varieties were accentuated by the mass evacuation of children from the cities to the countryside. In that climate, Compton (1941: vi) advocated training young people to speak in an 'easy, clear, reasonably exact, and friendly' way, and Trueblood (1933) viewed the spread of spoken mass media as something that could promote 'good' speech in the general population.

With the urgent need to train military personnel in foreign languages during wartime and the subsequent Cold War, demand for foreign language training had increased and the use of audio technology became more common in the USA, leading to the advent of the language laboratory. Language laboratories sprang up in the post-war years such that, by 1957 more than 60 secondary schools in the USA had them for the teaching of French, Spanish, German, Italian, Latin and Russian (Oberhelman, 1960), and more than 800 existed in US universities in the early 1960s; by the same time, the number of language laboratories in US secondary schools had topped 5,000 (Schaafsma, 1968). Prakken (1964) argues that it was not the invention of audio technology in itself that led to the enthusiasm for language laboratories; rather it was the existence of a 'language conscious public' (p. 301) and a publishing industry that harnessed and sold the technology, which was another example of grammar widening its scope beyond the universities and schools and occupying a place in the public marketing of foreign languages.

Language laboratories were an ideal technology for promoting the structuralist approach to grammar and the audiolingual approach in general: listening, repeating, drilling and using strictly controlled material were all possible in the laboratory booth where the student, wearing headphones, could individually control the tape-machine and the extent and timing of practice in a non-public environment. The labs served a dual purpose: they met the structuralists' requirement of an emphasis on spoken input and pronunciation, listening and absorbing the language before reading or writing it, and at the same time they offered the opportunity for pattern practice, with the student repeating and drilling targeted structures. Stack (1960), for example, gives examples of aural/oral grammar pattern practice for learners of French, English, German, Russian and Spanish.

In the late 1960s, while studying French as part of my university degree, I was sent to the language lab to improve my poor pronunciation. I spent long hours listening and responding to quite boring drills with no teacher present. I am not sure that I learnt anything or improved greatly, as I was not good at evaluating my own performance. The question for me as a student and for many a scholar and researcher at that time was: are language laboratories an efficient and effective way of teaching and learning languages? Commentators certainly argued that they were no substitute for live, face-to-face teachers, that the lonely student was ill equipped to be their own tutor and monitor, but also, on the positive side, they argued that they liberated time for the teacher to devote to more intensive work on grammar, essay-writing, etc. in class (Pimsleur, 1959; Kirch, 1963). Most were agreed that classroom time and lab time should be integrated and serve the same ultimate goals: grammar drills could be done in the lab, while discussion of grammar would best take place in class, which was an early manifestation of the 'flipped classroom' of recent models of blended learning.

Pimsleur (1959) argued strongly for the role of the language laboratory in grammar teaching: a grammar point studied in class could be practised orally in the lab, saving a huge amount of time compared with writing sentences in class. The assimilation of grammar, he argued, could take place more efficiently without the distraction of spelling. This debate on the relationship between in-class and out-of-class learning was set to re-surface with the arrival of blended and online learning in the early part of the 21st century (McCarthy, 2016). As with so much else in the field of grammar theory, description and pedagogy, the same preoccupations come back to challenge us, and we should never fool ourselves that we are the first to engage with them. 'Innovation' so often seems to mean 'renovation'.

By the mid-1960s the effectiveness of the language laboratory was being questioned. Green (1965: 369) reported 'strong under-currents of skepticism and incipient disenchantment among language teachers vis-à-vis the language laboratory', and by the late 1970s they were certainly falling out of fashion. The laboratories ultimately morphed into the Language Centres that we see today in schools, colleges and universities, where the technology is focused around computer screens and online and blended work, with more possibilities for class (under the teacher's control), as well as individual study. And even more recently, fixed terminals have been replaced by mobile devices which allow even greater independence and flexibility.

That was the 1960s. The fact that my grammar teaching was mainstream structuralist did not mean that the profession had not changed at all since the Second World War; it was just that I, and probably many like me, had no knowledge of the applied linguistics world or of any theories of grammar, nor were we expected to. In the next chapter we consider how the post-war period brought new developments in the worlds of linguistics and language teaching, and how innovative thinking gradually changed how grammar was taught and later led to a new emphasis and new ideas on how it was acquired by first and second-language learners. At the same time, the English language teaching industry moved towards capturing a global market.

5
INNOVATION
Major new grammatical theories

5.1 Noam Chomsky and his grammar

While J. R. Firth dominated linguistic study in the United Kingdom in the 1950s, an influence that continued into the 1960s and beyond (see 5.7), on the other side of the Atlantic, in the figure of Noam Chomsky, a fundamentally new and different approach to grammar was emerging. At the very same time that Firth was elaborating a theory of grammar which was firmly embedded in context and meaning, Chomsky was elaborating one in which context and meaning played no part. Chomsky's influence was massive in the USA and beyond, and it is impossible to understand how a particular type of second language acquisition (SLA) study emerged and developed without taking account of his work.

Chomsky's first work, *Syntactic Structures* (Chomsky, 1957) is not an easy read, but it repays careful attention to its main points. In its introduction, he lays out what he believes to be the purpose of a grammar, i.e. to provide a general method that will be valid for any language and which will generate all and only all of the grammatical sentences of a given language and none of the non-grammatical ones. The quest is purely formal, concerned with syntax. The native speaker of English can recognise that, although meaningless in relation to any reality, the sentence 'Colorless green ideas sleep furiously' is nonetheless recognisable as conforming to the *grammar* of English sentences, while 'Furiously sleep ideas green colorless' is both meaningless and ungrammatical (Chomsky, 1957: 15). The native speaker of a language is endowed with knowledge of the rules of the grammar of that language independently of any other aspect of language knowledge (e.g. lexis, phonology, etc.). What informs such knowledge is a universal feature of all languages, and Chomsky states that his interest is in 'the general nature of language' (p. 14). Here we see the centuries-old notion of universal grammar discussed in previous chapters coming to the fore again: the grammar of any individual language will be based on observations of the corpus of grammatical sentences of that language, but the set of all such grammars will comply with a universal theory.

Chomsky considers various possible ways of constructing grammars, from purely linear accounts, which he demonstrates simply do not work, to phrase structure and the breaking-up of sentences into their constituent parts, and he shows the limitations of that method. A typical phrase structure for a simple sentence would divide it into a noun phrase (NP) and a verb phrase (VP), where VP includes the verb and any objects or complements. Thus, a sentence such as *The teacher marked the essays* could be depicted in two ways:

Sentence
  NP + VP
  T + NP + VP
  T + NP + Verb + NP
  The + N + Verb + NP
  The + teacher + Verb + NP
  The + teacher + marked + NP
  The + teacher + marked + T + NP
  The + teacher + marked + the + N
  The + teacher + marked + the + essays
(my own sentence, after Chomsky, 1957: 27)

Each successive line of the process 'rewrites' the previous line until we reach the realisation of the actual sentence. Another way of looking at the same sentence is the familiar tree-diagram (Figure 5.1):

What we can see in this diagram is that the string *marked the essays* can be related back to *Verb + NP* and thence to *VP* and *Sentence*, but we cannot do the same for the adjacent words *teacher marked*, which are not a constituent of the sentence structure.

```
                        Sentence
                       /        \
                     NP           VP
                    /  \         /  \
                   T    N      Verb  NP
                   |    |       |    |
                  The teacher  marked the essays
```

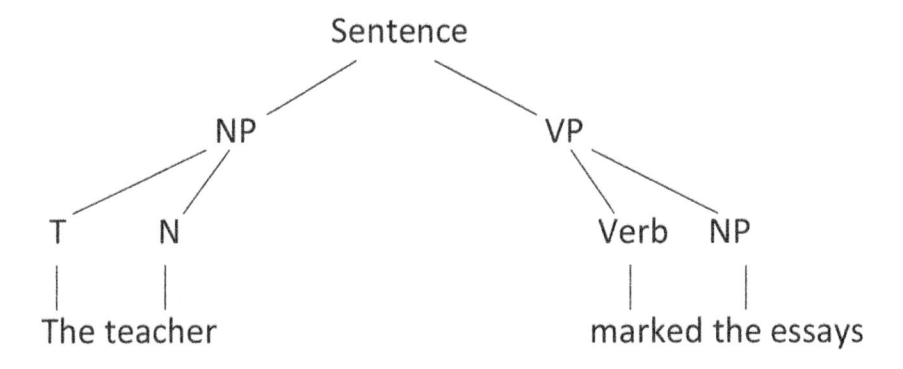

FIGURE 5.1 Phrase structure tree-diagram

5.2 Transformations

However, phrase structure procedures and diagrams such as Figure 5.1 cannot easily account for discontinuous relationships. Chomsky gives the example sentence 'the scene of the movie and of the play was in Chicago' (p. 35), where the receiver knows that *the play* has the same relationship to *the scene* as *the movie* does. The other problem that Chomsky discusses is the relationship between active and passive sentences. *The teacher marked the essays*, although it consists structurally of NP + Verb + NP, cannot be reversed to *The essays marked the teacher*, but has to undergo certain obligatory changes to produce the grammatically correct passive: *The essays were marked by the teacher* (NP + auxiliary + -*en* form of main verb + *by* + NP). Chomsky refers to this process of changes as a means to exclude the passive voice elements from phrase structure and instead 'reintroduce them by a rule', which states that if our original active voice sentence is grammatical, then a corresponding sentence adhering to the passive voice rules is also grammatical. Changes in form such as active to passive voice are 'grammatical transformations' (p. 44), hence the name *transformational grammar* (hereafter, TG). The passive voice, together with various other complex structures that Chomsky exemplifies in *Syntactic Structures*, are optional transformations, while the rules that create the sentences from which they are derived account for *kernel sentences* (p. 45), i.e. simple, declarative, active voice sentences with no complex verb or noun phrases (p. 107), which are the core of the language:

> 'Thus every sentence of the language will either belong to the kernel or will be derived from the strings underlying one or more kernel sentences by a sequence of one or more transformations'.
>
> *(p. 45)*

This statement considerably simplifies the grammar: phrase structure rules are needed only for kernel sentences; all other sentences can be derived by transformations that can be stated in the grammar (pp. 47–8).

The term *kernel* might echo in the minds of an older generation of English language teachers who recall teaching using O'Neill's highly popular coursebooks in the *Kernel Lessons* series published in the early 1970s. I recall using the higher-level *Kernel Lessons Plus* (O'Neill, 1973) in the late 1970s and getting my students to 'transform' pairs of simple sentences into a single sentence involving a relative clause (sentences such as *The boy broke the window* and *The boy had to pay for the broken window* become *The boy who broke the window had to pay for it*). I had no idea at the time why the coursebook was called *Kernel*, and I had never heard of TG, but by and large both my students and I survived the exercise, and I am sure that they learnt something. Having said that, it is fair to say that TG never had much direct effect on foreign/second language teaching, nor did Chomsky ever claim that it should. In fact, O'Neill's elementary level *Kernel One* (O'Neill, 1978) is hardly distinguishable from any other slot-and-filler structural course in its grammar exercises, especially in its *Review* units (pp. 117–24).

The basic notion of TG is very persuasive: Chomsky notes that the sentences *The wine was drunk by the guests* and *John was drunk by midnight* share the same structure on the face of it, but only the first can be derived from an active voice sentence, so we can have *The guests drank the wine*, but not **Midnight drank John* (p. 80), and trying to imagine a possible world in which such a sentence could be uttered is pointless. TG is a grammar of form; Chomsky dismisses any attempt to include meaning as 'relatively useless' (p. 101), given the lack of correspondence between formal and semantic features in language. Nevertheless, there are problems that seem to be intractable with regard to a purely formal account. I am indebted to my late friend, the grammarian Amorey Gethin, who many years ago challenged me to create a passive voice equivalent of the sentence 'Everybody loves somebody'. The moment that I had 'transformed' it into 'Somebody is loved by everybody', I realised that I had created an entirely different proposition. My personal anecdote does scant justice to Gethin's trenchant criticism of the whole edifice of Chomsky's theory (Gethin, 1999).

5.3 Competence and performance

In 1959 Chomsky published a critique of the behaviourist psychologist B. F. Skinner's *Verbal Behavior* (Skinner, 1957). The title of Skinner's book and Chomsky's reaction to its contents are telling. Skinner abandons terms such as 'speech' and 'language', preferring the term 'behaviour' (Skinner, 1957: 2). Humans react to external stimuli, responses and reinforcement in ways that are analogous to how non-human animals behave in experimental settings (e.g. obtaining food rewards for carrying out particular actions), and it was the extrapolation of the experimental laboratory and observations of animal behaviour to the human world that Chomsky objected to. For Chomsky, human language ability indicates 'that there must be fundamental processes at work quite independently of "feedback" from the environment' (Chomsky, 1959: 42). To understand these processes, the grammarian's job is to search deep into the human mind for the basic, universal predispositions which enable us to understand and create novel, well-formed sentences that we have never heard or uttered before. Furthermore, Chomsky says, 'The fact that all normal children acquire essentially comparable grammars of great complexity with remarkable rapidity suggests that human beings are somehow specially designed to do this' (Chomsky, 1959: 57). As he puts it, it is important to recognise that 'a grammar is not a description of the performance of the speaker, but rather of his linguistic competence, and that a description of competence and a description of performance are different things' (Chomsky, 1964: 35). Most significant here are the two terms *competence* and *performance*. All the false starts, stutters, rule-breaking and memory shortcomings of 'performance' are irrelevant to the quest for an understanding of the human capacity for language and the underlying system of rules of a language that speakers master (see also Chomsky, 1965: 4). This view is not without its problems, which we will return to later.

5.4 Deep and surface structure

The foundations laid in Chomsky (1957) were to find further elaboration in *Aspects of the Theory of Syntax* (Chomsky, 1965). There Chomsky states what linguistic theory should concern itself with:

> '… an ideal speaker-listener, in a completely homogeneous speech community, who knows its language perfectly and is unaffected by such grammatically irrelevant conditions as memory limitations, distractions, shifts of attention and interest, and errors (random or characteristic) in applying his knowledge of the language in actual performance'.
>
> *(Chomsky, 1965: 3)*

The grammar is not a model for a speaker or hearer; it simply attempts to be as neutral as possible and to describe the knowledge that underlies a speaker's use of the language (1965: 9). Linguistic theory is concerned with discovering a mental reality underlying actual behaviour. What we observe on the surface could offer evidence of that underlying reality, but cannot be taken to be the subject matter of linguistics (1965: 4). This stance is in contrast with structuralism in the sense that we saw it practised in chapter 4 and is also in contrast with grammarians for whom sentences and texts are sufficient in themselves without a need for recourse to some deep mental world – a stance where the best thing to do with any sentence or text is to relate it to its context to see how its grammar works. That theme we return to when we cross back over the Atlantic to examine British linguistics and how it evolved in the 1950s and 1960s. What I can say at this point is that my experience working with data in language corpora makes me doubt that I have ever met, or ever will meet, that ideal speaker-listener of Chomsky's acquaintance.

According to Chomsky, traditional grammars, despite their detailed examples and their listings of rules and exceptions, fail to discover the underlying principles that generate an infinite number of sentences, and modern grammars seem to have abandoned the notion of universal grammar (Chomsky, 1965: 6). We have noted in the course of this book how universal grammar keeps reasserting itself as a preoccupation of grammarians over many centuries, and in the 1960s Chomsky takes it up again. A generative grammar is based on the idea that below the surface of 'performance' lies a set of principles for generating an indefinite number of well-formed sentences and, once one has gone down to simplest, kernel sentences, the principles that underlie them are likely to be universal. For every sentence, syntax must specify a 'deep structure' which determines its semantic interpretation and a 'surface structure' which specifies the phonetic character of the sentence (1965: 16). To get from the deep structure to the surface structure is the purpose of transformations of elementary structures in the 'base' of the grammar. Hence, the grammar should be 'transformational-generative'.

5.5 Acquisition of grammar

The idea that the most basic level of the grammar corresponds to universal categories has important consequences for the study of language acquisition, whether first or second. The universal structures are innate, and the child experiencing the world around them has to work out which of the possible human languages with all their variations they are immersed in (Chomsky, 1965: 27). For a critique of innateness and other Chomskyan notions, see de Beaugrande (1991). First-language acquisition classically proceeds from single-word utterances (*spoon, teddy, book*) to pairs of words (*teddy-book*) that typically lack all grammatical function words, including copular verbs and can just consist of pairs of nouns, with no verbs. Schlesinger (1975) points out that such utterances are heavily dependent on context and are often open to several quite distinct syntactic readings. In this sense, they are no different from the myriad elliptical utterances in the everyday conversation of fully fluent adult speakers. The worker who turns to their assistant and says 'Right. Hammer!' will be fully understood in context as to whether they are asking for the hammer (noun) to be handed to them or directing the assistant to hammer something (verb). Adults often supply 'missing' words (grammatical and lexical) and expand the child's two-word utterances as a sort of checking mechanism, which exposes the child to more elaborated clause-patterns. Cognitive complexity rather than complexity of form then tends to dictate the progress to more demanding structures, such as interrogative clauses and conditional sentences (Schlesinger, ibid.).

Transformational grammar requires that we 'rewrite' the surface form of the sentence to arrive at the underlying phrase marker, which then undergoes the transformations that result in the surface form. However, it is questionable whether we need recourse to a notion of deep structure to understand the trajectory of grammatical acquisition: what we do need and hugely benefit from is contextual evidence of the child's actions and experiences in its environment and evidence of interaction between the child and its carers, so that we can understand *Teddy-book* in its different contexts (*Give me the book with Teddy in; Teddy is asleep on the book; the book shows pictures of Teddy; I'm giving the book to Teddy*, etc.). The same factors could be said to apply to second language acquisition, although they are clearly not the only ones.

5.6 The plausibility of TG

I have never found the TG view of grammar to be persuasive or applicable to the kinds of applied linguistics that I engage in. Chomsky himself notes the limitations on experiments to verify the linguistic intuitions of native speakers (1965: 19) but rests his case on the mass of evidence and knowledge, albeit often tacit, about grammaticality which the native speaker (and the linguist) can draw upon. The speaker's intuition is 'the ultimate standard' for determining the accuracy of any grammar (1965: 21). Milroy and Milroy (1991: 15–16) refer to plentiful evidence of the unreliability of speakers' judgements of their own usage. What do native speakers do when asked to judge grammaticality? Are they able to access some deep, innate competence in the grammar of their language? Could other factors such as schooling (what one has been told are the rules) or reflection on written standards at the expense of spoken norms muddy the waters? Here we enter the debate on *grammatical* versus *acceptable*, which, for Chomsky, were two different notions. His sentence 'colorless green ideas sleep furiously', discussed in section 5.1, is said to be judged as grammatical but meaningless by the typical native speaker. Is it to say that any noun phrase followed by a verb followed by an adverb is a formally 'grammatical' sentence in English? That says something about the accepted convention of typical declarative word order in English, but in what sense does it say anything deep or innate? Presumably, an informant asked to judge the grammaticality of a gobbledygook sentence in a non-subject-verb language will simply apply the word-order conventions extant in that language and, job done. And if *colorless green ideas sleep furiously* is meaningless, why would anyone wish to ever utter it anyway, other than in a largely pointless, abstract, hypothetical exercise? When presented with an out-of-context sentence, is it not the most natural instinct to try to contextualise it rather than immediately to judge its 'grammaticality'? Hopper says of out-of-context sentences:

> '... such sentences do have a context, but it is invisible. The problem, in other words, is the far more serious one of an unconscious *re*contextualization of sentences, rather than a sophisticated *de*contextualization in which supposedly accidental features of the environment are abstracted away'.
>
> (Hopper, 1988: 19)

This reminds me of a notice I saw while driving past the entrance to a farm in the region where I live a few years ago; it said, 'GOATS' MILK AND EGGS FOR SALE'. I joked to my travel companion, 'I didn't know goats laid eggs'. The point that struck me at the time was that nothing in the syntax revealed the relationship between *goats* and *eggs*. The reasonable assumption, given where we were, was that the eggs were laid by hens. Had the sign said *goats' milk and cheese for sale*, I probably would have assumed that goat cheese was available and not worried whether it was cows' or ewes' cheese. It was common-sense knowledge of the world of animals and of our local farm shops that enabled me to interpret the message; it was the linguist-analyst in me that led me to suggest a perverse interpretation. As an ordinary user of English, I needed no recourse to deep structure; all I needed was the surface structure and a bit of common sense. A well-worn joke in English is the following: 'He opened the door in his pyjamas – funny place to have a door'. The joke depends on a perversion of the common-sense notion that *doors* of the type that lead into and out of rooms and buildings are not found in pyjamas.

To take the argument further, let us consider poetic language. Poetry is full of strings of words that challenge us to create a meaning, and we often find that we can, however weird the syntax and vocabulary might strike us on first reading. The poet Gerard Manley Hopkins wrote this line in his poem *God's Grandeur*: 'There lives the dearest freshness deep down things;' (Hopkins, 1985: 27). The punctuation and lack of line-break suggest that it is a complete clause or 'sentence' in its context. It invites several plausible interpretations, each of which depends on a different syntactic analysis. Is *there* an adverb of place or an existential *there*? Is *deep down* an adverbial phrase modifying the verb *lives*? Or does *deep down* specify a location *in* certain things? Or does *deep down* act as an adjective phrase and describe a type of *things*? For me, when I arrive at these interpretations, I am simply applying different possibilities from the conventions of English usage and using my imagination. I am not at all sure that I could even identify any objectively valid kernel sentences that were truer or more plausible than any others, as each one, being invisible, is irrefutable by logic and only more or less plausible to a listener or reader if I expounded it in a considered critique of Gerard Manley Hopkins' poems. And we would hesitate to say that this line of poetry is 'unacceptable'. We either have to accept that poets such as Gerard Manley Hopkins and many other modern poets deliberately write 'ungrammatically' or that grammaticality, acceptability and semantic processability exist in a complex cognitive interrelationship which is mediated and made sense of in context. 'Poetic licence' is not a way of defying grammar; it is a way of creating grammar. Perfectly meaningful, useful but, by logical standards, ungrammatical utterances bombard us every day in ordinary conversation, as the evidence of spoken corpora show, and many are highly creative, exploiting the 'art of common talk' (Carter, 2004b). But Chomsky, in building the early edifice of TG, explicitly excluded sentences from a corpus as candidates for grammatical theory-building.

H. Sinclair (1975: 231) states the TG case that these three sentences all correspond to the same underlying structure:

The boy broke the window
The window was broken by the boy.
It was the boy who broke the window.

This immediately raises the question of which of these sentences we derive the underlying structure from, as each one would seem to be equally grammatical, acceptable, meaningful and plausible. H. Sinclair (ibid.) says further that the transformations that result in the surface structure do not change how we understand the basic meaning. Yet it seems to me that we gain little by positing a deep structure either of *boy > break > window*, or *boy > window > break*, albeit in real terms we might argue that both the boy and the window pre-exist the act of breaking, such that the second semantic structure might be more reliable than the first. This would seem to be plausible, despite the fact that the first semantic interpretation follows the subject-verb-object structure that English happens to prefer.

Of the many critics of TG, Givón is among the bluntest:

'... the traditional transformationalist approach to "independent syntax" is untenable on two grounds: First, it is derived from a set of data that is restricted and presanitized. Second, it does nothing to further our understanding as to why the grammar of human language is the way it is'.

Givón (1979: 207)

Here we have had recourse to a rather simplified version of TG, which underwent considerable elaboration and revision over the decades that followed Chomsky's first two, much-quoted works. One focus of this book is innovation. Going back to the original conceptions of different grammatical theories is important, as they were ground-breaking and innovative in their day, and they pushed the field forward. Their authors (in the case of TG, Chomsky) had a clarity of vision and challenged the existing paradigms. However elaborately their initial theories evolved, their first and early documents are where we most clearly observe the grammatical ground shifting. Chomsky achieved that in America in the 1950s and 1960s. In the United Kingdom, a shift in grammatical thinking also took place at that time, but in a different direction.

5.7 Innovation in British grammar: J. R. Firth and the neo-Firthians

Here we turn back to my home territory, partly because the United Kingdom is where I worked as a teacher and trained, 'after the event' as an English language teacher in the 1970s, and partly because a distinctly different thread of thinking about grammatical description and pedagogy developed in the post-war years parallel to what was happening in North America, with its dominant structuralist model and adherence to language-teaching technologies such as the language laboratory. Not that structuralism and language laboratories were only an American preoccupation. By the 1960s language labs were widely used in the United Kingdom in primary schools, secondary schools, universities, technical colleges and in industry, as reported in chapters written from each of these perspectives in Turner (1968).

Schaafsma (1968: 77) reported that British academics working in the United Kingdom and in universities abroad were prepared to pay lip-service to the idea of the language laboratory, but were 'a trifle reluctant to use it or design material for it'. The reality was that British linguistic thinking was never very strongly wedded to the structuralist paradigm and developed along a line that would lead to a quite different, rigorously elaborated description of grammar based on the interrelationships between form, meaning and context. This new way of thinking became, for me personally, a more persuasive description of English grammar and one of the cornerstones of my teaching of grammar to undergraduates and master's degree students over many years.

This approach to grammar, which consolidated its foundations in the 1950s and the 1960s, was spearheaded by a group often referred to as the neo-Firthians, owing to the pioneering work of the British linguist J. R. Firth and his pupils and associates. F. R. Palmer's edited collection of key papers by Firth covering the period 1952–59 is the source of citations in this section (Palmer, 1968). Firth was much influenced by the work of the anthropologist, Bronisław Malinowski, who had stated that 'an utterance has no meaning except in the context of situation' (Malinowski, 1923: 307), which was to assume great importance in Firth's and his disciples' approach to language description.

At the heart of Firth's linguistics is the notion of *levels*. The linguist considers not just the syntax or the phonology but takes each level into account, from the context of situation, to the text as an artefact, to relationships in collocation and syntax, to the forms of grammar and lexis, down to the phonemes and phonetics, and meaning is dispersed among the levels. The context of situation is not just a backdrop or setting; the text is an integral part of the context and the whole context of situation is a schematic construct enabling us to make sense of repeated, typical events in the overall social process (Firth; in Palmer, 1968: 175–6). This is a very different approach to the linearity of structuralism. It places Firth's theory in the social arena, although he explicitly did not dismiss mental aspects of language (ibid.). The essential features of the context of situation are the participants and the processes and events in which they engage.

One of the best early examples of these principles in action is seen in the work of Terence Mitchell, who had worked with J. R. Firth at the School of Oriental and African Studies in London. Mitchell (1957) reports his research into the language of buying and selling at markets and shops in Cyrenaica (part of modern-day Libya). He investigated how different aspects of the context of situation (the participants, the setting, goals, etc.) influenced the language used between buyers and sellers, resulting in a patterned form of interaction, just as Firth had outlined. Mitchell identified stages in the commercial exchanges. These included *salutation → enquiry as to the object of sale → investigation of the object of sale → bargaining → conclusion*, and at each stage, considerable linguistic variation could be observed, shaped by factors such as whether the transactions took place in a shop or a market, whether the markets were open-air or closed, what kinds of things the participants were doing, their social identities, their 'attitude' (1957: 33) and so on. Mitchell summed up this contextual variation:

> 'A text is a kind of snowball, and every word or collocation in it is part of its own context, in the wider sense of this term; moreover, the snowball rolls now this way, now that'.
>
> (Mitchell, 1957: 54)

Mitchell also notes that some activities are accompanied by very little verbal language, while others have a lot more. Although he was primarily concerned with the (at that time novel) notion of collocation, his observations presaged those of corpus linguists several decades later in that spoken corpus data would show variations in grammar in situations such as 'language in action' (Carter and McCarthy, 1997: 55–63). Mitchell's definition of the context of situation is that of Firth (whom he quotes) and he concludes that 'meaning must be sought in use' (1957: 32). His 1957 paper is largely uncited nowadays, but it remains one of the seminal works of Firthian linguistics and takes us a long way from the American structuralists and their 'mechanical procedures' (Palmer, 1968: 2).

Collocation – the relation of attraction and co-occurrence between lexical items – has long since ceased to be novel and is now part of the stock-in-trade of applied linguistics and language teaching. However, Firth also spoke of *colligation* – a relation of attraction and co-occurrence on the syntactic level. Colligations, for Firth, did not involve actual words but rather, the grammatical categories that they belong to and the syntactic functions that they perform. Firth (in Palmer, 1968: 181) quotes the sentence 'I watched him' and observes that the relation of colligation is here manifested in that between a first person singular subject pronoun, a past-tense transitive verb and a third person singular masculine object pronoun. Negating the sentence to 'I didn't watch him' attracts one of 22 syntactic operators (auxiliary and modal verbs); making the sentence interrogative requires a further syntactic operation of changing the word order. The 22 operators are 'colligated' (p. 182) with the negative particle *not*. It is necessary, says Firth, to work at the level of abstraction beyond words, as the expression of some grammatical functions might not involve words at all in some languages – word order is one factor in English colligations.

The neatness of Firth's levels becomes apparent only when we place grammar and lexis side by side, and then we see that both levels operate in a similar way, as shown in Table 5.1.

Michael Halliday, whose work we discuss in the next section, follows the same schema as Firth for lexis (Halliday, 1961: 276). Lexical collocations display varying degrees of restriction (e.g. *blond hair* but not *blond car*), while lexical sets offer choices within the set (e.g. *red* versus *blue* versus *green*, etc.). Colligations involve the kinds of restrictions discussed in relation to Firth's example sentence above (e.g. *Did you watch him?* but not *Watched you him?*), and grammatical categories offer paradigmatic choices (e.g. modal operators, pronouns). A word on its own cannot tell you much. When it collocates with another word, a meaning greater than the sum of its parts emerges. Likewise, colligations represent the interrelations between syntactic categories, and grammatical meaning emerges from those interrelations (see also Mitchell, 1966, 1971). Both lexis and grammar are only fully meaningful in phrases, clauses and sentences, which, in turn, are only meaningful in their phonological and orthographical realisations distributed in various ways across the clause/sentence (Firth; in Palmer, 1968: 103), and when located in their contexts of situation. All the levels are harmoniously present through the choices and requirements of each of them in successful texts. We shall see in the next chapter how, over the years, lexis and grammar were shown to be even more closely entwined when faced with the evidence of corpora.

TABLE 5.1 Levels of lexis and grammar

	structure	system
lexis	collocations	lexical sets
grammar	colligations	grammatical categories

5.8 Halliday's grammar

One of J. R. Firth's pupils, Michael Halliday, published a paper in 1961 on grammar. It was grounded in Firth's approach and laid out the basis of the territory which Halliday believed grammar to occupy. This included the statement that:

> 'The data to be accounted for are observed language events, observed as spoken or as codified in writing, any corpus of which, when used as material for linguistic description, is a " text"'.
>
> *(Halliday, 1961: 243)*

Text, in this quotation, includes the conventional notion of a text, but also allows for exemplifications and terminal generative strings (ibid: footnote 6). In the basic tripartite system of language, in its three levels, substance (phonic or graphic), form (lexical or grammatical) and context (non-linguistic features of the situation), lexis and grammar are seen as 'two related levels' (p. 244), which Halliday was to capture in the term *lexicogrammar* (Halliday, 1996: 4; see also Halliday, 1966). Formal meanings – the meanings of lexical and grammatical forms in their place of occurrence in the text – enable meaning in context to be created. Grammar involves 'closed systems' (p. 246–7). A closed system consists of a finite number of mutually exclusive items, and if any new item is added to the system, it changes the meaning of all the other items in the system. An example in the recent evolution of English grammar would be the addition of *they* (as a singular generic pronoun with male and/or female reference) to the now defunct system of *she* (female) / *he* (male or generic). In the new, gender-neutral system, *he* now, for most users, means 'only male, not generic'. For some, *they* and its inflexions can now be used about or by an individual who prefers not to identify as male or female (see, for example, the biodata of the scientist Annalee Newitz, *New Scientist*, 16 November 2019: 24). If these individual pronoun shifts become widely accepted, the whole pronoun system has changed.

The fundamental categories of Halliday's grammar in the 1961 paper are *unit, class, structure* and *system*. No single category takes precedence over another; they are all mutually defining. A unit is a stretch of language that carries a grammatical pattern, the patterns form structures, and these partake in a hierarchy of classes, from highest to lowest. Each higher-level class consists of units from the level immediately below; in other words, it is a *rank scale* (p. 251) – a key term not only in Halliday's grammar but also in the later account of discourse structure elaborated by Sinclair and Coulthard (1975). Made plain, the grammatical rank scale has a higher order unit of *sentence* and a lower order unit of *morpheme*. This can be expressed as in Figure 5.2.

Readers might be more familiar with the term 'phrase' than Halliday's preference for 'group'. The ranks in bold indicate the domain of grammar proper. The double-headed arrows indicate a two-way relationship: in the hierarchy, sentences consist of clauses (downward arrow), and clauses combine to form sentences (upward arrow) and so on for each rank. Beyond grammar, at the top of the scale,

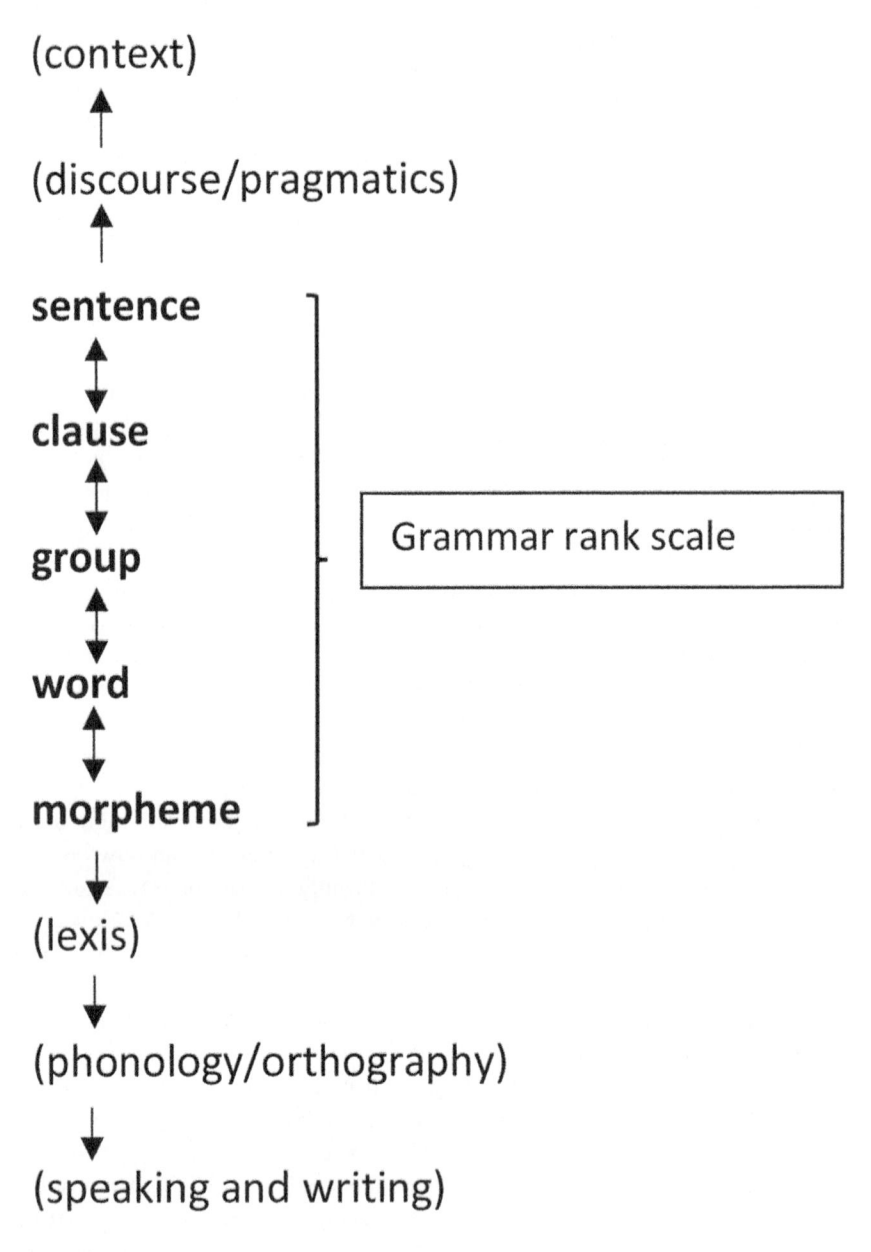

(context)
↑
(discourse/pragmatics)
↑
sentence ⎤
↕ ⎥
clause ⎥
↕ ⎥
group ⎥ Grammar rank scale
↕ ⎥
word ⎥
↕ ⎥
morpheme ⎦
↓
(lexis)
↓
(phonology/orthography)
↓
(speaking and writing)

FIGURE 5.2 Grammar rank scale
(after Halliday, 1961)

we enter the world of discourse and pragmatics and, beyond that, context. At the lowest point on the scale, we leave the abstract unit of morpheme and enter the lexicon of real words, which are subject to the rules of phonology and orthography and finally realised in phonic and graphic substance – the sounds spoken or characters written. Every element of a text can be viewed from any level of the grammar. Thus, a sentence is only a sentence in terms of its clause-structure, and a clause is only a clause in terms of the groups which constitute it. Elsewhere in this book, we shall see how the single-headed arrows can be converted into double-headed ones, enabling us to move, for example, from pragmatics to grammar in a meaningful way.

5.9 The clause

The clause is at the heart of Halliday's grammar. The functional elements of clauses are subject (S), predicator (i.e. verb) (P), complement (C) and Adjunct (A). The SPCA elements can appear in various sequences and combinations. (S) and (C) are associated with the participants in the clause, (P) with processes (which include actions and states) and (A) is associated with circumstances (Halliday, 1967: 39). Examples would be:

S P C A
(1) She | bought | a house | with the money her grandmother left her.
S P C
(2) That big tree in the garden | is | very old.
P C
(3) Have | some more coffee.
S P A A
(4) I | ran | down the stairs | in a great hurry.
A S P C
(5) With a big hammer, | they | smashed | the stone.

We can see that many sequences are possible (SPCA, SPC, PC, SPAA, ASPC and so on). But we also notice something else central to Halliday's grammar: the notion of *rankshift* (1961: 251). In example (1), the adjunct contains a noun phrase within it (*the money her grandmother left her*). These words form a nominal group with a noun head (*money*), but the nominal group has 'shifted downward' to become one of the elements of another group, in this case the prepositional group (*with the money her grandmother left her*). The prepositional group can be analysed as consisting of preposition (*with*) + complement of preposition (*the money her grandmother left her*). The nominal complement of the preposition in its turn is subject to the analysis of determiner (*the*) + noun head (*money*) + rankshifted clause post-modifying the head (*her grandmother left her*). These examples show how the complexity of everyday sentences is systematic: each element of each unit in each rank (like the players and their instruments in an orchestra) contributes equally to the symphony of the finished sentence.

The functions of the units are determined by their class, which is an abstraction derived by working top-down through the levels (1961: 261). The functional class *nominal group*, for instance, derives its identity from the class above – the *clause*. The functional element of *subject* (S) determines the identity of the level below: (S) must be a nominal group, and the predicator (P) must be a verbal group, and so on. Nominal groups must contain a *noun* or *pronoun*. A pronoun functioning as (S) must be in the subject-pronoun form. In English, this means making an appropriate choice within the system *I, you, he, she, it, we, they*. So, we move through levels of abstraction to actual words, while retaining always the identity of each word as it plays its functional role in each class at each level of the system, now looking bottom-up. The choices presented in the pronoun systems and other systems are 'the final requisite for the linking of the categories to the data' (1961: 265).

The clause, for Halliday, encodes three main types of syntactic choice: *transitivity, mood* and *theme* (Halliday, 1967b: 199). Transitivity represents the cognitive content, i.e. the relationships in the world between the participants and processes in events and states. So, the grammar must account for different clauses such as:

1. I washed this shirt yesterday
2. this shirt was bought yesterday
3. they laughed

The description is accomplished in terms of the relationship between the structural elements (S), (P) and (C). In (1) *I* am the actor, *the shirt* is the goal; in (2) *the shirt* is still the goal but is realised syntactically as subject (S), and there is no (C) present. In (3) there is only an actor, *they*, realised as (S) and no goal – what we commonly term an intransitive structure.

Mood is concerned with 'the organization of participants in speech situations' (Halliday, 1967b: 199). This includes whether a speaker is informing, questioning, commanding, requesting confirmation, etc. *Theme* is concerned with information structure. Halliday divides the clause into two structural parts, to which are given the functional labels *theme* and *rheme*. The theme is what comes first in the clause and, in an unmarked (typical, canonical) (S)(P)(C) structure, theme generally (but not obligatorily) coincides with given information, while the rheme coincides with new information. The theme is typically 'what I am talking about', and the rheme is 'what I am saying about what I'm talking about'. In our clause (2) above, the theme-rheme structure would be:

theme   rheme
this shirt | was bought yesterday

Put simply: I am talking about this shirt (given in the text or context) and I inform you that it was bought yesterday. The same applies in interrogatives (theme | rheme):

Did you | buy this shirt yesterday?
Who | bought this shirt?

Information structure also requires reference to given or new entities, typically through anaphoric (backward in the text) reference, ellipsis, i.e. non-realisation of otherwise obligatory elements of the clause, as in A: *Which cake do you want?* B: [I want] *That one* and substitution (e.g. *She intended to sell the house but never did so*). These examples presage the full elaboration of textual cohesive devices given in Halliday and Hasan (1976), which we examine more closely in chapter 7.

Simple examples like those given here are only a sketch of the complexity of the elaboration of transitivity and theme, which are laid out in monumental detail in Halliday (1967a, b and c), but within the limited scope of this book, they are offered as providing something of the flavour of Halliday's grammar and to indicate how different it was from the linearity of conventional structuralism.

5.10 Systems

Halliday's grammar is appropriately known as a *systemic* grammar, where 'the grammar takes the form of a series of "system networks"' Halliday (1967a: 37), and as it deals not just with the forms but simultaneously with the functions of all these elements in terms of the rank scale, it is also known as *systemic-functional* grammar.

In any system, there are 'entry conditions', that is to say a choice must be made in any system which will then lead to further choices in other systems and so on. Halliday gives various graphic representations of systems, like the one in Figure 5.3. In the first system (1), *a* or *b* must be chosen. If *a* is chosen, it becomes the entry condition to system (2), where a further choice must be made. In this case, the

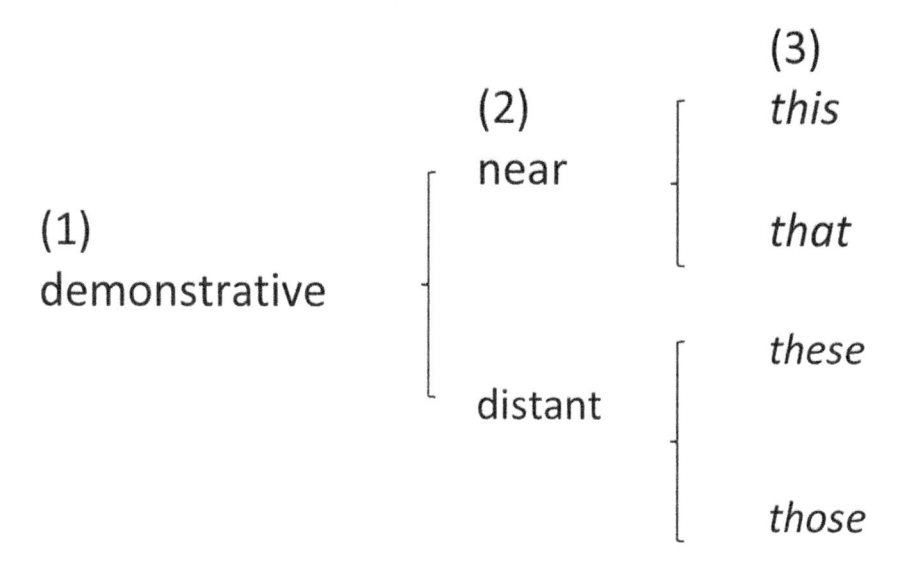

FIGURE 5.3 Systemic choices: English demonstratives
(after Halliday 1967a: 38)

English demonstrative system (*this, that, these, those*) offers a choice at (2) between *near* or *distant*. If *near* is chosen, then there is a choice at (3) between *this* (singular) and *these* (plural), but not *that* or *those*. The movement from left to right in Figure 5.3 can be construed as an increase in 'delicacy' or depth of detail (Halliday, 1961: 248, 258). As the delicacy of the description increases, there comes a point of ultimate delicacy where no further systems present themselves; grammar runs out, so to speak (see also Sinclair, 1966). It is there that grammar yields to lexis, and lexis has to be seen as existing on a different level from 'most delicate grammar' (Halliday, 1961: 268), with its own theory.

5.11 Language and society

Halliday's 1961 and 1967 papers laid out most of the essential territory of systemic-functional grammar, but his work continued to evolve throughout the 20th century. His book *Language as Social Semiotic* (Halliday, 1978) – and in particular the chapter of the same name in that book – adds to the picture by relating features of language form to features of meaning and to features of the context of situation. In this respect it is in the tradition of J. R. Firth's theory. The main situational categories are *field, tenor* and *mode*, and these correlate with semantic features. The field, put simply, is the *what* of a text, its content and argument – it activates *ideational* features of meaning. The tenor accounts for the *who*, the relationship between sender and receiver, activating *interpersonal* features of meaning. The mode refers to the *how*, the channel of communication (e.g. speaking versus writing), activating *textual* features (Halliday, 1978: 115–7).

When we view these situational and semantic features alongside the categories of the grammar, we see a tripartite macro-system at play, The ideational/experiential meanings of situations in the world (manifested in fields) find their functional correlates in transitivity and the (S)(P)(C)(A) options within the clause. The tenor – the vehicle of interpersonal meanings (sender-receiver relationships) – finds expression in such features as mood (declarative, interrogative, imperative) and modality. The textual world is expressed through various modes of meaning: speaking and writing, information organisation by theme and rheme, and cohesion manifested in features such as reference, substitution and ellipsis. All these systems operate at once in every text, be it spoken or written.

Halliday did not confine his work to theorising, and he applied it in various ways, including by tracking the acquisition of English by his son, 'Nigel', as he acquired the grammatical system from the age of nine months to three and a half years (Halliday, 1975). The child, at just under two years old, has developed considerable communicative skills, but his grammar is fluid; he has still not fully grasped the pronoun system, for example, alternating between using *I/me* and *you* for first person reference and not mastered the interrogative features of the mood system in the questions that he asks (Halliday, 1978: 116; see also 211–16). Halliday (1978: 231) also looks at the role of language in institutions. A school, like other institutions, is a 'communication network' where the structure of the institution 'will be enshrined in the language' and the different types of interaction that take place in the institution. Halliday referred to his approach as 'appliable linguistics' (Halliday, 2007: 16), and in the 1960s he worked with teachers from all levels in British schools on mother-tongue education to produce teaching materials, and then in the 1980s and 1990s in Australia along similar lines. Halliday argues that the teaching of mother-tongue English is perhaps the most important school subject, and one that should not be left in the hands of untrained practitioners (often teachers of literature) – a fact that the second-language teaching profession has taken on board over the years (Halliday, 2007: 26).

5.12 Halliday's enduring influence

Halliday's work saw its fullest elaboration in the *Introduction to Functional Grammar*, the third, revised edition of which, written in collaboration with Christian Matthiessen (Halliday, 2004), has become a standard reference work to match the great grammars we reviewed in previous chapters. Its readership is primarily in universities. It brings together all of Halliday's systematic approach, centred around the clause but also bringing in the above-sentence features of cohesion. It is not a reference grammar in the traditional sense; it is rather one to be read from start to finish as a testament to a half-century of innovative thinking. Coming in just shy of 700 pages, it is not for the faint-hearted. However, two very practical spin-offs of Halliday's work have found enthusiastic audiences among undergraduates whom I have taught: Margaret Berry's *Introduction to Systemic Linguistics* (Berry, 1975, 1977) and the second edition of Angela Downing and Philip Locke's *English Grammar: A University Course* (Downing and Locke, 2006), originally published in 1992.

Halliday's theories have been put into practice in various ways, not least in corpus linguistics from its earliest times (Halliday, 2007: 18). Corpus linguists have realised dividends from the perspective not only of lexis in the neo-Firthian tradition of a focus on collocation, but also in the concept of lexico-grammar and the delicate patterning of lexical and grammatical forms. In my own research and teaching, time and time again I find myself returning to his *Language as Social Semiotic* as my *vade mecum*.

5.13 Conclusion

In this chapter, two major innovations in grammatical thinking have been surveyed. The brief treatment given in the chapter to each one can barely do justice to their founders and the complexity of their work elaborated over half a century of scholarship. As with the previous historical chapters, we can only hope to get a taster of the great works. However, in both cases, going back to the earliest documents where Chomsky, Firth and the neo-Firthians first laid out their thoughts is a most rewarding pursuit, imbued as their seminal works are with clarity and vision that is at times less easy to capture in later elaborations of their theory and adaptations by others. The Chomskyan and neo-Firthian are two very different ways of looking at grammar – one looking into the human mind and the other looking at texts and contexts, but both have enjoyed a solid following among academics and beyond. The Atlantic Ocean is an apt metaphor for the distance between the two, with Chomsky's influence being strongest in North America and the neo-Firthians in the United Kingdom and Europe (as well as in Australia). Although I personally get more from Halliday's way of thinking, I could certainly not write this book without acknowledging the influence of Chomsky's work in the construction and maintenance of the edifice of SLA theory and research.

6

GRAMMAR AS DATA

Corpus linguistics

6.1 Let the data speak

So far in this book we have considered various theories and models of grammar dating back to ancient times. All of them could be said, in one way or another, to have recourse to data. The data may be the works of great writers, the speech of the educated population, how well or badly English texts comply with the rules of Latin grammar, the historical evidence of grammatical development and change, the evidence of newspapers and letters, the native speaker's introspection and judgements on whether sentences are correct or not, conversations carefully written down in market-places together with information on their contexts of utterance, observations of structural patterns in different languages, observations of little children making sense of grammar, and so on. Although these sources of insight are quite distinct from one another, they are all data, all raw material for the grammarian. In most cases, the data are called upon to prove or support a theory, model or framework elaborated by the grammarian, albeit sometimes it is called upon selectively while ignoring other available or possible data. There is nothing fundamentally wrong with that. However, as Carter (2004a: 2) put it in defending the approach of corpus linguistics, the Chomskyan tradition was characterised by 'invented, decontextualized sentences designed by and attested by the researcher only to substantiate the identification of structures, mainly grammatical structures, which are then claimed to be of universal significance'. When it comes to genuinely attested data, Halliday does not mince his words:

> 'We are only now beginning to get access to a reasonable quantity of data. This has been the major problem for linguistics: probably no other defined sphere of intellectual activity has ever been so top-heavy, so much theory built

overhead with so little data to support it. The trouble was that until there were first of all tape recorders and then computers, it was impossible to assemble the data a grammarian needs'.

(Halliday, 1996: 24)

As the physicist Stephen Hawking said in relation to scientific theory, 'the real test is whether it makes predictions that agree with observation' (Hawking, 1988: 137). But what does 'observation' entail in the case of language study? What happens if we eschew theory and just start with a mass of attested language data and very few preconceptions about what it might tell us about grammar? And what if, instead of introspecting and applying our intuitions and prior experience of grammar, we let a computer and its software loose on collected data and ask it to do what it is best at, i.e. count things? After all, computers do not (yet) have theories or intuitions, do not have any prejudices as regards grammar, do not get into a moral panic, are not irritated by 'bad grammar' and have never been to school. This approach would represent a strong version of corpus linguistics, where the data speak, and we listen respectfully and try to make sense of what the machine is telling us. Such a view was continuously adhered to by my great mentor, Professor John Sinclair, who believed that a lack of sufficient empirical evidence could only lead to speculation rather than an honest encounter with the facts (Sinclair, 2004: 9). Sinclair's position was always 'trust the text' (the title of his 2004 collection of essays). Yet it is very difficult to divest oneself completely of theory and preconceptions and the body of existing observations we have inherited, as Sinclair admits (ibid., p.10); nonetheless, he favours doing our best to reduce those effects.

When I first became a colleague of John Sinclair's at the University of Birmingham in the early 1980s, I bore with me the baggage of a decade and a half of English as a foreign language (EFL) grammar teaching under a broadly structural umbrella which steadily gave way to a more communicative approach. In an unforgettable series of informal lunchtime seminars, Sinclair inspired me and my colleagues to approach data with an open mind. I found this at first difficult, challenging and almost threatening and wondered if anything he said had any great relevance to my principal concern at that time: language teaching. I had a feeling that busy language teachers would just find it all too unnerving and impractical – an unnecessary rocking of the solidly built boat of the well-tried English language teaching (ELT) grammatical canon. For what we were seeing in the data was an apparently inseparable relationship between grammar, lexis and meaning. What is more, the machine was telling us loudly and clearly that the more data that it was fed, the more patterns were emerging, which were visible in the strikingly repeated configurations of forms in multiple concordance lines. In the end, the notion of meaning being attached to a single word seemed to dissolve before our eyes, to be replaced by units consisting of two, three or more words congealing into meaningful chunks, which Ron Carter and I later investigated in spoken data (McCarthy and Carter, 2002). Similarly, structural configurations seemed to be strongly conditioned by colligational and collocational factors, resulting in grammatical patterns that leapt out from the computer screen (for example, see Hunston, 2001). It meant that we all had to start thinking in a new way about lexis and the relationship between lexis and syntax. This all left 'grammar' in the sense of an independent level of linguistic form in a very precarious position.

6.2 Grammar in corpora

In the early days of corpus linguistics, it was difficult to tease out facts about language use from the data, with long strings of complex commands needed to get the computer to produce word lists, concordances or anything that the linguist could make sense of. Unless specialist help was at hand, the hapless applied linguist had to have a knowledge of computational syntax. However, computational analysis of texts was seen to be an extremely useful and illuminating process in the two main areas of language study that adopted corpus-based approaches in the late 1970s and early 1980s: literary stylistics and lexicography. Both areas were quick to recognise the power of concordances for retrieving patterns in their data. Literary stylistics and literary study in general realised the potential for getting at authorial fingerprints and traits of style: for example, the concordances to works of Joseph Conrad produced by Higdon and Bender (1983, 1985). Meanwhile, the pioneering COBUILD dictionary project at the University of Birmingham, under the direction of John Sinclair, broke the mould of dictionary compilation by observing the meanings of lexical items in concordances rather than through introspection or the received wisdom of existing dictionaries. Concordances became the stock-in-trade of subsequent corpus-based lexicography projects, and soon became the raw material for projects in grammar (COBUILD, 1990; Greenbaum, 1996; Biber et al., 1999; Huddleston and Pullum, 2002; Carter and McCarthy, 2006; Carter et al., 2011).

Frequency based on corpus data played a role in the evaluation of grammatical acceptability from the 1980s onwards (e.g. Quirk et al., 1985). Frequency lists are more often than not the first thing that corpus linguists look at, as they enable us to distinguish between the core of the language and the periphery, but they can also yield surprises or anomalies which are then followed up in concordances. And it is the sheer visual impact of concordances that very often reveal the most striking patterns of lexis and grammar. Corpus output in the form of raw frequency lists, key wordlists, collocation information and concordances can say a great deal about different modes of communication (e.g. writing versus speaking), different varieties of a language (e.g. native versus non-native), different contexts of use (e.g. public versus private, lecture versus seminar) and language change (data collected at different historical times), as well as distinguishing social factors such as age, gender, class and so on. They can also lead us to reflect on the very nature of grammar.

6.3 Grammar and frequency

Some grammatical forms and configurations are more frequent than others. It is uncontroversial to assert that in English, the present simple aspect is more frequent than the subjunctive mood, or that modal *can* is more frequent than *ought*. However, other items and features are more difficult to access from intuition. One example is the alternative negative forms for third-person singular present tense of the English verb *be*. In writing grammar materials for the *Touchstone Level 1* course (McCarthy et al., 2005), my co-authors and I were uncertain about which of the negative forms of *be*, *(s)he isn't* or *(s)he's not*, to present. The publisher's pressures on available space and time and the teaching/learning burden suggested that one of them would do, but which one? Both seemed equally correct and acceptable. We were, at that time, writing materials focusing on speaking, for a predominantly American English market, but the results that we obtained by searching a spoken American corpus are paralleled in these figures from the more up-to-date 11.5-million-word spoken British National Corpus (hereafter Spoken BNC2014; see Love et al., 2017).

The *(s)he isn't* forms total 98 occurrences; the *(s)he's not* forms total 2,588 – some 26 times greater. So, the difference is not marginal and suggests, at least for general spoken English, that the *(s)he's not* forms should take priority in presentation. My co-authors and I also found that the *isn't* form was often found in the environment of full noun subjects, as in *our address isn't registered / the driver isn't responsible / the oven isn't consistently delivering heat* (Spoken BNC 2014). Not only was this, for us at least, an unpredictable set of observations; it also provided us with useful advice to pass on to learners. It was not a 'rule of grammar' in the conventional sense, but a rule of thumb in terms of probability of occurrence. But probability is not just a convenient means of avoiding definitive statements. 'Frequency in text is the instantiation of probability in the system' (Halliday, 1991a: 42) and a corpus-based grammar is a statement of a series of probabilities, where grammaticality and acceptability are based on overwhelmingly repeated patterns of use in the speaking and writing of many thousands of users. Probabilities, in the Hallidayan sense, are not just statistical features of the data; they are a feature of the system itself. Halliday (1991a: 57) makes the point that the practice of measuring probability of occurrence of *lexical* items is generally accepted and that the same can be done for grammar. Probabilities of occurrence are realised in the grammatical choices made by myriad speakers and writers. Probabilities do not predict individual choices but state what the odds are that a specific grammatical configuration will occur, and this may vary in different contexts. Indeed, the notion of register is simply an observation of the instantiations of restricted sets of choices brought about by individual configurations of field, tenor and mode (Halliday, 1991b). And the probabilities are liable to change over time as contexts, societies and cultures change.

TABLE 6.1 Spoken BNC2014: Negative forms of third person singular present tense *be*

	no. of occurrences
she isn't	42
she's not	1,037
he isn't	56
he's not	1,551

Another example of frequency and probabilities of co-occurrence concerns the English subjunctive, mentioned above. The English non-inflected subjunctive (i.e. where the verb ending is always the base form) has a long and somewhat up-and-down history going back many centuries (Turner, 2008). It was notably in decline in the 18th century but, at the same time, grammars of that era seemed to be inviting its revival, and not without some success (Auer, 2006). There was debate among 18th-century grammarians, including those whose work we sampled in chapter 3, such as Brightland, Harris and Lowth, about its syntax and status, questions such as its relationship with modal *should*, its use after *if, though, lest* and similar subordinating conjunctions, as well as its status as a feature of polite style. Fowler (1926: 574) considered it moribund and did not at all like some of its uses in his day. In more recent times, attested data suggest that the subjunctive is more frequent in American English than in British English (Zandvoort, 1969: 87; Johansson and Norheim, 1988; Leech et al., 2009: 52–61; Kjellmer, 2009). Aarts (2012: 4) says 'In the United States the subjunctive is very much alive'. Not only has the subjunctive survived in educated usage, it has entered the ELT canon as an expected ingredient in advanced level pedagogical resources, especially those that originate in American English, where it can be found in various forms.

Typical treatments of the subjunctive in grammar practice books and pedagogical grammars take as their point of departure the formal constraints of the pattern *subject + reporting verb + (that) + subject + base form of verb (for all persons)*, with the reporting verb types dominated by meanings connected with requesting, demanding, suggesting, advising, etc. e.g. *they recommended/suggested that the match be postponed* (see similar examples in COBUILD, 1990: 324–5). Instinctively, this seems like a sound approach. Yet corpus output on frequency and significance of collocation with subjunctive clauses shows a number of nouns and adjectives with similar meanings to the reporting verbs governing the subjunctive. These include *stipulation, proviso, requirement, imperative, recommendation, suggestion, condition,* and *preferable, desirable, vital, essential* (collocational statistics from English Web 2015 enTenTen15 corpus, accessed via Sketch Engine, 2019).

Zandvoort (1969: 86–7) gives nouns and verbs that are used with the subjunctive, but no adjectives. Eastwood (1994: 322) gives a list of seven reporting verbs and six adjectives that can govern the subjunctive, but no nouns. Murphy (2004) includes one adjective (*essential*) in his presentation of the subjunctive, and no nouns (p. 68). Hewings (1999) offers a list of nouns in addition to the reporting verbs but no adjectives. Azar and Hagen (2009) list eight reporting verbs and six adjectives, but no nouns. Carter and McCarthy (2006: 635) give examples of reporting verbs and add conditional subordinators (*if, lest, on condition that*). These sources represent a mixed bag of priorities; their decisions on what to include are probably based on pedagogical instincts and experience and the age-old pressures of time for learning, and not least how many pages a publisher looking over your shoulder will let you have! And we seem to be no better at sorting out the ragbag of observations than were our 18th-century forbears. As with any relatively higher-level or more complex structure, there is a noticeable lack of consensus, unlike the more uniform items of the EFL canon for elementary learners (McCarthy, 2013). However, the comprehensive, corpus-informed grammars of Quirk et al. (1985: 157) and Greenbaum (1996: 268) list reporting verbs, nouns and adjectives in their sections on the subjunctive, as does Swan's superbly useful pedagogical handbook for learners, albeit only offering one noun: *advice* (Swan, 2005: 567). Another feature of the English subjunctive is its relative infrequency in informal spoken data; in the Spoken BNC2014 it is almost non-existent. McCarthy et al. (2014), with the benefit of extensive corpus research into American English data, include 17 verbs, nouns and adjectives and a note to learners about the rarity of the subjunctive in conversation (pp. 109 and 163). The sorts of insights discussed in this section would be difficult to achieve solely through introspection; evaluating the corpus evidence is a good case of 'letting the data speak'.

6.4 Concordance, pattern and meaning

Electronic concordances (manual ones have existed for centuries) are a fascinating innovation, both in terms of their form and content. Their typical form – the key word in context (KWIC) display – places the target word(s) in a vertical central column with a variable amount of text on either side and usually some code available on each line, which identifies the source of each example. The co-text around the target word(s) can be alphabetically sorted leftward and/or rightward. KWIC concordances enable the analyst to read the assembled lines in a different way, not just each one horizontally from start to finish, as we might do in the text of an English novel, but also horizontally and vertically, at once hopping back and forth from one to the other mode. What we get from this way of reading the data is a visual sense of pattern. Figure 6.1 takes the example of a search for the word *moment* in the Spoken BNC2014 and shows 13 lines from a random sample of 100 of the total 2,000+ occurrences.

Without any further sorting, in a 'vertical' reading, our eye is already drawn to the nine occurrences of *at the moment*. We could perform a leftward sort and make the pattern even more visible. Each context for *at the moment* seems to point to a meaning

t really mess up my nice schedule that I have at the	moment	I "m a little bit annoyed about it if that "s th
e roads are then how slow the traffic is going at the	moment	well it updates itself does n"t it ? yeah hand
ackhand is perfect your forehand is I- is great at the	moment	your who do you think is quicker around the
does n"t seem to be that much actual down for the	moment	? no well it might fill up a bit more as it gets
chool is she ? yeah she was she "s on holiday at the	moment	but erm yeah but at the end of that mm nex
ep breath I "ve not got enough teaching work at the	moment	to keep me busy and not bored mm in the n
s own play and also do all the music if I hop off for a	moment	it "s cos I "ve got to change the CD oh god oh
yeah they are yeah so they "re only on lease for the	moment	well some some of the youth hostels have
anish yeah and because of the EBac that is in at the	moment	is being brought in yeah you know a languag
ith himself because he "s getting away with it at the	moment	and erm --UNCLEARWORD --ANONnameM g
as just gone to get a cup of tea so she "ll be back in a	moment	and we can carry on from there ah yes yes o
ither be pronounced err or er but he does n"t at the	moment	cos he "s learning that he will because he "l
to have about a hundred and eighty missiles at the	moment	well and they do n"t kn- admit to it but Israe

FIGURE 6.1 Extract from concordance of *moment*, Spoken BNC2014

of 'right now' or 'at the time of speaking'. But there are also three lines where the governing preposition is *for* + *a* or *the*, not *at*. This tempts us to see if there are more examples with *for* in the 2,000+ hits for *moment*. A straightforward search using the string [*for*] [] [*moment*] to accommodate the occurrences of *for a moment* and *for the moment*, where the empty brackets indicate 'any word', yields 33 occurrences of *for the moment*. Here the meaning accords with 'for now' or 'temporarily'. Figure 6.2 shows a 13-line sample of *for the moment* from 71 hits of the search string.

The evidence presented by these expressions with *moment* is a classic example of the different things that a corpus analysis can achieve. It could well be that nothing I have said about *at the moment* and *for the moment* comes as a surprise to you, and introspection might be sufficient to light upon the different forms and meanings. A corpus can confirm (or refute) the analyst's intuitions, which in itself is a valuable exercise. Corpus analysis can also, as already illustrated, inform us of relative frequency, which is a more difficult thing to pin down through introspection alone. In this case, *at the moment* (1,735 occurrences) turns out to be some 50 times more frequent than *for the moment* (33 occurrences) in the Spoken BNC2014 — a fact that might be helpful to someone selecting items for language teaching materials. I personally would have been unable to come up with such a figure from intuition or introspection. This simple example demonstrates the close tie between form and meaning, which the patterns in concordances underpin.

The form—meaning relationship often challenges the ELT grammatical canon. Consider the use of the future perfect tense-aspect forms, i.e. forms such as *(s)he will have arrived* (simple) and *they will have been working* (continuous/progressive). These are well established in the ELT canon. Azar and Hagen (2009: 73) offer a description of the simple form typical of many grammar books for learners: 'The future perfect expresses an activity that will be *completed before another time or event in the future*' [their italics]. Murphy (2004: 48) offers the same description, as does Hewings (1999: 30). Greenbaum (1996: 274) has similar examples, while COBUILD (1990: 255) states that the future perfect simple form can be used for 'something that has not happened yet but will happen before a particular time in the future'. All of these descriptions are true and are borne out by intuition and

you write notes ? no you can just sit and listen	for the moment	--UNCLEARWORD carry on --ANONnameM ar
yeah there are a lot of jobs that are at risk but	for the moment	she seems to be she "s alright alright yeah G
rammes and stuff well I "ll not think about that	for the moment	although that "s funny but I certainly want to
e darling ? yeah yeah stay on the inside I think	for the moment	we can go up any one of these for parking to
ly be primed to adrian took it out so it it "s safe	for the moment	yeah is that has that been run yet or ? no we
or two pieces left mm oh I "ve given up playing	for the moment	you were playing yesterday no I was just stu
I "ll know it yeah but like from using it but like	for the moment	I "ll just persevere with what I know and I do
our money back from Barclays yeah that "s fine	for the moment	see what what I "m frightened of now the ne
ome crisps in there --ANONnameM I "m alright	for the moment	oh do n"t tell my dad open them though yea
like some ? or it "s not your thing yeah I wo n"t	for the moment	cos I "ve just had a glass of wine so I "m ah ye
ttom that "s it oh that "s no you "re okay I think	for the moment	yeah I "m alright your dad was n"t very hairy
ome more as well --ANONnameM ? I "m alright	for the moment	I "ll get oh he "s going and coming back dear
h that ? um salt sorry I was just I I "ll leave that	for the moment	I was just uh coriander you "re saying like co

FIGURE 6.2 Extract from concordance of *for the moment*, Spoken BNC2014

examples, yet when we look at concordances, we see a different picture. Figure 6.3 reveals another typical use of the future perfect that seems not to refer to the future at all. Of the 20 lines sampled here, 15 seem to have more to do with confident speculation and assumptions about a present state or situation already achieved. These include examples such as 'I expect the well the roads will have improved since then', 'he will have read George Orwell presumably', and 'if he's been in Morse* I will have seen him' (*a popular British TV detective series). None of these looks forward to a point in the future when something at present incomplete will be completed – quite the opposite; they refer to things in the past that have relevance or consequences in the present. *Will* is good for speculation, and *have* is good for present relevance; neither is bound to future time.

The concordance illustrations here have been compressed, owing to space considerations and for better readability; the display on a typical computer screen offers a wider view, with more co-text and the option to see the codes that indicate the contextual origin of each line (e.g. text source, speaker information). In most software packages, it is also possible to click on any line to expand it into a full sentence or longer. In this way, we are being true to a neo-Firthian approach of adducing meaning in context, as discussed in chapter 5, relating the target item to its colligational and collocational environment and drawing inferences from each level of realisation, from the grammatical morphemes through the clauses out to the context of utterance. The future perfect seems to occupy two principle colligational environments – one governed by adjuncts of future time (e.g. *after three months, a thousand year's time, by the time they got old*) and one conditioned by adjuncts of past time (*since*

he Star Wars films but if he "s been in Morse I	will have seen	him yeah he would have yeah he played h
what cats are like yeah like like they will they	will have learnt	instantly and they will never need to have
February ? theoretically speaking the alcohol	will have burned	off in all that heat but it did cross my mind
UNCLEARWORD is less than forty grand so you	will have paid	off the house yeah but I do n"t know what
was a big queue outside ? is that cos the sales	will have started	? yeah do you remember that lovely thing
lution of language no single present day word	will have survived	a thousand years " time but we "re speaki
ch --ANONplace and if they did these people	will have moved	away but you know you have like in Yorks
million ? no Martin Sorrell how old is he ? dad	will have heard	of him have you ? have you heard of Mart
ssume that by that stage hopefully something	will have happened	for him yeah yeah and and I it "s it "s not j
s like a track ha ha I expect the well the roads	will have improved	since then but they were n"t bad in those
ee it yeah you "d like t- all everyone at school	will have seen	it well but with all of the expectations I th
ed by the whole thing did I tell you about it ? I	will have told	you about it oh yeah when I was like a tra
ah so well they will all have at least I hope all	will have got	the message that they "ll need this oh we
vhenever it was by the time they got old they	will have paid	lots of money in mm and they "re not allo
t youth these days a large proportion of them	will have heard	of the Nargle Song erm Charlie the Unicor
n our our ancestors my side or your mother "s	will have travelled	as far as you ha- have because we would h
e back after three months because the money	will have run	out mm yeah but it does mean I mean she
vell "s idea of a good pub and you know he he	will have read	George Orwell presumably because he di
e yeah maybe I do n"t imagine an extra week	will have given	them much of an advantage no no I do n"t
-ANONplace I was thinking of going but I oh it	will have changed	a lot recently you know I do n"t know wha

FIGURE 6.3 Random sample concordance lines for future perfect simple form, Spoken BNC2014

then, recently), as well as other colligational and collocational features indicating hypotheticality (*if x, then y will have happened, presumably, I expect/hope x will have happened*). As before, these are probabilistic statements, but in the neo-Firthian/Hallidayan perspective, they are also statements about the system. The solution to the distinct form-function correlates could well be to abandon the term 'future perfect' altogether for the *will-have* forms, and just call them *will-have* forms and focus on their different colligations. Swan (2005: 218–20) describes both the future and present/past certainty meanings of the *will-have* forms but keeps them separate, with the certainty function coming under *will* in the section on various future forms, and the future function getting its own traditional heading of 'future perfect'. McCarthy et al. (2014: 150), informed by extensive American English data, devote a section in the grammar to the present/past certainty meanings.

When we examine corpus data, we often discover meanings of grammatical forms that we know subliminally and use naturally and automatically but cannot easily access from introspection alone. This is one of the major contributions of corpus linguistics to the study of grammar; the corpus is an innovation with profound implications. It is no longer just a question of the native speaker making a judgement of grammaticality of individual sentences in the Chomskyan sense, but a genuine portal into users' language competence based on attested utterances gathered from a huge range of times, places, users, texts and contexts. Chomsky (1965: 18) had asserted that the speaker-hearer's linguistic competence was not amenable to direct observation, 'nor extractable from data'. This could be true if we believe that drilling down to some unconscious cognitive domain – the 'underlying linguistic structure' (ibid.) – is the only way to construct a grammar. However, corpora allow us to partake in a kind of exercise akin to the mass observation social research project undertaken in the United Kingdom in the 1930s, which Timmis (2016) uses so effectively to get at spoken language data observed and jotted down in an era prior to the availability of easy audio-recording. When we are in possession of enormous corpora of data amounting to tens of millions of words carefully collected from many thousands of sources, we observe the usage of 'the masses' in the form of grammatical patterns repeated hundreds, often thousands of times. This is all we need to write a reliable grammar: the usage of the masses *is* the grammar. We need apply no other test of acceptability or grammaticality. Of course, the corpus must be carefully collected to be as representative as possible of the target language; size alone is a not a sufficient criterion (Leech, 1991: 10–12). And it will be necessary to organise our observations into a coherent and usable account for anyone interested in accessing it, for which a neo-Firthian/Hallidayan model (as described in chapter 5) provides a potential framework of organisation. As Halliday says:

> '... the corpus does not write the grammar for us. Descriptive categories do not emerge out of the data. Description is a theoretical activity; and ... a

theory is a designed semiotic system, designed so that we can explain the processes being observed'.

(Halliday 1996: 24)

Notions of deep structure can be intellectually interesting and challenging, but they are by no means necessary.

6.5 Spoken and written grammar

Some of the most significant insights to emerge from the study of grammar in corpora concern the differences between the grammar of speaking and the grammar of writing. Many of these insights come from the study of individual grammatical items and features using corpus evidence. The starting point is often a noticeable difference in frequency of grammatical items (function words) when spoken and written data are compared. Putting two frequency lists side by side can immediately show up noticeable differences in the ranking of an item. Table 6.2 compares the 30 top-ranking words in the written texts of the BNC 1991–94 (BNC Consortium, 2007) and the Spoken BNC2014 in their normalised occurrences of per one million words (whole words only; contracted morphemes, e.g. *'s, n't* are excluded).

Although the definite article *the* appears in both lists in the top five, its frequency per million words is almost one-and-a-half times greater in the written corpus. This could be related to the fact that no pronouns appear in the top ten of the written list, while three appear in the spoken top ten; the written data are likely to be noun-heavy, and the spoken pronoun-heavy. A search for all the words tagged as nouns and all those tagged as pronouns in the two corpora shows that the written data are indeed noun-heavy, with full nouns over 20 times more frequent than pronouns, while in the spoken data, the frequencies are much closer, with a ratio of 1.3 nouns to every pronoun.

The spoken list has *I* and *you* in the top five, while the same two pronouns languish at 13 and 23, respectively, in the written list. This is indicative of the highly interactive nature of face-to-face conversation: when we talk with friends and intimates, the world is seen through the lens of 'you and me'. If this was all that we could learn from the frequency lists, their value would soon be exhausted, but in fact they yield almost inexhaustible pathways into grammatical differences between the two datasets. Some of these, which are chosen for what they tell us about the special nature of spoken grammar, are explored in the next section. These also lead us to more wide-ranging conclusions about the nature of grammar itself.

6.6 The *get*-passive: pattern and context

The lemma *get* (i.e. all the forms of the verb *get*) appears at number 17 in the spoken list in Table 6.2; it is down in the 70–80 rank in the written list, which represents a big difference, by any standards. *Get* is also a highly ranked positive *key* word in the spoken data (i.e. an item occurring with statistically significant greater frequency when compared with the written BNC). Its high frequency and

TABLE 6.2 Top-ranking frequencies in writing and speaking

BNC written			Spoken BNC 2014	
	lemma	per 1m words	lemma	per 1m words
1.	the	56,435.04	I	39,740.27
2.	be	35,313.50	be	35,470.18
3.	of	28,741.68	it	32,211.55
4.	to	23,650.72	you	28,319.73
5.	and	23,600.05	the	27,080.09
6.	a	19,626.17	and	25,045.45
7.	in	18,043.20	yeah	23,638.82
8.	have	11,155.88	do	21,039.09
9.	that	8,933.88	that	20,982.36
10.	for	8,135.41	a	19,669.64
11.	it	8,021.92	to	18,209.18
12.	he	7,049.98	like	14,534.82
13.	I	6,632.37	of	12,010.27
14.	on	6,499.42	have	11,862.09
15.	with	6,127.79	they	11,428.73
16.	as	6,116.38	in	10,329.45
17.	not	5,942.00	get	9,531.273
18.	by	4,958.12	so	9,472.818
19.	at	4,755.90	but	9,404.455
20.	they	4,588.01	he	8,863.818
21.	she	4,020.59	oh	8,782.636
22.	from	4,017.27	no	8,515.909
23.	you	3,996.18	know	8,382.182
24.	this	3,961.32	we	8,337.909
25.	his	3,957.59	just	7,772.273
26.	but	3,806.66	go	7,615.091
27.	do	3,663.74	mm	7,495.091
28.	which	3,433.97	what	6,749.364
29.	or	3,330.78	well	6,738.909
30.	an	3,178.67	there	6,527.818

keyword status are hardly surprising, given its nature as a delexical verb, i.e. a verb whose meaning in context is construed through its collocating complements (Stein and Quirk, 1991 give many examples of such delexical verb-noun combinations for common verbs). In the case of *get*, the spoken corpus shows that *get back/out/ up/on, get there, get away, get a job* and other everyday combinations all feature in the list of statistically significant collocates.

Get has had a bad name among prescriptive grammarians in the past, most probably because it has long been redolent of informal speaking and thus had no place in the elegant writing that pedagogically oriented grammars and usage manuals generally aimed to underpin and foster (for examples of such discussions in the 19th century, see Anderwald, 2016: 224ff). Some readers might recall their schooldays and exercises foisted upon them by over-zealous schoolteachers keen to rid compositions of the dreaded verb, with instructions to substitute occurrences of *get* with verbs like *obtain, arrive, understand*, etc.

Exploring the verb *get* in the spoken corpus, as well as providing ample evidence of its delexical nature, yields numerous examples of the so-called *get*-passive, i.e. constructions such as *get damaged, get paid, get chosen*, etc. The *get*-passive has generated a number of studies over the years; see those surveyed and cited in Carter and McCarthy (1999). In the research that I did with Ron Carter for our 1999 paper, we found that a great majority of our sample of *get*-passives from a sub-corpus of the CANCODE spoken corpus (see McCarthy, 1998 for details of that corpus) occurred in the context of negative or undesirable events. In our data, people got arrested, killed, criticised, deported and ripped off, together with various other misfortunes and calamities. Only in very few cases did speakers report positive events such as getting awarded something, getting upgraded, getting picked for a team, etc. In searching the data, one first has to manually filter out cases where the complement is adjectival with the meaning of 'become' (e.g. *get bored, get addicted to, get dressed*) rather than a true passive meaning, something that the computer is not always good at. Nonetheless, a random sample of 200 concordance lines of *get* + past participle generated from the Spoken BNC2014 reinforces the point that Carter and I made in our 1999 paper, namely that the preferred environment of the *get*-passive correlates strongly with undesired events. There are positive events recorded in a few cases; we can explain this by the shared context of 'newsworthiness', in the full knowledge that bad news is always more exciting and newsworthy than good. Samples from the Spoken BNC2014 include: [1]

Example 6.1
[complaining about poor medical treatment]
<0198> ah you can **get fobbed off** too easily can't you?
<S0230> yeah
[SRGR]

Example 6.2
[discussing a cultural festival where dangerous activities take place]
<S0454> mm people **get injured** every year
< S0579> oh there's always somebody hurt yeah
[SPG4]

A further observation made by Carter and McCarthy (1999) was the infrequent occurrence of a *by*-agent in the *get*-passive construction (see also Collins, 1996; Downing, 1996); this is borne out in the Spoken BNC2014: only three *by*-agents occur in our 200-line random sample. The *get*-passive is an example of how a corpus can be the basis of contextual grammar, and of the role that probabilities can play in assessing items. The innovative approach of corpus linguistics gives empirical substance to observations made by linguists such as Halliday and the earlier neo-Firthians in an era before software for linguistic analysis was widely available and easy to use. The syntactic and contextual characteristics of *get*-passives are elements of a systematic description of the form, not just adornments. The *get*-passive is a candidate for full treatment in a corpus-informed, probabilistic grammar of spoken English, which is what Carter and McCarthy (2006: 5–7) call a grammar of choice in contrast to a deterministic grammar.

6.7 Like

Computer software trained to tag data (i.e. to label each word with a word class) does not generally get on well with the word *like*. The quest for a proper classification of English words is, as we saw in chapters 2 and 3, centuries old. Apart from the relatively straightforward classes of noun, verb and adjective, other classes such as particles, adverbs, conjunctions and interjections have been something of a ragbag into which everything else is tossed, or, as Hopper calls them 'graveyard categories' (Hopper, 1998: 147). A good principle with ragbags – one instilled in me by my mentor John Sinclair – is that once the ragbag is full, it is likely to contain enough items to require further classification. Inside the ragbag of items in everyday spoken data we find words that operate outside of the sentence structure – words that organise the discourse or that reflect the speaker's stance towards the talk, now generally accepted as the class of discourse markers (Schiffrin, 1987 and others referred to in chapter 7). Rather than forcing every word into the word classes that quite effectively label almost everything in formal written data, we have to rethink the notion of word class for everyday informal speaking, and the notions of discourse/pragmatic markers have contributed greatly to pulling related objects out of the ragbag and giving them their own categorical identity. The class of discourse/pragmatic markers, like conjunctions, is a relatively open set in comparison with closed sets such as demonstratives or modal auxiliaries and ranges from single words such as *well, right* and *so*, organising and managing the talk, to chunks such as *to be honest* and *the trouble is* expressing speakers' stances. It also includes markers such as *look, listen* and *remember*, which focus the listener's attention. These markers stand freely in the flow of talk, with no requirement to be syntactically integrated into clauses in the co-text.

In the spoken list at Table 6.2, *like* is at rank 12 – a very high position. It can operate as a lexical verb (*to like*) as a function word (preposition *like*, conjunction *like*). The highest ranks of frequency lists for general English data are normally populated by function words, with lexical words pushed way down the list. *Like* has acquired the properties of a discourse marker, prefacing and creating focus on a preceding or following segment of talk and, used with the verb *be*, functioning as a speech marker. The Spoken BNC2014 has more than 9,000 occurrences of the string *I/(s)he was like*. In a random sample of 200 occurrences, no fewer than 177 introduce a direct speech report. Here are some examples:

> **Example 6.3**
> <S0441> he text me saying oh you can use my green bin* if you want because it's empty so **I was like** okay that's great so I text him back at like seven **I was like** yeah that would be really good thank you ...
> [S2AJ] *green bin: a rubbish container for organic waste only

> **Example 6.4**
> <S0235> what did she say? **she was like** oh erm <pause dur='short'/> you need to go downstairs and speak to the librarian downstairs ...
> [SUVQ]

> **Example 6.5**
> <S0439> ... the week beforehand when I was doing the Great North Run* **he was like** erm I'm so proud of you you know like you mean the world to me like I can't describe how much like I like how like impressed I am by you and how much you mean to me ...
> [STKV] * a half-marathon run held annually in north-east England

Does this use of *was like* simply mean 'said'? Romaine and Lange (1991) in an early study of the phenomenon, noted that what is framed by the *be like* construction does not necessarily imply a verbatim report; it can also be used to represent the speaker's thoughts or stance on a situation, as in Example 6.6, which can be heard as a 'dialogue with the self':

> **Example 6.6**
> <S0441> it's a lot of hours
> <S0439> yeah and
> <S0441> −[unclear word]
> <S0439> full time work and then obviously I was training for this half marathon I just couldn't fit it all in and **I was like** I'm not going to do it justice cos I don't want to waste my money so I decided not to do it
> [SD62]

6.8 Grammaticalisation and the evidence of spoken corpora

Example 6.7, below, reveals something fundamental about the use of *like* as a 'frame' for a segment of talk. In this example, as well as the speech-reporting *like*, there are seven other occurrences. Similarly, Example 6.5 above has five other examples of *like*. These other examples seem to frame segments of significance in their narratives (in Example 6.7 the hoped-for destination − a Bed and Breakfast), an odd turn of events (driving through an industrial area) or unexpected/disturbing sights (garages, kitchen and bathroom showrooms). Here, *like* is acting as a marker focusing attention on the important or newsworthy events. This is an illustration of how words from other word classes (nouns, verbs, adverbs, etc.) evolve to become used as markers, the process of 'grammaticalization' (Hopper and Traugott, 1993). In this case, *like* has metamorphosed into a marker of speech reporting and as a focus marker. A similar process has resulted in the lexical verb *go* becoming a speech-reporting marker (here also bolded):

Example 6.7
<S0336> I can't I can't speak any German I get to the conference the conference is fine and then they've given me the address of this **like** B and B so I get into a taxi and **I'm like** oh <S0343> take me there
<S0336> <overlap> this this is the address and **he's going** oh I d- I don't think there's a B and B there **I'm like** <pause dur='short'/> well this is the address I've got <vocal desc='laugh'/> so shall we just check it out? so we're **like** driving through this industrial estate there's **like** Ford garages and **like** **like** big **like** kitchen and bathroom **like** showrooms and stuff ...
[S3LE]

This case of grammaticalisation is not confined to British or American English and is older than many people might think, especially those who see it as a recent, irritating speech habit of teenagers. Irish English examples are pertinent. Irish English is often characterised by utterance-final *like*, as in this example from the Limerick Corpus of Irish English:

<$3> So I've no lectures I've to do the research myself.
<$2> You've to do it yourself.
<$3> Which is harder **like**.

(cited in Clancy and McCarthy, 2014)

In a corpus-based study of orality in Irish English emigrants' letters home from the mid-18th to the mid-20th century, Amador Moreno (2019: 112–16) gives examples of discourse marker *like* in clause-initial, clause-medial and clause-final position (the second most favoured position after clause-medial). The grammaticalisation of *like* has a long history from its original uses as an adjective, adverb, conjunction and preposition to its emergence as a discourse/pragmatic marker from the 18th century onwards, as citations in the *Oxford English Dictionary* (OED), as well as in Amador Moreno's work, testify. For further discussion, see also Amador Moreno (2012). Schweinberger (2012) is a study of recent changes in the sociolinguistics of *like* in Irish English (based on the Irish sub-corpus of the International Corpus of English), and for a relevance-theory perspective on *like* as a marker, see Andersen's (1998) study, based on the Bergen Corpus of London Teenage Language. All these works cited show *like* as a grammaticalised discourse/pragmatic marker, and we see why *like* is at home in a frequency list that we would normally expect to be populated at its highest ranks by function words rather than lexical ones.

Grammaticalisation is an important notion in the study of language change, and it has a central place in the approach of this book, as it opens up the whole question of the stability and validity of our conceptions of word classes and of the *a priori* status of grammar in relation to discourse. Nowhere is this more clearly in evidence than the grammar of everyday speaking, and corpora are the key to observing phenomena that might otherwise remain subliminal and on the margins of consciousness in the native speaker's usage (Watts, 1989; Milroy and Milroy, 1991: 15–16).

6.9 Grammaticalisation: *You know* and *I think*

Further evidence of grammaticalisation is seen in the presence of the lexical verb *know* in Table 6.2, at rank 23 in the spoken list and nowhere to be seen in the top 30 written list. It quickly becomes clear that its high rank is due to the frequency of the expression *you know*, which is the number one most frequent bigram (recurring combination of two adjacent words) in the Spoken BNC2014. It is followed closely at third place in the ranking by *I think*. *Know* is traditionally seen as a transitive verb, i.e. a verb that requires an object, yet in a random sample of 200 occurrences from the almost 46,000 total occurrences of *you know*, 172 have no object. In these cases, *you know* is used as a freestanding pragmatic marker expressing assumed common ground, shared knowledge or understanding, where the question of transitivity is irrelevant.

I think evidences a similar process of grammaticalisation (Palander-Collin, 1998). A speaker who says, 'I think she works on Sundays', in seeking confirmation or agreement from an interlocutor, might well use a tag and say, 'I think she works on Sundays, doesn't she?'. It would be bizarre to say, 'I think she works on Sundays, don't I?'. *I think* has become an epistemic pragmatic marker signalling the speaker's stance towards the truth, certainty or reliability of their utterance (Weinert, 2012), and we gain nothing by analysing the clause *she works on Sundays* as the object of *think*.

6.10 The significance of grammaticalisation

Grammaticalisation has been summarised as the process whereby 'lexical or less grammaticalized linguistic expressions are pressed into service for the expression of more grammaticalized functions' (Heine, 2003: 578). We have seen how this applies to lexical verbs such as *think* and *know* and the word *like* – an already hardworking item on both the lexical and grammatical levels. It also applies to more than single words, as in the example of the collocation *go to* becoming grammaticised to the 'going to' future (Traugott, 2003). The notion has a long history: Heine (2003) traces it back to the works of 18th-century philosophers and 19th-century historical linguists and their attempts to explain the evolution of grammatical morphemes by reduction and change in lexical items (see also Hopper, 1996 for further historical background). Lexical items lose or suffer reduction of their semantic content and gain extension to new contexts with gradual change in their status within the word-class system. An example from English is the modal auxiliary *will*, at various times in its long history having a fully lexical meaning of desiring or wishing for something, using one's will, wanting and intending, etc., remnants of which can be found in expressions such as *say what you will, God willing, where there's a will there's a way*, and so on. It is now used to supply a meaning of future time, alongside *shall, going to, be to* and other forms that are put into service in the absence of an inflected future tense in English. Swedish still retains the lexical meaning of desiring/wanting and its inflexions in the equivalent verb *vilja* (*jag vill* = *I want, jag ville* = *I wanted*), but also shows evidence of grammaticalisation in the fixed expression *det vill säga*, which is equivalent to English *that is to say* or its Latin abbreviated form *i.e.* (*id est*). English has grammaticalised *will* to a far greater extent: its lexical content has been drained, and the more abstract, functional meaning expressing a grammatical notion of future time has come to dominate its use. Such processes can be slow, but by Shakespeare's time (late 16th to early 17th century), *will* is attested in the OED as being in transition from the ancient to the more modern sense. *Go* has likewise undergone grammaticalisation from a lexical verb of motion to supply a future meaning in *be going to* (Hopper, 1996: 228–9). Similarly, historical trajectories have been traced for English *really* and its French equivalent *vraiment*, where the authors refer to *pragmaticalisation* as a distinct step in the change of an item's function, from major word class membership (here adverbs) to their present-day functioning as pragmatic markers (D'hont and Defour, 2012). Heine (2003) points to the diachronic overlap of meanings and functions and gradual transition as inherent to grammaticalisation. And similar processes of grammaticalisation are found in other languages, for example, the grammaticalised *la verdad es que* in Spanish and its Catalan equivalent *la veritat és que*, meaning 'the truth is', used as pragmatic markers (González, 2015). Other Hispanic studies examine the grammaticalised use of Spanish *como*, which parallels English *like* (Kern: 2014), the grammaticalised Spanish *verás* ('you'll see'), functioning as a pragmatic politeness marker (Chodowroska-Pilch, 2008), and *pues*, functioning in a similar way to English *because/cos* (Traugott, 1982: 255). Aijmer (2018) looks at the multifunctional uses of the Swedish modal *ska(ll)* (in some but not all respects similar to English *shall*) and also acknowledges its grammaticalised character. In these and many other cases in various languages we can observe a process of what Traugott (1995) refers to as *subjectification*: the process whereby grammaticalised forms encode the speaker's subjective stance rather than the original 'objective' meanings of truth, reality, temporality and so on.

Grammaticalisation brings us back to one of the central assertions of this book: far from being built on solid and unshifting foundations, grammar is more like a flowing river, although admittedly it can appear to flow sluggishly compared with the speed with which the vocabulary cascades into a well of new words and phrases and fads and fashions of lexical usage (Aleksandrova et al., 2017; McCarthy, 2017). In chapter 9 we shall look again at examples of grammatical change and discuss the social and historical forces that bring about change in grammar. For the moment, it is worth considering where grammaticalisation fits into a general theory of grammar that we have not touched upon up to now: emergent grammar. This view of grammar is one of the most interesting and potentially ground-shifting innovations of the past 20 to 30 years.

6.11 Emergent grammar

In the cases that we have focused on, the noticeably high frequency of what may be thought of as English lexical words (*go, know, think*) alerts us to some special property of theirs. Frequency is by no means a side issue in the question of grammaticalisation; Bybee, who uses the alternative term grammaticisation, sees it as a central feature of the process:

> 'Frequency is not just a result of grammaticization, it is also a primary contributor to the process, an active force in instigating the changes that occur in grammaticization'.
>
> (Bybee, 2003: 602)

A similar observation, although not directly attributed to grammaticalisation, can be seen in Aijmer's (2002: 27) discussion of the relative frequency with which discourse particles can be analysed purely on the level of discourse or on the propositional level, the results of which can be interpreted as indicative of grammaticalisation in action. An increase in the number and types of contexts in which the item in question is used boosts its overall frequency. Constant repetition solidifies an instance of usage, and we are left with the trace of myriad occasions of use; we call that trace 'grammar', and we mark the behaviours of words with word-class labels. In this view, grammar does not exist *a priori*. We see the after-effects of discourses that survive in the form of texts and memories collectively shared, with their choices of form and function made by their countless creators; all of these instances gel into recurrent patterns. Grammar *emerges* rather than exists before the fact. Sooner or later, we all agree that future time in English is adequately expressed by *will, shall, going to, be to*, present simple and continuous, etc. In the early stages of grammaticalisation we can expect resistance from those whose view of grammar is more conservative: we need go no further than the nearest online forum to see the kinds of heat generated by public debates over the use (usually condemned as overuse) of items such as *like* and *you know*. The condemnations are typically aimed at the people who use such forms rather than the forms *per se*, and those stigmatised are usually members of various groups which are marginalised from the sociopolitical establishments of power, class and profession: groups such as the young, the working class or certain ethnic groups, a recurring theme in Peterson's (2020) thought-provoking investigation of the notion of 'bad English'. The heat usually dies down over time to be succeeded by begrudged acceptance, not necessarily because light has been shed on things by researchers and academics, but simply through the inertia of habit and familiarity. In chapter 9 we shall see further examples of these public debates that testify to how unsettling grammaticalisation and consequent changes of usage can be for many people.

Hopper sees the growth in interest in discourse and pragmatics as one of the factors that led to a resurgence in the study of grammaticalisation in the 1970s after a period in which it languished in the doldrums. He offers the view that grammar can be understood as 'a historical process embedded in use rather than as a purely abstract synchronic state' (Hopper, 1996: 220). Use is *prior to* grammar; grammar emerges from use, not the other way around. If the other way around were true, grammar would never change; change is evidence of use in different and new discourse contexts. For Givón, putting it in slightly different terminology, there are two modes of communication, the pragmatic mode and the syntactic mode, and it is the latter which emerges from the former, not the other way around (Givón, 1979: 222). And it is probably uncontroversial to say that current changes in British English grammar are greatly conditioned by the shrinking world of global communications and global mobility, alongside social changes within the United Kingdom and the ever-present creativity in everyday usage (e.g. see Carter, 2004b: 97–100). All of this we return to in chapter 9.

Hopper's work on emergent grammar stresses the state of flux and the temporary nature of grammatical phenomena. As regards speech, he criticises the 'reduction of a temporal medium to a fixed, stable, and timeless one, articulated in a terminology of parts and units' (Hopper, 2011: 23). In that same 2011 paper, in an illustration of the repetitive nature of linguistic phenomena, including what might conventionally be termed clauses and phrases as well as fragments, Hopper shows how most of a conversational transcript can be accounted for by strings that return hits ranging from hundreds to millions when entered into an internet search engine. Informal dialogue, says Hopper, 'consists not of sentences generated by rules, but of the linear on-line assembly of familiar fragments' (Hopper, 2011: 26). Here we are reminded of the idiom principle expounded by Sinclair (1991), mentioned in chapter 4; Sinclair's corpus insights amount to the same conclusion as Hopper's: most (or all in Hopper's view) of what we say is drawn from a collectively sanctioned and massively repeated repertoire of words that routine use has sedimented into clumps of form and function strung together, which we interpret as 'grammar'.

6.12 Conclusion

In this chapter, we have been guided by the data, rather than starting from a ready-made model of grammar. We saw that words convey meanings in distinct patterns of form and function, that items from the pedagogical canon of English grammar and the way that they are described and taught can be at odds with what we find in corpus data, both in terms of formal distribution (our example was the subjunctive) and range of meanings (exemplified by the future perfect tense-aspect form). We also saw how a simple set of frequency lists can lead us down pathways that illuminate questions of grammar in surprising and often unanticipated ways, which are difficult to find via intuition alone. Certain banal words prominent in the frequency list of our everyday spoken data and notably absent from our written data give us a window not only into how everyday speaking is organised and managed differently from formal writing, but also into how grammar is forged in the crucible of ordinary interaction. The process of grammaticalisation that a word such as *like* has undergone and is still undergoing suggests that people exploit linguistic resources to respond to the pragmatic requirements of their current communicative situation. They do not take grammar ready-made off the shelf. Hopper is highly critical of the assumption of an 'abstract, mentally represented rule system which is somehow implemented when we speak' and which has assumed the status of 'virtually an official dogma' (1987: 140). We observe grammar after the fact; it is the trace left on the written text or the transcript, on the audio record or in the collective memory, by repeated interactions over long periods of time and uttered by countless numbers of the language's users. The key, then, to understanding grammar lies in discourse and pragmatics, not vice-versa, and so it is to the world of discourse that we next must turn.

But before we conclude this chapter, we should ask the question: what does all this mean in practice? In other parts of this book we have seen how very different approaches to grammar have been applied (or not) in reference resources, usage manuals and materials for language pedagogy. This chapter has rested on three premises: that corpora can tell us much about the workings of language that is difficult to access through intuition or native-speaker competence, that the grammar of informal speaking is distinctly different from the grammar of formal writing, and that spoken grammar throws into sharp relief significant aspects of language change through the process of grammaticalisation. However, the information on spoken grammar offered by corpus linguists had by no means an easy ride among pedagogical applied linguists and language teachers in the early days. When my colleagues Ron Carter and Rebecca Hughes and I travelled to the USA to take part in a symposium with Douglas Biber and his co-researchers (who were working in similar areas to us) at an international conference in the mid-1990s, our presentations on corpus and spoken grammar left our audience underwhelmed, to say the least. Later, we even encountered resistance and open hostility to the idea that the settled, consensually compartmentalised world of the ELT grammar canon might be disturbed by the evidence of the ubiquity of chunks, the extra-syntactic phenomenon of pragmatic marking and indications of previously unnoticed lexicogrammatical patterns and uncharted meanings for familiar grammatical features. You would have thought that we were preaching armed insurrection, so strong was the reaction on occasion. One member of the audience at an event in the United Kingdom, when we explained that our corpus data was compiled from recordings of ordinary people, including our families and friends and members of the public at large, stood up during the Q&A session and said that they did not want to hear about the grammar of our 'semi-literate friends'. I wanted to point out to our audience that we chose our friends carefully but that nobody could choose their family, but that would probably have been dismissed as facetious. The serious point was that what corpora were revealing about the grammar of everyday speaking was, for some, proving to be very unsettling.

It was not only language teachers from the wider world of the ELT industry who were unhappy. Academics began to criticise us and others (generally in more civilised tones) for advocating an important role for corpora in describing the usage of native users of English. Cook (1998) was understanding of, and politely generous to, my colleague Ron Carter's support for the contribution of corpora to language teaching (Carter, 1998), but Cook claimed that 'immense damage' could be done by those taking a hard line on the use of corpora. Not that Carter and I were ever hardliners, nor were we ever naïve enough to think that corpus evidence was a silver bullet for language teaching and learning. Cook argued that the ways that grammarians organise the language also constitute facts about the language, which is another assertion with which I cannot disagree, or else I would not have devoted such space and praise in this book to the work of Halliday. 'A good deal of actual language use is inarticulate, impoverished, and inexpressive', says Cook (1998: 61), but should applied linguists set themselves up as arbiters of 'good' language, as heirs to some of the more prescriptive grammarians whom we have cited in this book? However, Cook offered a well-balanced set of arguments overall and never charged the work that Carter and I were doing with taking a hard line; for anyone interested, he names and shames those he considered to be hardliners.

A more trenchant criticism of corpora that Cook (1998) and others made was the equation between 'real' English and native-speaker English. Such evidence, it was argued, was increasingly irrelevant in a world where most users of English were non-native speakers. They had a point in terms of the numbers of English users. However, Carter and I had never advocated either that native-speaker evidence was the only evidence that should be adduced in the construction of grammatical syllabuses, or that anyone should be forced to adopt any model of English that they felt unhappy with, whether it be British, American, Australian, Irish or whatever, or any non-native-speaker model of English (see Farrell, 2020 for a recent discussion of models of English in ELT). We liked to think that people were intelligent enough to make their own choices based on as wide a range of information as possible. We were delighted to see corpus projects being launched into learner English, into varieties of English outside the so-called inner circle countries and into English as a lingua franca. However, we felt confident about our own work for several reasons: spoken corpus transcripts were showing us fundamental aspects of *human* interaction, not just English-speaking ones, and corpus studies of other languages were steadily supporting this belief by revealing similar distinctive phenomena in their spoken grammar, albeit with different linguistic realisations. Furthermore, when we persuaded our publishers to let us develop resources that included a focus on spoken grammar, by and large, teachers and students liked them and gave us positive feedback, and the publishers achieved commercial success with them (e.g. Carter and McCarthy, 1997; Carter, Hughes and McCarthy, 2000; McCarthy et al., 2005; Carter and McCarthy, 2006; Carter et al., 2011). Above all, we were gaining dispassionate insights into the workings of language from computers that knew nothing about syllabuses, exams, commercial pressures, attitudes, prejudices, fads and fashions, ideologies, canons or orthodoxies. Trained by our mutual mentor, John Sinclair, we let the data speak, we trusted the text, and we drew our own conclusions.

Note

1 Unless otherwise indicated, the spoken corpus extracts in this book are all from the Spoken BNC2014. Each extract is followed by a document ID in square brackets indicating the source of the transcript. All extracts from the Spoken BNC2014 used in this book are owned by Cambridge University Press and are reproduced under licence. Where appropriate and where they do not alter interpretation, computational annotations have been removed or simplified for ease of reading.

7

GRAMMAR AND DISCOURSE

7.1 Beyond the sentence

Many of the discussions about grammar over the centuries have been seen from the point of view of items and structures that can fit into the grammar of sentences; that is to say, the grammar that can fit between full stops in writing or, in a looser but more satisfactory sense, the grammar of clauses and clause combinations. This latter designation is more satisfactory, as the notion of 'sentence' is especially problematic when we look at transcripts of speech and types of informal writing, such as advertising copy and social media posts. We do not speak in capital letters and full stops, and as Brazil put it, as regards the grammar of speaking, '…we do not necessarily have to assume that the consideration of such abstract notions as 'sentences' enters into the user's scheme of things at all' (Brazil, 1995: 15). Hopper is blunter in his rejection of the notion of sentence:

> 'It seems to me, and it has seemed so to others also, that the sentence is an artifact of some historical accidents, including most prominently the Western rhetorical and grammatical tradition and the development of a written language'.
>
> *(Hopper, 1988: 19)*

The notion of the sentence as forming the boundary of grammatical study is also problematic for a neo-Firthian approach to grammatical description and modelling, with the addition of the paradigm-shifting notion of emergent grammar as a safeguard against falling into the trap of trying to explain the fabric of discourse in terms of sentences (Hopper, 1987). None of this is easy to achieve, as we lack, at the time of writing, an appropriate and agreed metalanguage to capture the complexities that contexts and discourses present to us and through which we can adequately describe grammatical features in discourse environments.

With its emphasis on semiotic systems and the context of situation, a neo-Firthian grammar takes us 'above' the sentence in the visual metaphor of the vertical rank scale (see p. 78), but also 'beyond' the sentence in terms of going outside the limits of morphology and syntax to consider choices from the patterned lexico-grammatical repertoire in their contexts of use. Both terms – *above* and *beyond* – are current in approaches to language description. Here I shall stick to *beyond*, as I hope to show that conventionally labelled phrases and clauses and the ways that they combine can be fully apprehended only by bringing in features of co-text and context, outside of the limits of the immediate spoken utterance or written sentence and by going conceptually 'beyond'. In other words, we are dealing with discourse, the creation of meaning in context and with an innovation that came about in the late 20th century and that is broadly covered by the umbrella term of *discourse grammar*, although *grammar in* (or *and*) *discourse* and *the grammar of discourse* are also current. In an emergent view, the last term, *the grammar of discourse*, perhaps more closely aligns with the idea that discourse is prior to grammar and not the reverse.

Zellig Harris (1952a), in a paper entitled *Discourse Analysis*, won the term widespread attention. Harris sought to get at the structure of a text by looking at how sentences in the text fell into classes of equivalence and how they were strung together cohesively to compose the text. He eschewed the reduction of sentences to phrase structures such as NP + VP, dismissing the activity as 'one that could be applied to any set of English sentences, whether they constitute a continuous discourse or not' (Harris, 1952b: 477). He was interested in features such as repetition of grammatical elements in identical environments, substitution and co-reference (e.g. pronoun reference), terms that were later to become central to the study of how sentences related to one another in texts. Harris's analysis is a rather abstract exercise; he was Noam Chomsky's teacher, and we can see his influence on Chomsky's abstract approach to sentence structure.

7.2 Discourse analysis and textual cohesion

The term *discourse analysis* has been applied to the analysis of both written texts and spoken ones. Since Harris's time, discourse analysts have shifted their attention to accessing the functions and meanings immanent in texts, focusing on the linguistic devices in the text and/or taking into account the context of utterance, whether it be the social or ideological context. Our focus will be on the contribution of grammatical (i.e. non-lexical) choices within the text in its context. The most basic statement we can make initially about the relationship between grammar and discourse is that grammatical choices play a role in the cohesion and coherence of the text, i.e. they help to 'stick the text together' and help it to make sense by providing various types of links across units of meaning.

Halliday and Hasan (1976) are credited with the most innovative and comprehensive account of textual cohesion in their description of how linguistic elements connect clauses and sentences in continuous texts. The details of their later revision of cohesion (Halliday and Hasan, 1989) need not concern us here, as the basic

1976 grammatical framework remains valid and suits our purpose. They showed how reference by pronouns could look backward in text (anaphora), forward (cataphora) and out of the text into the immediate context (exophora). It was thus possible to categorise the following uses of demonstrative *this* as having different types of referent. The first two examples are from the British National Corpus (BNC Consortium, 2007); the third was seen on a sign on a door:

    (1) The asking price was £3,500. **This** was a considerable sum of money. [BNC 1991–1994: A7C]
        (anaphora: *this* refers to the asking price of £3,500)
    (2) **This** is what her letter said: My dearest Victor, I am so happy that you will soon be home. [BNC 1991–1994: H8G]
        (cataphora: *this* refers to the whole clause after the colon)
    (3) **This** door must be kept closed at all times. [sign on a door]
        (*this* refers 'out' from the text into the context)

Here we see ways in which the internal choices in the clause/sentence can be understood only by going beyond the clause/sentence. However, example (1) above allows for at least two alternatives which retain the coherence of the text:

    (1a) The asking price was £3,500. **It** was a considerable sum of money.
    (1b) The asking price was £3,500. **That** was a considerable sum of money.

Elsewhere (McCarthy, 1994) I have commented upon this three-way choice in terms of their functioning as signals of the sender's stance. Pronoun *it* in (1a) seems to simply continue the current topical focus in a neutral way. Pronoun *that* (1b) distances the sender somewhat from the previous sentence. Pronoun *this* (1) closely aligns the sender with the evaluation of the previous sentence, shining a spotlight on it, perhaps with the intention of elaborating upon it. These are interpretations that I backed up in my 1994 paper with support from the literature (e.g. Lakoff, 1974; Thavenius, 1983; Geisler et al., 1985) and an analysis of a sample of 50 examples of the target items and textual extracts from British newspapers and magazines. I revisited the question using spoken examples in McCarthy (1998: 69–72). I hope that my interpretations were plausible ones, but my purpose in citing my paper here is that, around that time, I began to realise that the data were saying something more fundamental about the relationship between grammar and discourse. Conventionally, *this* and *that* belong to a paradigm (or system in the Hallidayan sense – see p. 82) of four members, shared with *these* and *those*; you choose one of them when the moment arises. They enable the speaker to express the primary distinction between people and things near and those further away (but see Tao, 1999 for a detailed survey and a challenge to this rather simplified view, using Mandarin Chinese data). Pronoun *it*, however, is typically grouped in a system with personal pronouns (*I/me, you, she/him, our,* etc.), which distinguish person, case, gender and number. Thus have grammarians stated the relationships among pronouns for centuries. However, Brazil (1997: 23) provides us with a new term for the *it* vs *this* vs *that* paradigm. He refers to 'existential paradigms' – sets of choices dictated by the discourse at appropriate points within the text which re-arrange the decontextualised paradigms found in standard grammar reference books. From an emergent viewpoint, this tripartite choice exhibits the subjectification discussed in chapter 6. They are grammatical choices, but they respond to discoursal conditions, not the other way around.

7.3 Cohesion and speaking turns: conjunction

Halliday and Hasan (1976) also listed conjunction and ellipsis as cohesive devices. Although these are all found in written texts, it is their occurrences in spoken texts that prove most illuminating in terms of the grammar–discourse relationship. Conjunctions such as *and, but, or* and *so* frequently occur in writing at clause- and sentence-initial positions (e.g. see Bell, 2007), but they also occur in spoken transcripts at the beginning of speakers' turns. In this way, they can perform a cohesive function not only between clauses, but between contributions of different speakers or between successive elements of the same speaker's discourse where a contribution by another speaker has intervened. In Example 7.1 we see a number of turns beginning with conjunctions (*and, so but*):

Example 7.1
[The speakers are discussing the treatment of different types of wood and objects made from them.]
<S0094> I mean different woods are involved <pause dur='short'/> although that's teak
<S0021> ah very nice yeah
<S0094> **and** that's a eucalyptus as well
<S0021> mm mm mm mm
<S0094> **so** it's actually you know it's fine<S0021> mm<S0094> **but** like we thought these bits would come up quite nice as contrast-y<S0021> <overlap> mm<S0094> I, when it oiled
<S0021> yeah
<S0094> **but then** this is really nice not oiled <pause dur='short'/> I mean you could just oil bits of it this'll come up nice
[S23A]

And (*and that's a eucalyptus* ...) performs its core additive function, but it also confirms speaker 0094's status as main floor-holder, while speaker 0021's turns are confined to back-channel *mm* and *yeah* and a brief non-minimal response *ah, very nice, yeah*. Speaker 0094's utterances are typical of informal speaking in that increments are added in real time and in a linear fashion (see Warren, 2015 for further examples and discussion). There is no evidence that the speaker is attempting to construct 'sentences' by their use of conjunctions. *So* seems to be prefacing an evaluation and, in combination with *actually* and *you know*, suggests signalling an end to this particular segment of the discourse (see Handford, 2010: 111–13 for examples from business meetings). Bolden (2009) offers an interesting discussion of various functions of turn-initial *so*, and González (2005) presents a number of examples in oral narratives in English and its equivalent(s) in Catalan. *But* is a little more elaborate: the first *but* seems to suggest a shift to a new segment/sub-topic (the possibility of oiling items), while *but then* indicates a contrast with the (unstated) implication of oiling the whole of an item. If turn-initial *but* is often a signal of a challenge to a previous turn (Channon et al., 2018) or objecting to a proposal that is implicit in the context (Zeevat, 2012), then the best that we can say here is that the speaker is setting up a self-initiated pseudo-challenge and thereby continuing to hold the floor and to manage the discourse. Another, more illuminating interpretation is that speaker 0094's use of *but* sets up what Fillmore (1982) would call an 'alternate framing', i.e. seeing the discourse as a series of cognitive-interactive frames whereby participants make sense of the situation and segment the talk accordingly. Speaker 0094 is suggesting an alternative frame for judging the merits of oiling or not oiling the wood. In this way, the conjunctions can be seen as cohesive not at the inter-clause or inter-sentence level but at the discourse level of connected frames.

A similar phenomenon can be observed in the turn-initial use of *cos/because*, which in written discourse would typically signal a cause-effect cohesive relation. Stenström (1998) shows how what she calls disjunctive uses of *cos* do not express cause-effect relations in informal talk. Schiffrin (1987, 191) also sees *cos/because* as a discourse marker and observes its ability to refer to a unit of talk rather than just as a subordinator attaching to a main clause, while Schleppegrell (1991) sees it as a way of signalling further elaboration on what the speaker has already said. A similar argument is present in Stirling's (1999) study of isolated *if*-clauses (i.e. *if*-clauses not attached to any main clause), opening up the whole question of the viability of the traditional notion of 'subordinate clauses' in informal speaking.

Example 7.2 shows how speaker 0315 uses *cos* to explain/justify asking the question *did you enjoy it?* in a next turn overlapping with speaker 0255's response, and *cos* seems to operate in the way suggested in the discourse analysis literature:

Example 7.2
<S0315> did you enjoy it?
<S0255> really did yeah really nice
<S0315> <overlap> **cos** I enjoy doing it as well
<S0255> yeah
[S28F]

Conjunctions such as *and, but, so* and *or* can also occur in the turn-final position (Norrick, 2009). Example 7.3 below shows two turn-final occurrences of *but* – first immediately after a question – and second as the final word in a question. These cases represent what Hata (2016: 138), working within a conversation-analytical (CA) framework, refers to as 'pragmatic turn-completion without syntactic accomplishment'. Given our discussion of emergent grammar in chapter 6, one must ask why 'syntactic accomplishment' is even needed as an explanatory notion for what is perfectly normal spoken grammar, and which does not seem to be 'without' anything. In context, these turn-final conjunctions can be interpreted as leaving the option open for an opposing proposition or frame, in the first case that the situation may be temporary, and similarly, in the second case, the speaker is suggesting the opposite of *not right now* may be in the listener's mind (perhaps at some point in the future); the contrasts remain implied but unsaid, simply because they do not need to be said:

Example 7.3
<S0262> so then so you're not working at the moment then? **But**
<S0334> no
<S0262> you like you but you not obviously not but are you gonna thinking about you know eventually I mean not right now **but**?
<S0334> <overlap> yeah <pause dur='short'/> yeah I don't know erm <pause dur='short'/> don't know what to do really
<S0262> mm <pause dur='short'/> just see what happens <pause dur='short'/> yeah
[SFG3]

Likewise, with turn-final *so*, a speaker can project a conclusion from what they have just said, without saying it (Example 7.4):

Example 7.4
<S0018> I've not seen him for must be two or three years <pause dur='short'/> seems like he's grown since then
<S0131>no he's a good lad <pause dur='short'/> he cooked me a nice curry on Sunday night
<S0018> how did it turn out?
<S0131> he's a great cook <pause dur='short'/> he loves <pause dur='short'/> all three of them love cooking **so**
<S0018> fantastic <pause dur='short'/> you've brought them up so well
[S2XV]

In all these cases, the use of turn-initial and turn-final conjunctions plays a significant role in turn construction and turn management. We can see a parallel with the cohesive role of conjunctions in written text, but we see more: an interactive dimension that enables speakers to manage their contributions while not excluding contributions from their listeners and effectively linking segments of the discourse. Our conjunctions may well be grammatical (in the sense of 'non-lexical') items, but ones that have undergone grammaticalisation to become turn-construction markers. This is the grammar of turn-construction and cohesion across turns, not of sentence construction and cohesion across sentences. It is grammar in the service of discourse, not in the service of well-formed sentences.

7.4 Ellipsis

Typologically, if we start from the conventions of formal writing, English is a language where a subject is compulsory in an indicative verb phrase, so an exchange along the lines of *A: Who's Sandra? B: She's my cousin* is acceptable, but *A: Who's Sandra? B: Is my cousin** is not. However, principles that conventionally apply in formal writing as to what must be included and what need not be do not apply in informal speaking if we are to believe the evidence of corpora. Example 7.5 has a question that can be understood as synonymous with *Do you want some seconds?* and a response interpretable as synonymous with *I'm alright for now thanks*; yet there is no evidence in the corpus transcript that the participants have any problem interpreting the question and answer as uttered.

Example 7.5
<S0548> want some seconds?
<S0551> alright for now <pause dur='short'/> thank you
[SWU6]

I have avoided making reference to anything 'missing' or 'omitted' from Example 7.5. There is nothing omitted. The questioning nature of speaker 0548's utterance is clear in the context (and was obviously clear to the transcriber, who marked it with a question mark), and 0551's response is obviously a first-person reference (it would be odd if it referred to a different, articulate guest at the table), and the question is clearly seen as an offer. Are the utterances 'grammatical'? The term usually applied to explain such utterances, *ellipsis*, is unfortunate, for it is often conceived as meaning that something is omitted from the grammar (as in the current *Oxford English Dictionary* [OED] definition), albeit that even 17th-century citations in the OED show that it referred to 'things understood' rather than 'things missing'.

Computers are not good at helping us to retrieve phenomena that are conventionally labelled as ellipsis from data, as it is much easier to retrieve and count what *is* there rather than what we think is not (see Greenbaum and Nelson, 1999, who performed a considerable amount of manual annotation of their data). The problem tends to lie in machines that have been trained on written language rather than spoken transcripts (Caines and Buttery, 2010), as writing typically adheres to more elaborated forms, given that most (but certainly not all) formal written texts are composed with a view to their being read at times and places different from those of their production. It is more illuminating to say that written texts tend to *add* elements for that very decontextualising purpose, rather than to suggest that informal spoken transcripts miss things out.

Example 7.5 is a case of *situational ellipsis* (Carter and McCarthy, 2006: 181–88), where the immediate physical situation itself provides all the contextual cues needed to interpret quite short and economical utterances (the speakers are at a dinner table, the first servings have just been consumed, S058 is the host, etc.).

Rühlemann (2007: 55–58) sees situational ellipsis in terms of the shared context that is characteristic of face-to-face conversation and the real-time processing that interlocutors engage in. It is different from textual ellipsis, where elements can be understood by reference within the text itself, as in example 7.6:

Example 7.6
It was suggested that they call the police, and they did. [understood: 'and they did call them/the police']
[BNC 1991–1994: doc 964]

In our 2006 grammar, in the section on situational ellipsis, Carter and I give corpus examples where all sorts of elements supposedly 'obligatory' in phrases, clauses and sentences are simply not there, including pronouns, auxiliary verbs, determiners and copular verbs. Likewise, Caines et al. (2016) give numerous examples from the BNC of progressive/continuous verb phrases where no auxiliary is present, and Caines and Buttery (2010) showed that 27 per cent of questions in their data with *you*-subjects (e.g. *What you doing? You been working?*) had no auxiliary, compared with only 5.4 per cent of such patterns in a comparable written dataset. They argue that this sort of ellipsis does not occur randomly and that contextual features such as the subject pronoun type and certain tense-aspect forms can be used to create a predictive model for machine-training in natural language processing. Caines et al. (2018) is an updated version of the 2010 work based on the Spoken BNC2014.

What appears on the transcript can resemble a series of fragments, but fragments that are perfectly communicative and pragmatically appropriate in their contexts. Often, it is a fruitless exercise to try to fill in the so-called 'missing' elements and difficult to do so with any certainty. For example, Carter and I quote a speaker saying, 'Lots of things to tell you about the trip to Barcelona' (Carter and McCarthy 2006: 181). How do we make this 'syntactically complete' (as if we need to)? Should it be *There are lots of things …?* or *I've got lots of things …?* In one interpretation we would have an *existential subject* + *copular verb* + *complement* structure; in the other, a *personal subject* + *lexical verb* + *object* structure. In other words, we can read at least two different types of transitivity in the Hallidayan sense (Halliday, 1967a, b and c) into the utterance, and it is an example of what Thomas (1987) calls 'verbally indeterminate' ellipsis, where interpretation depends on the context rather than any co-text. But it would be a mistake to think that verbally indeterminate ellipsis is some kind of oddity thrown up by people speaking in heavily embedded contexts; such contexts are the everyday norm; people talk while doing things. The participants know what is meant and do not need to fill in any gaps or complete any syntax, and probably could not give two hoots which of the interpretations is more valid. The examples of what we term situational ellipsis are the clearest indications of grammar serving the purposes of the discourse, not vice-versa.

7.5 Heads or tails?

We noted the high frequency of pronouns in the spoken data in chapter 6 and attributed this to the interactive dimension of dialogue and face-to-face talk. Personal pronouns have deictic meanings, locating speakers, listeners and others in the discoursal world: put simply, *I* means speaker, *you* means listener(s), *(s)he/it/they* mean other(s), including non-human animals and things; *we* can mean speaker and listener or speaker and other(s). There are further deictic possibilities which contexts offer: *you* can mean everyone (speaker included), *we* can mean a single author in academic writing, *they* can mean 'the powers that be/the authorities', *one* can mean speaker or people in general, *I* can mean writer and reader in philosophical discourse, and so on; see Kitigawa and Lehrer (1990). As always, the meaning of the grammar depends on the context.

Description conventionally tells us that the subject of an English verb can be a noun phrase or a pronoun; this is the assumption that virtually all pedagogical grammars and grammar practice books for English follow. Indicative verb phrases must have a subject (but see 7.4, above); you can select a noun phrase or a pronoun, but not both at the same time. And yet, when we look at spoken corpus data, we find numerous examples where noun phrases and pronouns seem to compete side by side for interpretation as subject of the verb. Consider these examples:

Example 7.7
<S0255> **my nephew he** really likes all the different cheeses <pause/> [intervening words] **me sister she** eats lots of raw peppers but she only likes double Gloucester*
[S8GL] *a type of English cheese

Example 7.8
<S0417> ... erm **my cousin X*** **she**'s had twin girls they're about one year's old now
[S3C6] *people's names are anonymised in the corpus

In the real-time world of informal face-to-face interaction (the context in which most of the world's language production at any given moment takes place), items such as *my nephew, me/my sister* and *my cousin X* need not be classified as subjects but rather as topics: these are the people or things that the speaker will talk about. They are cues for the listener. Phonologically they typically occupy their own intonational group which marks them out as a kind of 'headline' for the newsworthy information that follows. Carter and McCarthy (2006: 192–94) call them *headers*. In addition, in Example 7.5 they act as framing devices for the contrast between two people (the nephew and the sister). They are in a psychological sense simultaneously the subjects of the verbs that follow (*likes, has had*) and co-referential with the 'extra' pronouns (*he, she*), but this assignment of the label 'subject' is after the event; it is an account of the trace of the interaction rather than the unfolding of it. Furthermore, there can be more than one topical noun phrase (Examples 7.9 and 7.10) or intervening matter (Example 7.11), with or without a following pronoun:

Example 7.9
A friend of mine, his uncle had the taxi firm when we had the wedding.
(author's own data, cited in Carter and McCarthy, 2017)

Example 7.10
His cousin in London, her boyfriend, his parents bought him a Ford Escort* for his birthday.
(author's own data, cited in Carter and McCarthy, 2006: 193)
*popular model of car at the time

Example 7.11
And **my grandmother**, I've never forgotten, when we were small my sister and I, **she** used to take us down, stand on the cliff there and we'd sing to the seals.
(Heir to the British throne, HRH Prince Charles, speaking on a BBC television broadcast, 3 September 2005; http://news.bbc.co.uk/1/hi/uk/4212394.stm)

Example 7.10 acts like a series of lexical stepping-stones, designed to get the listener into the topic; there is no requirement for the three noun phrases to be syntactically linked. Indeed, a fully syntactic version such as *his cousin in London's boyfriend's parents* or *the parents of the boyfriend of his cousin in London* would in both cases be quite a mouthful, difficult to produce or process, except for in the temporally displaced and more reflective media of writing and reading.

A mirror-image of the noun phrase + pronoun at the end of a clause is seen in these examples, where there is a consistent pattern of evaluation. The evaluative element (in these cases the underlined adjective phrases) are brought into greater prominence, and the grammatical subjects are represented by lexically weak pronouns:

Example 7.12
<S0024> **they**'re lovely **my friends**
[SP6E]

Example 7.13
[speakers are talking about cherry tomatoes]
<S0199> **they**'re nice **the ones you grow yourself**
<S0192> yeah I bet they are
[SQHY]

Example 7.14
<S0327> and **they**'re so beautiful **the kestrels**
[S2ZU]

Example 7.15
<S0454> I find **fish and chips they**'re so greasy **the chips** now
<S0579> yeah they're so thick they er they're covered up very little fish inside
[SPG4]

McCarthy and Carter (1997) call these *tails* (see also Carter and McCarthy, 2006: 194–96). There is an extensive literature on what we called headers and tails, examples of which are cited in Carter and McCarthy (1995) and the two references just mentioned above. That literature does not need to be rehearsed here, but it often falls prey to the metaphors of *a priori* spatial syntax, referring to left dislocation (headers) and right dislocation (tails). We rejected those metaphors as failing to reflect the fact that speaking is temporal, not spatial (Pekarek Doehler, 2011); we see them as hangovers from the study of grammar in writing and the confines of the sentence. Hallidayan grammar employs the spatio-temporally more neutral terms *preposed* and *postposed* themes (e.g. Downing and Locke, 1992: 234), which capture far better the notion of topics and variable prominence given to them rather than the formal notion of shifting or dislocating grammatical elements. In the data presented here, nothing is dislocated; items are simply delivered in common-sense sequences, which are communicatively efficient and effective – 'a convenience alike to the hearer … and speaker' (Quirk et al., 1985: 1417).

A related phenomenon to tails is a type of repetition wherein the evaluation is topicalised after a pronoun and repeated after a co-referential noun phrase:

Example 7.16
<S0525> … I mean **they** were lovely **the kids** were lovely
[SB7R]

Example 7.17
<S0199> **they** were weak **my defences** were weak
[SJB4]

Example 7.18
<S0278> you pay to go in erm they've got a lovely shop <pause> and and **it**'s fair **the prices** are fair
[SDXW]

Example 7.19
<S0013> **it**'s all rusty **the wires** were all rusty
[S7RA]

Seen from a conventional syntactic viewpoint, some of the ways in which speakers arrange their messages are a struggle to analyse. It is no wonder that corpus taggers and parsers have such trouble with naturally occurring spoken data. In the Prince Charles example (7.11, above), it is not at all clear how the phrase *my sister and I* relates to the rest of the utterance syntactically:

> And my grandmother, I've never forgotten, when **we** were small **my sister and I**, she used to take **us** down …

The bold noun phrase acts as a tail to *we*; it is also co-referential with *us*, to which it could be a header, or it could be both tail and header. The transcription includes a comma after *I*, but this too is ambiguous – headers are often followed by commas in written contexts such as quoted speech. We could resort to interpreting Prince Charles's utterance as an *anacoluthon* – a rather spectacular piece of terminology meaning the collapsing of two sentences into one, with *my sister and I* facing in two directions, as it were, but that would not get us very far, as we are likely to bump into such utterances all over our corpus data. The OED citations suggest a somewhat negative connotation of the term *anacoluthon* (incoherence, disconnected), and yet rarely if ever do we find overt evidence in corpus data that listeners experience strings like our royal example as incoherent or disconnected.

7.6 Grammar in spoken and written discourse analysis

In this chapter, I have placed the emphasis heavily on grammar in spoken discourse and the innovations in description made possible by corpora. This is not because I wish to ignore the work scholars have done on written discourse, among which we find innovative work on pattern grammar, the recurrence of form-meaning correlations in linguistic strings of various kinds; e.g. Hunston and Francis (2000), lexico-syntactic priming, the strong associations of items with particular positions in texts, e.g. Hoey (2005) and Hoey and O'Donnell (2015), who show that quite long texts can be subject to close analysis, and critical discourse analysis, which seeks to expose the undercurrents of ideologies in texts, e.g. Fairclough (1995), Wodak and Meyer (2009); see Baker (2015) for an interesting corpus-based discussion. Then there is the impressively original work of Biber on multi-dimensional features of texts, revealing how a wide range of grammatical items and features are unevenly distributed across different registers of writing and in conversation, providing lexico-grammatical fingerprints of texts in different languages (Biber 1988, 1995; Biber and Finegan, 1991) and culminating in the register distinctions that permeate the Biber et al. (1999) reference grammar; all these have been innovative in their distinct approaches and have shed light on texts beyond the sentence.

My own research has long been dominated by the study of everyday spoken interaction, for two principal reasons: one linguistic, one ideological. The linguistic reason is by now, I hope, becoming clear: everyday spoken interaction is, par excellence, the site of emergent grammar in Hopper's sense, and of language deeply embedded in its contexts of use, in the Hallidayan sense: two views of grammar to which I adhere – the first based on open-minded observation of use and the second offering organising principles for making sense of the endless complexity of grammar and enabling a coherent record of it to be formulated for reference and pedagogy. For me, the two are not incompatible, whereas a Chomskyan approach to language is compatible with neither. Then there is ideology: for centuries, as this book has demonstrated, grammatical description and prescription were dominated by the language of the upper classes, the educated, the great writers and orators. It was the view of 'good grammar' as a moral aspiration reflecting social hierarchies that have not gone away even today, although the privilege of pronouncing on orthodoxy has, in the case of my own country, shifted from the upper to the middle classes. The value of corpora such as the CANCODE corpus (McCarthy, 1998) and the demographic spoken data of the BNC has been that they have brought the grammar of the plain people to the fore, the ordinary users, those whose grammar is often undervalued or even disdained (the 'semi-literate friends', see p. 104). What could be more universal, more ordinary and more frequent in our everyday experience than social conversation? It is to this that we return in the final sections of this chapter by looking at the everyday activities of turn-taking and responding, and what insights we can gain about grammar in discourse from those most ordinary of activities.

7.7 Special discourses, special grammars

Another area where grammar has been seen in a beyond-the-sentence context is that of specialised discourses. Much work has been devoted to the grammar of domains such as business discourse and academic language. Professional domains develop their own ways of wording their contexts and collectively adopt grammatical conventions that suit their goals. In this section, we focus on academic language, with a briefer mention of business English.

In the academic domain, corpus-based work by Biber and his associates has been at the forefront. Biber's work gives us both the detail of the occurrence of individual grammatical features as they are present in academic discourse and also, thanks to the multi-dimensional type of analysis that looks at how individual features cluster and interact, gives us a discourse-level, bird's-eye view of academic speaking and writing in its different contexts. For example, he shows how the major word classes – noun, verb, adjective and adverb – are significantly differently distributed across the spoken and written contexts of academic life, with writing being noun- and adjective-heavy, the noun phrases often being long and complex, while speaking depends more on verbs and adverbs (Biber, 2006: chapter 4). Similarly, personal pronouns *I, you* and *we* display different distributions across different spoken activities such as lectures and classes (see also Buttery et al., 2015 on pronouns in spoken academic discourse). What is more, the chunks or clusters characteristic of any dataset and indicative of the idiom principle which we touched on in sections 4.3 and 6.11 turn out to have different fingerprints in everyday conversation and academic writing, with academic discourse tending to prefer frames consisting of function words with an intervening slot filled by content items, and conversation preferring a greater occurrence of frozen formulae (Biber, 2009). In addition, Hyland (2008) discusses variation in the use of chunks across academic disciplines. More recently, Biber and Gray (2019) argue for a dynamic and less conservative view of change in the grammar of academic writing, which is shown to have evolved over the centuries.

At a more detailed level, multi-dimensional analysis can show how features interact to serve different discoursal functions within local events (e.g. Csomay, 2004). At the local level, the patterns formed by grammatical use become discoursal patterns, and must be interpreted in their local contexts. Directives in academic writing, for instance, which could be face-threatening in other contexts, can be far more nuanced in their pragmatic functions and reception within academic contexts (Hyland, 2002). We are again in the presence of emergent grammar, where grammar as a static entity is replaced by grammaticalisation and pragmaticalisation to serve the dynamics of discourse. As Hyland (2009: 7) expresses it, 'The discourses of the disciplines ... work to interpret the world in particular ways, each drawing on different lexical, grammatical and rhetorical resources to create specialized knowledge'.

In all respects, Hyland's comment on academic English applies equally to business English, especially in its spoken manifestations, where we find further examples of the grammaticalisation of items in the recurring contexts that shape participants' understandings. Handford (2010: 41–3) provides interesting examples of the contextual interpretability of the semi-modal *have to* in the functions of *you have to* in different contexts, with different pragmatic force in intra-company and inter-company meetings. McCarthy et al. (2009) put some of the grammatical insights from spoken business data into a grammar practice book for businesspeople, for example, the use of future continuous tense-aspect form for politeness. These 'special grammars', such as are manifested in academic and business contexts, are often overshadowed by the special vocabularies that evolve in institutional and professional contexts; corpus evidence of regular patterning at the discourse level suggests they are part of the fingerprint or DNA of communities of practice every bit as much as are their specialised lexicons.

7.8 Taking the turn

The activity of turn-taking involves a couple of basic principles: how 'the floor' (i.e. who is the current speaker) is acquired and relinquished and how the turn itself is constructed. There is now a huge literature on all of this, going back to Sacks et al.'s (1974) seminal paper and beyond, in the CA tradition, where transcripts are examined in minute detail to chart the unfolding and ongoing nature of the interaction. Much CA has little or no recourse to the frameworks of grammar, nor does it need to, since it is concerned with social actions. However, research has shown that grammatical strategies are also involved in turn-taking and, as we shall see, turn-construction and turn-management show much evidence of grammaticalisation.

We begin with a quote from Schegloff, who points to the importance of what happens at turn-openings:

> 'Turn beginnings are an important initial place, and an important initial resource, for the projection of the turn-shape or the turn-type of the turn that is being begun at that turn beginning. Such projection is a critical resource for the organisation of the turn-taking system for conversation'.
>
> *Schegloff (1987: 71).*

In this connexion, Tao (2003) took a novel approach to counting things in corpora and observed the frequencies of items that begin speaking turns. His analysis showed that only 20 distinct turn-initial forms accounted for 60 per cent of all turn-openings in his data. The turn-opening slot is mostly populated by pragmatic markers (e.g. *yeah, no, well, right,* okay) and pronouns introducing fixed expressions such as *I think, you know, I mean, that's* + adjective (*that's right, that's true*), etc. We have already observed how common conjunctions serve as pragmatic markers at the turn beginning (section 7.3, above). Tao also notes a functional hierarchy: for example, a turn-opening such as '*Oh, no, so...*' would suggest a hierarchy of a change in the knowledge state, followed by an assessment or acknowledgement, then an item completing the all-important 'tying' function (linking the new turn to the previous turn). In this respect, *yes/yeah* and *no* are interesting examples of grammaticalisation. As well as providing positive and negative answers to *yes-no* (polar) questions, they have grammaticalised into topic-management devices (Lee-Goldman, 2011), in that they can mark shifts in topics or pre-empt implicit assumptions or stances on the part of interlocutors. Schegloff (2001) observes how *no* frequently operates to return the discourse from humorous side-sequences to more serious business. It is clear too that *no* commonly occurs to signal a shift in topic, for example to a sub-topic or to close or sum up a current topic:

Example 7.20
<S0603> are you looking for anything in particular for the house?
<S0492> erm always looking for <pause dur='short'/> erm
<S0603> a new dartboard <laugh>
<S0492> well <pause dur='short'/> **no** I just kind of like funny little finds for the house would be quite cool
<S0603> **yeah?**
<S0492> yeah <pause dur='long'/> but erm **no** so I like a good I like a good market
<S0603> I might crack that er chutney open
[S78P]

It is evident in the final turn of 7.20 that <S0603> feels that the sub-topic is sufficiently complete to enable the talk to shift to the subject of opening some chutney. Used with *oh, no* can express disbelief or a shocked reaction:

Example 7.21
<S0255> but he died on before he even left the air ambulance came but he was dead before
<S0315> **oh no**
<S0255> <overlap> they didn't even take him
[S28F]

Yeah and *no* often occur together, either as *yeah-no* or *no-yeah*, doing multiple work in bracketing speaker responses to particular utterances in the discourse or to longer segments of talk (Lee-Goldman, 2011).

Example 7.22
<S0590> cos I've had the same hairdresser
<S0588> <overlap> random really
<S0590> <overlap> for years now I I
<S0588> <overlap> it's terrible because
<S0590> <overlap> at thirty-five pounds a shot
<S0588> I usually
<S0616> <overlap> right
<S0590> yeah
<S0588> <overlap> find someone and then they move to Italy or something
<S0616> <overlap> **yeah no** well that's it
<S0588> <overlap> it's really annoying
[S263]

Yes/yeah and *no* are complex, adaptable items which have grammaticalised to carry out a variety of strategic acts in discourse. In Example 7.22, we see a number of overlaps, which rarely seem to be a problem in conversational transcripts: the whole process of talk just flows along. The linking function that these turn-openers perform contributes greatly to the discourse 'flow', or *confluence*, that jointly constructed fluency, which we all miss when it is absent or breaks down. Interestingly, apart from its occurrence in fixed expressions such as *the trouble is*, the definite article was not prominent as a turn-opener in Tao's (2003) study or in McCarthy (2010). This is in stark contrast to written discourse, where the definite article commonly begins sentences: in 100 million words of written texts in the BNC, some 470,000 sentences start with *The* (4,700 occurrences per million words). After taking into account turns starting with fixed expressions such as *the thing / trouble / problem is*, the Spoken BNC 2014 shows only roughly 1,000 occurrences per million words of turns starting with *the*. In everyday spoken interaction, we see a preference for grammaticalised markers carrying out the functions necessary to create smooth turn-taking and to manage the topical progress of the conversation (Koops and Lohmann, 2015). Furthermore, turn-openers reveal a remarkable consistency of grammaticalised functions across different languages (Heritage and Sorjonen, 2018).

One of the most striking features of conversational transcripts is the prevalence of short responses from interlocutors which do not constitute the taking of the floor (McCarthy, 2002, 2003). These are often just one or two words, and they are often fully lexical. Morphologically, they are often adjectives (*great, fine, good, cool*) or adverbs (*definitely, absolutely, quite*). These are in addition to back-channel responses (*mm, ah, uh-huh*), exclamatory reactions (*wow! gosh! no way!*) and words such as *yes/yeah, no, okay*. The adjectives often combine with *that's*, as in *that's good / right / fine / great*. Examples 7.23 to 7.25 show these forms in action, sometimes in combination:

Example 7.23
<S0269> the parish counc-
<S0268> <overlap> but they they might
<S0269> X Parish Council* aren't allowed to speak the opposition group
<S0268> **oh right okay**
<S0269> has got three minutes objectors<S0268>
<overlap> **okay got you**
<S0269> right?
<S0268> <overlap> **got you** <pause dur='short'/> **yeah okay**
<S0269> <overlap>and if there's a lot of objectors
<S0268> **yeah**
<S0269> the three minutes is split
<S0268> **right**
* place name anonymised; a Parish Council is the smallest unit of local government in England
[S9HC]

Note also in 7.23 the repeated use of *got you*, another grammaticalised item involving *get*.

Example 7.24
<S0252> the the thing is whether it's local government or national government it has got to be run as a business you know
<S0369> **absolutely**
<S0252> <overlap> have to get your funds and get money in in order to pay for all the services
[S4QF]

Example 7.25
<S0007> and then when I was asked I was like I really don't fancy that <pause dur='short'/> cos er just I don't know <pause dur='short'/> I just didn't

<S0018> [laughs]
<S0007> didn't think it'd be for me <pause dur='short'/> but but I do love it <pause dur='short'/> it's one of the best things I do here
<S0018> **cool**
[S32W]

What we may take from these examples, apart from the fact that they reinforce the notion of grammaticalisation, is that the morphology of the items in bold is largely irrelevant. Labelling them as adverbs or adjectives does not fully capture their ability to respond to whole turns or even longer stretches of discourse. The problem is that we do not have a shared metalanguage for these items. *Response token* would seem to capture their discourse function and the fact that they do more than merely acknowledge incoming talk attaches to them a significant role in the expression of active listenership. The same phenomenon is prevalent in other languages (for Spanish, see Amador Moreno et al., 2013).

Grammars of speaking need to jettison some of the metalanguage inherited from written grammars. We could also point, for example, to the difficulties in the morphological classification of 'double modals', such as *might could* and *should oughta*, which are heard in informal speech among native English speakers in different parts of the world (Lebedeva and Orlova, 2019). Common spoken features prompt a rethink of the whole set of word-class labels. In the emergent view of grammar, syntactic and morphological labels do not exist *a priori*; they simply show us how words adopt noun-like, adjective-like, verb-like or adverb-like shapes and functions in strategic use in discourse.

7.9 Grammar, discourse and co-construction

In everyday informal conversation, often what can be seen as 'sentence-like' phrasal or clausal combinations are the work of more than one speaker. Co-construction has attracted a good number of studies in recent years (e.g. Lerner 1991, 1996; Ferrara 1992; Helasvuo 2004) and, as with other features, it challenges the notion of *a priori* syntax in the speaker's mind as they construct their turn. As Ono and Thompson (1996: 90) put it, syntax is 'constantly being modified by conversational encounters, and is drawn on in innovative ways to achieve satisfying interactions'. Clancy and McCarthy (2014: 430) refer to 'items that seem to be, on the face of it, hooked on, on-the-fly, to the contribution of the previous speaker'. Examples from their data include speakers adding a *then*-clause to a previous speaker's *if*-clause, jointly creating the common *if x, then y* clause relation, and second speaker adding a *when*-clause to temporally modify a previous speaker's clause. Tao and McCarthy (2001) looked at *which*- comment clauses at turn-beginnings, and although they found that the *which*-clause was typically uttered by the same speaker after a brief contribution by an interlocutor, there were also cases where a different speaker added a *which*-clause. Example

7.26 shows a second speaker adding a which-clause and 7.27 shows both speakers adding such clauses.

Example 7.26
[speakers are discussing an old people's home]
<S0230> ... it's run as a business
<S0192> yeah
<S0230> erm a money-making business
<S0192> **which is terrible**
[SN98]

Example 7.27
[speakers are discussing current bad weather conditions with ice and snow]
<S0084> so you it's more than likely that you won't have to go to school tomorrow
<S0157> **which would be amazing**
<S0084> **which would be great cos you could just stay in bed**
[STJD]

7.10 Conclusion

The examples in sections 7.5, 7.7, 7.8 and 7.9 of this chapter reveal the complexity of grammar in interaction and how syntax is flexible, adaptable and emergent rather than taken off-the-shelf. Phenomena that would be considered inappropriate in formal writing are common and normal in everyday conversation. Speakers' skills in adapting grammar to the conditions of discourse are not inferior to those of writers who wrestle with the grammar of well-formed sentences on the page or screen; they are simply different. The very special quality of ordinary spoken interaction is that participants work on it together, jointly supporting each other's talk and creating the complex, extraordinary but largely unnoticed workings of the artefact of a satisfactory conversation.

In the next chapter we return to the theme of grammar in language teaching. As before, the focus will be on English language teaching, as it is the activity to which I have devoted many years of my life, however, where I can, I shall attempt to bring to bear insights from other languages. The chapter will be framed in terms of the positions that I have taken in this book so far.

8

GRAMMAR, LANGUAGE TEACHING AND LANGUAGE LEARNING

8.1 The canon

I have already mentioned the English language teaching (ELT) canon as an invisible orthodoxy – invisible, because it is not written down anywhere but exists as a compact between materials writers, teachers, publishers, curriculum designers, examining boards, official bodies (e.g. the British Council, government ministries), teacher trainers, students, care-givers and other stakeholders, together with academic researchers and applied linguists of various sorts. Obviously, it did not appear out of the blue and has been with us a long time (O'Keeffe and Mark, 2017; Burton, 2019). It has evolved over several centuries, with elements of its ancestry traceable to the grammatical projects of the ancients in their attempts to systematise word-classes and morphology and partly to the more recent concerns with sentence construction and syntax. It has passed through the structuralist era (chapter 4) and picked up a lot of its present-day character from that way of thinking. It is also the result of collective pragmatism. Those of us who have taught a language such as English know that it makes sense to begin with basic words and structural patterns – things such as subjects, copular verbs and their complements in simple situations embedded in the here-and-now, hence the typical focus on presenting personal information and verb forms such as the present simple and continuous forms. *My name is X, I am a student* is as good a place to start as any, after which increasing complexity is added into the mix (Nunan, 1988). And certain areas of grammar seem to attract similar levels of attention from different authors of materials, even though such selective attention might not be reflected in actual usage as evidenced in corpora, for which Biber et al. (1994: 171–4) offered the example of the treatment of post-nominal modification in English (and see the discussion of conditional sentences, below). Although, as I have mentioned in this book and elsewhere (McCarthy, 2013), the advanced level sees a greater disunity in what is considered essential in the grammar syllabus for English, at the earlier levels there is a remarkable consistency that would almost lead one to believe in a conspiracy theory.

The problem with an uncritical acceptance of a canon for the teaching of any language (and English is not unique) is that it permeates so much of what feeds into the experience of the end-users. For example, if you want to study grammatical acquisition by a group of learners, it is likely that you will seek to measure the degree to which what they have been taught has been understood and retained. If what you have taught them is discrete items from the canon, and if your experiments select those items for investigation, then there is a danger of a self-fulfilling prophecy. For one can easily shut out the possibility of how acquisition might have proceeded if the target group had been taught in ways different from what the canon and its artefacts encourage, or what grammar they have acquired through means other than your direct teaching, or if looking at the acquisition of discrete items rather than how items interact is a mistake. If, however, you assume nothing about what learners learn and how they learn it, you might wish to examine actual data of learners' use of the target language in and out of class. In the sub-discipline of second language acquisition (SLA), all of these avenues and more have been considered over time (see 8.2, below).

Burton's (2019) study is the most thoroughgoing investigation to date of the origins of the ELT grammatical canon, from its historical beginnings in the evolution of pedagogical grammars, via the perceptions of it provided by stakeholder informants, and in case studies of the treatment of favoured canonical items (conditional sentences, relative clauses and forms expressing future time) in a selection of contemporary course books. He concludes that the persistence of a grammatical canon for ELT is driven by publishers' commercial ends and that writers of such materials have less freedom now than they enjoyed in the past. As Thornbury (1998: 19) puts it, publishers 'have been falling over themselves to produce copycat courses'.

In Burton's view, certain texts were milestones in the solidification of the grammatical canon. One was Palmer's (1924) grammar, which we examined in chapter 4.4 of this book. Another was William Stannard Allen's 1947 book *Living English Structure* (Allen, 1947/1974), which achieved remarkable longevity, with new editions and reprints taking it into the 1990s. In his introduction, Allen states:

> 'An English schoolboy [sic] does "grammar" as an analytical exercise, but the foreign student needs to learn the mechanics of the language. Many existing grammar books were designed originally for the English schoolboy, and even a large number of those that are intended for foreigners have not managed to free themselves entirely from the purely analytical point of view'.
>
> *(Allen, 1947/1974: vii)*

This statement makes a distinction between analysing grammar (which native speakers do during their education) and the learning of the language by the foreign-language learner, which involves a different sort of engagement with the workings of the language. That view has stuck, and the grammar charts and their accompanying exercises in contemporary English as a foreign language (EFL) course books are graded to correspond with different levels of proficiency and explicitly lay out grammatical paradigms and rules, together with the discrete items that realise them, often with advice on pitfalls to avoid. Native-speaker education in countries such as the United Kingdom, however, bases grammar teaching on age groups, with primary school children typically practising identifying basic word forms such as nouns and adjectives, leading on to textual and more stylistically oriented analysis at secondary level, while foreign language primary age learners might engage in games/songs, etc. to encourage the experience of using the target language, with older, more advanced groups manipulating complex grammatical structures in exercises and essay-writing. The official British government documents for England on the subject make this clear as regards the first language learner:

> 'The grammar of our first language is learnt naturally and implicitly through interactions with other speakers and from reading. Explicit knowledge of grammar is, however, very important, as it gives us more conscious control and choice in our language. Building this knowledge is best achieved through a focus on grammar within the teaching of reading, writing and speaking. Once pupils are familiar with a grammatical concept [for example "modal verb"], they should be encouraged to apply and explore this concept in the grammar of their own speech and writing and to note where it is used by others'.
>
> *(Department for Education, 2013)*

Under the English national curriculum, seven-to-eleven-year-olds engage with terminology such as *prefix, direct speech, determiner, possessive pronoun*, which, by any reckoning, are demanding concepts for children so young.

Allen explicitly relates the different levels of his exercises to the different levels of the Cambridge Examinations, which is a mutually supportive circular exercise in the sense of the invisible canon: neither of the two systems was originally fully objectively or empirically founded. However, Allen admits that students can only be 'very roughly graded' (Allen, 1947/1974: viii). This is one of the many problems with the canon, in that any of its stakeholders can lean on any other stakeholder to validate its position. That is not to deny the immense amount of research into issues of validity that examination bodies have carried out over the years.

A. S. Hornby, who was a major figure in the EFL world in the 1940s and 1950s, dedicated himself to both dictionary and grammar work for learners. I picked up a copy of the first edition of *A Learner's Dictionary of Current English* (1948), signed by Hornby, for just a couple of pounds in an antiquarian bookshop and I treasure it. But Hornby's 1954 student grammar is of greater interest to us here. It focuses on grammatical patterns, especially those around the verb, rather than traditional syntax and inflexion. It has numerous substitution tables in the structuralist tradition, which are reminiscent of those that we saw in Harold Palmer's books. It is also interesting in its division of conditional sentences into just two main types: 'A, those with clauses that contain a condition that may or may not be fulfilled, and, B, those with clauses in which theoretical condition is put forward' (Hornby, 1954: 231–7).

Another important figure in the evolution of the canon was L. G. Alexander, whose influence was enormous when I began my career as an EFL teacher in the mid-1960s and who remained a key figure in the profession into the 1980s. He was one of the co-authors of *English Grammatical Structure* (Alexander et al., 1975), a basic syllabus for the grading of English grammar and a touchstone in the evolution of the ELT canon. He not only authored English courses and grammar books but was also involved in the pan-European project of the *Threshold Level*, one of the central features of the Common European Framework (CEFR), corresponding to level B1 of the current system (Council of Europe, 2001).

Alexander's (1988) grammar is comprehensive in its coverage of word classes and clause- and sentence-types. It included three types of conditional sentences, the classic types 1, 2 and 3 (Alexander, 1988: 273–83). These had already been laid out by Allen (1947/1974: 152) and became deeply entrenched in the ELT canon (Burton, 2019: 180). But research based on actual usage showed a much greater variation in the realisations of conditional meanings (Maule, 1988; Fulcher, 1991), and in fact Alexander (ibid.), working in the pre-corpus era, gave a great many variations on the three basic types, but the three basic types persisted in the collective mind and in syllabus organisation. The dilemma, which is probably not resolvable by a simple recipe, is whether to be as faithful as possible to attested usage or to reduce the learning load to a manageable core, which is itself a conundrum, as there are several ways to define a 'core' (frequency? conceptual simplicity? register neutrality? learnability?).

We saw in chapter 6.3 on the subjunctive how different pedagogical grammar texts presented the same feature in a variety of different ways, with nouns, verbs and adjectives governing subjunctive use given very uneven treatment. This is another aspect of the canon: the canon dictates what its adherents feel should be taught in terms of a series of headings, but the devil is in the detail. However, it might not matter that the detail lacks uniformity, and there could be all sorts of practical constraints on what, precisely, each section or sub-section includes in its description of the feature, whether subjunctives or conditionals. As Hinkel (2016: 369) points out, some features could give 'too low a return on the investment of precious time'.

A sensible approach to a problem such as conditional sentences is taken by Jones and Waller (2010). They present an array of some 40 variations on the conditional sentence pattern based on BNC data, but conclude that the most useful insight for pedagogy from their analysis is the prevalence of 'real' conditionals (a fourth type beyond the traditional 1, 2 and 3, e.g. *If its energy level falls to zero, it dies and disappears.* [BNC 1991–1994 FNR]). These should be given greater emphasis compared with the traditional categories, and a discoursal approach where context offers the choice of possible forms for expressing conditionality is recommended. This would seem to be an enlightened and feasible approach to the numbing orthodoxy of the canon.

Burton (2019) takes all the factors and constraints on board and shows what a complicated thing the ELT grammatical canon is – a bottom-up creation for which nobody has had general oversight. He does not dismiss the collective wisdom of centuries – indeed, he is a true ELT historian who respects his sources and the views and recollections of his distinguished informants – but he does believe that a more empirical, corpus-informed approach to the canon will yield better sources of information on content and sequencing for the future.

In this last regard, the English Grammar Profile (EGP) would seem to offer a way forward. However, before we examine more closely the pioneering work of Mark and O'Keeffe in creating the EGP, we should consider ideas pertaining to second-language development and acquisition and what role errors and difficulties play in our perception of learners' proficiency.

8.2 Make no mistake

Another credo of ELT grammar during the years that Allen's book and others were in the ascendency was that the purpose of the grammarian was to help the user to avoid falling into error; Allen mentions grammar in connection with 'problems' three times in his preface (1947/1974: v). We illustrated this in chapter 3.3 (also chapter 4.2), where, in the 18th century, Bishop Lowth saw his duty as stating 'what is right, by showing what is wrong' (Lowth, 1762/1799: viii). When I began my career as a language teacher, Lowth's prescription was immanent in the approach to teaching at that time: the job of the materials was to model correctness, and the teacher's job was to present that model and to correct errors if and when they occurred. Errors derived from interference from the first language, obviously, so what was needed was an effective contrastive analysis of the learner's L1 and the target L2. However, it soon became clear that things were not that obvious, that contrastive analysis lacked sufficient predictive power, and that the systematic making of errors (regular departures from native-speaker conventions) might be seen instead as part of the normal process of learning a language (Norrish, 1983: 7); error analysis was a more fruitful path to pursue (Corder, 1967). Elsewhere, Corder says: 'language learning is a creative activity-it is a process of discovering some sort of regularity in the language data presented to the learner' (Corder, 1975: 410).

There might be more to errors than just interference from the learner's first language, or even learners' creative strategies for manipulating the L2, and this is where the centuries-old recurring theme of universal grammar rears its head again (see chapter 2). If there are, indeed, grammatical universals, then acquisition of an L2 grammar might take its own pathways and be unaffected by the sequence of teaching and practice as typically dictated by the canon. Rather in the way that Chomsky described for the first-language learner (Chomsky, 1965: 27), the L2 learner would not be a blank sheet but would come to the task with a predisposed set of innate universal principles and knowledge of their own L1, which required exposure to the data of the L2 to become realised, via hypotheses regarding L1-L2 differences, as competence in L2. This led to several guiding concepts. First, at any given stage of development, the learner's grasp of the L2 system was partial, fluid but systematic; it was an *interlanguage*, influenced by both L1 and L2, but independent of both (Selinker, 1972). Second, it should be possible to determine an ideal or universal order of acquisition of grammatical items which could inform the grammatical syllabus. This was the era of the so-called 'morpheme studies', which grew to encompass, for English, experiments aiming to demonstrate orders of acquisition of discrete grammatical items and features.

Morpheme acquisition studies appeared in the 1970s, with many researchers keen to show that there was a universal, fixed order of acquisition of basic English morphemes among child and adult L2 learners. The features chosen for investigation included articles, present- and past-tense endings, plural endings, the possessive 's', etc. (Dulay and Burt, 1973, 1974; Bailey, Madden and Krashen, 1974, among others). The efforts of these researchers suggested that there were similarities in the order of acquisition regardless of L1, but they were never sufficiently watertight to demonstrate that the order was convincingly universal. Hakuta's (1976) case study showed up the potential weakness of the strong claim to universality, while Larsen-Freeman (2010) urged a broader, more varied and contextualised approach.

Morpheme studies suffer from serious shortcomings, not least in their assumption of grammar as a set of static entities that have to be loaded into the operating system like a set of apps, so to speak, rather than a dynamic, contextualised, meaning-making process which the neo-Firthian and emergent types of grammar that I have argued for in this book suggest is a more accurate picture. Grammatical features are in constant interaction, one with the other, in the creation of discourse. Even if we take a more deep-structural approach to languages, the work of language typologists such as Hawkins (1987) argues for an intricate fabric of interrelations among features and a hierarchy of syntactic preferences in languages that suggests that atomised approaches to the acquisition of grammar are doomed to tell us very little of any use.

A change in focus came about in the 1990s, owing to what came to be known as the aspect hypothesis – a series of research studies that developed into a veritable cottage industry (e.g. Andersen, 1991; Bardovi-Harlig, 1992, 2000; Shirai and Andersen, 1995; Salaberry, 2000, among many others). In this research, a distinction is drawn between aspect as a grammatical function of the verb and the lexical meaning of the verb, which may cause confusion for the learner at early stages of proficiency. English, for example, has two tenses marked on the verb, present and past, and three aspects: simple, continuous (progressive) and perfect. The English simple past does not inflect, whereas Spanish past tense has inflexions. Swedish has no inflected continuous form, and other languages show different characteristics. It is often not easy to disentangle these, as they are marked simultaneously in verbal groups. A Hallidayan systemic approach would capture the choices available in English. For any English verbal group, the speaker chooses between present and past, simple and continuous, and perfect or non-perfect, such that the clause *I had been working all day* has chosen simple past tense auxiliary *had*, continuous main verb *been working* and perfect *have* + past participle *been*. However, one of the difficulties is grasping the meaning of tense-aspect, and not just for learners. The simplest way to look at it is that tense marks events in time (present, past, future), while aspect marks the speaker's perspective on events in time.

In English, simple aspect locates the speaker as observer, like an astronaut standing on the moon, from where planet earth looks like a perfect circle, the circumference of which forms a boundary around all the goings-on down there on the surface, yet the planet is still moving in time from its past to its future. The person down there on the planet is 'continuously' immersed in its events and is observing them from the inside looking outwards, and they can choose how to express the temporality of those experiences. From their perspective, the earth is moving through time, but has no boundary; one can move in any direction without falling off the edge. As the physicist Stephen Hawking put it: 'Reports of people falling off are thought to be exaggerations' (Hawking, 2001: 85). Thus can we observe events from the inside and leave their start- or end-points open, or from the outside and see events as more like facts bound in time, and we can decide how we interpret movement through time according to the context of utterance. This metaphor of the external observer for simple aspect and internal observer for continuous aspect has served me well over the years in my English teaching; not that I habitually turn my grammar lessons into Physics for Beginners!

Some verbs, however, seem to force an observer's interpretation. Often quoted in the literature are *arrive*, which suggests a point in time where start and finish happen at once, and *run*, where start and finish are separated by movement through time. The aspect hypothesis sees acquisition typically moving from an association of the lexical meaning of certain verbs with specific aspects towards a more sophisticated understanding of the separability of the lexical semantics and the grammatical perspective. However, as with the morpheme studies, results of experiments turn out to be mixed, with some studies suggesting that L1-L2 similarities influence the speed of acquisition of aspect, some suggesting that acquisition is not reliably predictable as the student's proficiency increases, while others suggest that classrooms and materials play a role in how aspect is acquired (see Thane, 2018 for an interesting discussion). One could argue that if the model of aspect adhered to is flaky, learners may be under-exposed to everyday uses. For example, in EFL course books, orthodoxy traditionally dictates that speech reporting be taught via simple past tense verbs followed by back-shifted reported clauses (*She said she was going to change her job*). However, one common discourse strategy in English is to use past continuous forms to report newsworthy re-tellings (*He was saying he thinks the factory will close / she was telling me they're getting a new boss*); only a discourse-based or corpus-informed grammar is likely to suggest attention to such matters (McCarthy, 1998: chapter 8).

None of this uncertainty and diversity of viewpoints should really surprise us. If we see language acquisition as taking place in a black box in the brain, there will always be many variables battering on the lid of the box and threatening to falsify the theory. If, however, we see language acquisition as a social process, achieved through engagement with discourse, and if we see grammar not as a series of *a priori* items into which discourse must fit, but rather as a resource for meaning making, then the field opens more widely. All sorts of preconceptions about aspect could be open to question. For example, the canonical idea that stative (non-dynamic) verbs such as *like/love* and *want* in English are not used in continuous aspect is contradicted by corpus evidence: the Spoken BNC2014 has 51 examples of *want* in present and past continuous form with a personal pronoun subject. If teaching materials fail to reflect such usage, then learners could have an impoverished exposure to the range of lexical verb and tense-aspect forms, and this might well affect their perception of what is and is not allowable.

8.3 Outside the black box: from grammar to grammaring

So far, the morpheme and aspect studies have focused on a view of the learner as someone struggling to make mental representations of the L2 grammar, to 'get it right', and acquisition is seen as equivalent to arriving at control and mastery, the achievement of native-like usage. However, five decades of teaching experience have taught me that the acquisition of grammar is a complex affair, differently achieved in the different countries and contexts where I have taught it. In general, grammar teaching was an easier task for me when I worked in Sweden and the Netherlands than in Spain or when working with groups of Russian and Chinese speakers in the United Kingdom. That might suggest that I am happy to rest my case on good old-fashioned contrastive analysis. That is not so. Sweden is not only the home of the Swedish language, whose syntax is mostly like English; it is a social context where people are surrounded by subtitled English on television, where the general use of creative media in English is high, where speaking a foreign language is seen as a natural and necessary thing, and where language education for adults (the context in which I worked) was taken seriously by the government and society as a whole and schools and universities were (at that time, the 1970s) well provided for, and where, in my teaching context, communication was emphasised over the dry learning of rules. These social and classroom contexts are all-important for the understanding of how successfully people learn grammar.

Some versions of second language acquisition theory take these concerns on board and move out of the domain of the mental black box where grammar rules are processed and stored for future use and into the external, social environment of learning (Pekarek-Doehler, 2006). Constructivism is one such departure: in this perspective, 'multiple realities or multiple ways of knowing are to be expected in the classroom' (Blyth, 1997: 51), leading to a more nuanced approach to grammar pedagogy, where the grammar is not seen as a monolithic object, all to be transmitted in the same way. Numerous studies, inspired by the communicative movement in language teaching, have investigated behaviours such as the negotiation of meaning among learners working on tasks in different settings and modifications of meaning in interaction (Long, 1996). Another perspective is to see grammar as an ongoing process to be explored through interaction, where the revelatory power of the analysis of transcripts involving learners communicating strategically with the resources at their disposal can be explored to observe grammar in action. Such a re-alignment of SLA was proposed by Firth and Wagner (1997). Alongside this shift in thinking is the Vygotskian perspective of scholars associated with sociocultural theory, where individual development 'begins in the social relationships both framing and framed by extended participation in our communicative practices' (Kelly Hall, 1997: 302; for a wider discussion, see Lantolf and Appel, 1994).

The problem is that we are trapped in the metaphors through which we construct our epistemology: grammar is reified in a series of nouns (*grammar, noun, verb, tense, voice,* etc.) (see Thornbury, 2001: chapter 1 for a discussion); grammar becomes a thing, rather than a dynamic, flexible and evolving strategic resource which provides tools for performing social actions. One attempt to get away from this reification in grammar pedagogy is Larsen-Freeman's notion of 'grammaring' (Larsen-Freeman, 2003), which is a conscious use of the dynamic, activity-oriented *-ing* ending for English verbal nouns, at the same time expressing the temporally 'boundless' character of the English progressive/continuous verb form in *-ing*. Larsen Freeman brings together in her thinking chaos and complexity theory and a dynamic view of language and language change (Larsen-Freeman, 1997). Chaos theory deals with the way that relatively simple systems can change in unpredicted ways, while complexity refers to complex systems in which many parts interact and which can produce unpredicted order in the system. The non-predictability of the resultant changes is at the heart of the theory. Chaos and complexity are non-linear processes, constantly in flux, always 'becoming' rather than 'being'. Language changes through the actions of its users, even though we might not notice it, and even when we do, the novel typically soon becomes the normal. This is not far off Halliday's position on language change, where the 'text', any instantiation of language, is an open, dynamic system which interacts with its environment (the context of culture), and both are constantly changing. These interactions are nothing more mysterious than 'just those of people talking and listening' (Halliday, 2005: 44). Alongside this view come usage-based approaches to SLA, which hold that grammatical competence builds up from frequent exposure to form-meaning associations, with frequency of usage being the key to what is acquired (Ellis and Ferreira-Junior, 2009). In this approach, the learner's mental representation of the language is seen more like a corpus of all the utterances that they have experienced than a static set of grammatical entities internalised and stored like items in a reference grammar. Thus, although coming at the question from different angles, there seems to be a commonality of thinking between the Hallidayan/neo-Firthian view of text and context, the emergent grammar of Hopper, sociocultural theory, constructivism, usage-based theories of SLR and Larsen-Freeman's translation of chaos and complexity theory into the notion of grammaring. This is a very satisfactory conclusion as we move towards the end of this book.

Grammaring sees the acquisition of grammar as a constant, creative process of activity and interaction among learners and their teachers, and its development can be both chaotic and complex at once and could involve the learner's L1 as well as the L2 (Levine, 2014). This would suggest that changes in the learner's internalisation of the conventions of the language system can occur in real time but non-linearly. As Larsen-Freeman says: 'individuals may not intentionally seek to change language, but they do so by their day-to-day interactions in using it'

(Larsen-Freeman, 2003: 30), which would seem to apply as well in the language classroom as in the street. Language acquisition is 'a dynamic, complex and non-linear process' (Larsen-Freeman, 1997: 142). For this reason, the recent focus on interaction in the language classroom offers opportunities to observe not just the teaching of the 'static' grammatical system as input (comprehensible or otherwise), but to see how teachers and learners engage in interaction, presenting a different locus for SLA studies to the experimental set-up (Markee and Kasper, 2004; Mondada and Pekarek Doehler, 2004). A system of real-time observation such as Walsh's, which distinguishes talk of different kinds in the classroom and applies the rigours of conversation analysis provides a window on the interactional flow and moments of learning opportunity (Walsh, 2006).

8.4 Staying outside the black box: Learners, grammaring and corpora

One of the most illuminating developments to arise from the availability of learner corpora is the grammatical profiling of learners at different proficiency levels. We would undoubtedly expect learners to possess a greater repertoire of grammatical features if they have been rated at a higher level of a system such as the CEFR or passed examinations at higher levels parallel to or linked to the CEFR. Therefore, it should be a straightforward exercise to show that stepwise input based on the ELT canon is reflected in the stepwise output of learners. However, the picture seems not to be so straightforward. The pioneering work of Mark and O'Keeffe on the English Grammar Profile (EGP)[1], working with the Cambridge Learner Corpus (CLC), reveals a more nuanced picture. Their project builds on and advances in a very practical way the work of Hawkins and Buttery (2010), who also used the CLC, on 'criterial features' of learner performance, the positive and negative occurrences and distribution of particular structures in learners' writing as compared with their occurrence and distribution in native-speaker usage. The researchers set out 'to investigate what learners at each of the six CEFR levels "can do" with grammar in English' (O'Keeffe and Mark, 2017: 459), based on a huge database of learners' writing from around the world. The EGP is not concerned with what learners cannot do (for example, through error analysis), but with what learners can do, through analysis of their production, at different levels.

The results of the EGP shed light on some key aspects of L2 grammatical acquisition and raise questions in relation to the canonical input. One example is the unexpectedly frequent use of *would* at A1 level. It turns out that some 80% of its occurrences at that beginner level are in the chunk *I would like*, which is indicative of the strategic potential of such easily acquired fixed forms to enable communication without involving syntactic analysis. This initial stage quickly gives way to a range of complex uses of *would*, colligating with conditional contexts and certain adjunct types and tense-aspect contours. This example and others led the researchers to conclude that there is little evidence of one-to-one correspondence between forms, their range of meanings and levels of attainment (O'Keeffe and

Mark, 2017: 468). Instead, forms are first evidenced at a certain level and then control of pragmatic functions emerges, but evidently not in alignment with the static elements of the canon. Learner grammar development seems to be a process leading to greater complexity and dexterity in use and pragmatic purpose (O'Keeffe and Mark, 2017: 479), not a set of lock steps storing the discrete items of the canon in mental compartments. The EGP shows grammaring in action.

8.5 Conclusion

This chapter has skimmed across the surface of a vast enterprise that has informed language teaching for more than a century: the teaching and learning of grammar. The chapter has necessarily been selective in its focus and driven in its purpose by what I perceive to be major innovations and their concomitant challenges. Like the rest of this book, it is a personal view. It concludes at a point that I feel we have reached through many years of research and practice, experimentation and observation, experience and our never-failing optimism that things get better. It also represents a conclusion to the whole book – almost. It started with where we came from and how we got here, which is a long journey of two millennia. What follows in the final chapter is not so much a 'where we are' as a 'where we might be heading' in terms of grammar.

In my five decades as a language teacher and researcher, I have been inspired by a series of threads that have woven the fabric of my professional knowledge and stance, which, on the face of it, seem unconnected at first, but which, to my mind, point towards a shared north for our professional compass. The next and final chapter carries out a brief reconnaissance of the field of 'grammar out there', that is to say beyond the world of theory and weighty grammar books, into the world of the public – a world of attitudes and practices, of tensions and conflicts. It is a grammatical jungle out there.

Note

1 The EGP, with examples of learners' grammatical output at the different CEFR levels, is available as a free online resource at www.englishprofile.org/english-grammar-profile.

9
GRAMMAR AT LARGE

9.1 Variety: standard and non-standard

I was born and raised in Cardiff, south Wales, and grew up speaking the English of that city. I was not aware that my English was special or different and certainly did not think it in any way deficient. I was aware that some people (especially on radio and television) spoke 'posh' English and sounded their aitches, but if you had asked me what, if anything, marked out the *grammar* of my part of the world, I would not have had a clue. It was only when I went to university in England that it dawned on me that nobody around me used *there's* with an adjective (*there's lovely/ awful*, etc.), or asked someone *Where to is it?* if they wanted to know the location of something, or said *leave it by here*, if someone was delivering a parcel, or said that *they played great / she speaks really clear*, and that they only used the present tense *-s* ending with third person subjects rather than all subjects (*I likes, you likes*, etc.). The anthem that I grew up with was: 'I'm Cardiff born, Cardiff bred, and when I dies I'll be Cardiff dead' (local ditty). You may understand, therefore, why I felt quite at home sitting on this bench on a footpath in Northern Ireland (figure 9.1).

Grammatical variations of this kind are well documented in the comprehensive *World Atlas of Variation in English* (Kortmann and Lunkenheimer, 2012), which includes a section on Welsh English (Penhallurick, 2012) that fills me with nostalgia, with its familiar non-standard tense-aspect forms and non-standard reflexive pronouns. Coupland (1988) documented the dialect of Cardiff – another source of nostalgic connection with my lost identity. I do not refer to identity lightly or because it is, at the time of writing, a buzzword. Our grammar, wherever we got it from, is part of our identity. Yet often we give it up, adapt it or consciously change it under the subtle but relentless pressure of alien establishment values, of current vogues and social forces and a desire to accommodate to our surroundings. It is only relatively recently that the grammar of Irish English has been given due attention in its own right – a development paralleled by the

FIGURE 9.1 'Grammatical benchmark'
Photograph © Michael McCarthy 2019

increased confidence and pride in Irishness and a new post-colonial attitude to academic matters seen at the turn of the 20th and 21st century (Filppula, 1999; O'Keeffe 2006, 2011; O'Keeffe and Amador Moreno, 2009; Migge and Ní Chiosáin, 2012; Farrell, 2020; O'Sullivan, 2020).

Grammatical variety is inherent in language, and the idea that there is a single, homogenous grammar for any language is a fallacy. What usually happens is that one variety becomes dominant for political or historical reasons. In the case of English, we can look at the influence of the printing press, brought to England by William Caxton in the 15th century. Caxton chose one particular dialect as his model for printing, and it happened to be the English East Midland dialect, which was familiar to and suitable for the aspiring middle and upper classes of south-east England. The problem was that then, and later, standard speech was equated with correct speech and correct speech with sophisticated speech, and sophisticated speech with good speech – the persistence of the age-old link between grammar and morality which we traced in chapter 2. The aim in 16th-century England was to forge an English vernacular capable of expressing the same depth of intellectual ideas as Latin was supposed to possess (Drury Hall, 1977).

The variety that took on the mantle of superiority and survived, which is generally referred to as educated standard English, spread its tentacles around a world dominated by the British Empire and more recently by other sociopolitical agents (Phillipson 1991, 2001), and it took a very long time for any of the vibrant local varieties of English that evolved in countries other than the United Kingdom to receive recognition from the literary and educational establishments of the old English-speaking world and to receive their due titles as local languages rather than just the offspring of the mother-country still attached by an umbilical cord (Talib, 2002). As Carter showed, the notion of 'good' English with a moral element was alive and well in the early 1990s when the National Curriculum for English was being promoted and attacked, including by HRH Prince Charles, who saw 'writing proper English' as a feature of educating 'for character' (Carter, 1997: 7).

In the area of England where I now live, some interesting grammatical variations on the educated standard can be heard on a daily basis. Local dialect speakers routinely use *that* in preference to standard *it* (*that rained yesterday*), use third person present singular without the *-s* ending (*I think he want a biscuit*), exchange *was* and *were* relative to the standard (*you wasn't well, was you? / she weren't there last night*) and have non-standard agreement tags (*A: It was cold last night B: That it was!*). I hear all these forms in my village on a daily basis (see also Vasko, 2010). These examples of British variations on the standard, sometimes overlapping in form, demonstrate the arbitrariness of grammatical convention and the local, social compacts that are emergent in speech communities rather than existing a priori as a set of abstract rules. I encountered further examples of grammatical variation when I lived in Malaysia in the early 1980s, with everyday examples such as *I don't think so he'll come today*, or shopkeepers saying *Don't have but can get* when an item was not in stock – just a couple of features of a living grammar evolving to suit its local conditions and the discourses of its people (for further background and discussion of Malaysian English, see Yamaguchi and Deterding, 2016). It is another reminder that the grammar of educated standard British English is as arbitrary as any other.

9.2 Grammatical change

The vocabulary of English changes rapidly. It is not uncommon for the *Oxford English Dictionary* (OED) to incorporate hundreds of new words and new senses of old words every few months, and old items fall into desuetude. Grammar seems to change at a slower rate, to the extent that we do not often notice it – something that undoubtedly contributes to the lay perspective that it does not (and should not) change. But change it does, and corpora can be very useful in tracking such changes (see below). Grammar changes because people change; they say and do and hear different and novel things in different and novel situations, a premise on which the notion of emergent grammar rests. One of the changes in British and other societies, helped along by the advent of mass media and more recently social media, is what has been labelled 'conversationalisation' (Fairclough, 1995), which is something of a mouthful, but a term that captures the move towards more informal, conversation-like public discourses as old social hierarchies become more permeable.

Would that we could shake off that pernicious link between using 'good', standard grammar and being a better human being. Where power is vested in one group of people, it can be denied to others, as has been argued in relation to the implicit goals of 16th-century Latin pedagogy in England, where the texts in use portrayed a subtle, exclusive social stratification (Sullivan, 2008). A standard language is more than just a language; it gives access to a 'standard language culture' (Peterson, 2020: xvii). The standard and its culture can be stubbornly resistant to change until new powerful and influential groups emerge. And emerge they do; the 'standard' never stands still. Southern British English and its grammar was the behemoth that I struggled with when I began my career as an English teacher in the mid-1960s; never would it have occurred to me at that time that in a mere few decades, standard American English (AmE) would, numerically, be the world's preferred variety and that such was the demand from the language-teaching industry that I would be commissioned with my co-authors to write a course for learners of AmE (McCarthy et al., 2005, 2012, 2014). Peterson (2020) makes a keen observation in this regard:

> 'It is interesting that given its status as a European variety of English, as well as being considered the "birthplace" of English, the British standardized variety is often associated with school and formal learning for students in Europe, whereas American English seems to evoke more personal and private realms of use'.
>
> *(Peterson, 2020: 6)*

Outside of Europe, AmE has been the variety of choice for learners for a good many years. So ubiquitous has the spread of American economic and social influence been in the world that even those who see themselves as speakers of standard British English are often not aware of how much AmE grammar and vocabulary they routinely use (see 9.3 below); I know this from personal observation, social media exchanges and shameless eavesdropping. This is partly because the general public, by and large, thinks that grammar does not change – or at least that it should not change – and that therefore it does not. Anything that deviates from the public's sense of the norm is considered aberrant and to be resisted. As Peterson (2020: 29) points out, it is typically the people who use non-standard forms rather than the forms themselves who get the blame (e.g. the young, certain ethnic groups, uneducated people, one gender or another, hyper-posh individuals). This was true even in the 18th century, when Lowth blamed the users, not the language, for grammatical neglect (Lowth, 1762/1799: vi). Grammar simply does not and should not change; it is logical, immutable, our heritage from great writers and orators and the bedrock of sensible thinking. Or so the story goes.

Leech et al. (2009: 1–6) point out that grammar does change and that there is plenty of historical evidence of change. However, they cite the various possibilities for post-modification of noun phrases by relative clauses as an example where purists home in on the issue of *who* versus *whom* at the expense of other, more subtle changes over time. In relative clauses and elsewhere, *who* and *whom* seem to have become a magnet for debate and controversy. Google® Ngram Viewer facility shows a decline in the use of *whom* in written documents over the course of the 20th century, down by more than a half.

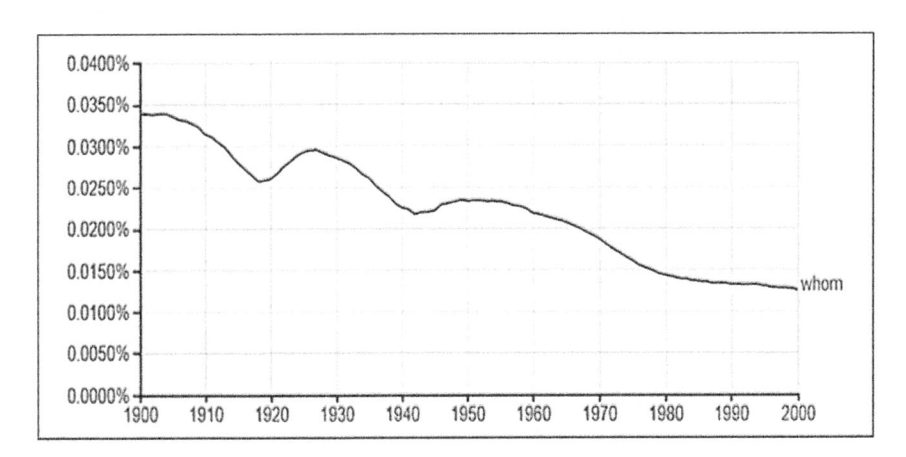

FIGURE 9.2 Use of *whom* in written documents 1900–2000
(Google Books Ngram Viewer http://books.google.com/ngram © 2013 Google)

Fowler (1926: 723–6) has plenty to say about *whom*: English speakers are 'very little conversant with case forms' (p. 723) and so are bound to make mistakes, including the use of *who* in relative clause where *whom* should be, 'giving the educated reader a shock' (ibid.). That was in the 1920s, but *who* versus *whom* still taxes people almost a century later: the internet returns tens of thousands of hits if one types 'Who or whom?' into a search engine. A British tabloid newspaper in 2019 reproduced a grammar quiz from as recently as 1984. The readers were invited to fill the gap in the sentence: 'Joanna kissed _____ last night?' The correct answer was *whom* (Mulroy, 2019).

Other grammatical changes are more subtle and less visible on the public radar. In the Google® Ngram Viewer facility, the modal verb *ought* shows a similar rate of decline to *whom* (i.e. down by more than one half) over the 20th century. Likewise, the BNC (1991–94) shows a steep decline in the use of *ought* between 1960 and 1993, and the Spoken BNC2014 shows only half as many occurrences as those in the 1985–1993 BNC texts (see also Leech et al., 2011: 80–3). At the expense of *ought to*, the semi-modal *need to* seems to have gained ground, with almost three times the occurrences in the Spoken BNC2014 compared with the spoken transcripts of the BNC 1991–94. Yet there is little evidence of public lamentation or anger over the decline of *ought to*. Another change that has been observed in English is a growth in the use of generic *you* and shifts in its pragmatics (Haas, 2018; see also Myers and Lampropoulu, 2012). Such subtleties rarely generate great debate or moral panics in the United Kingdom, often because the changes are a result of people's immersive experiences in the language of broadcast and social media and the world of films and music and other cultural contexts, where items of the grammar of other native varieties of English (American, Caribbean, Australian, Irish) and non-native ones may be adopted subliminally and without resistance. The influence of American English is the most salient example.

9.3 Americanisation

American English (AmE) and British English (BrE) vocabulary differences are well known, and many are widely accepted in the United Kingdom and Ireland: in my experience I have rarely heard anyone complain if someone refers to *standing in line* rather than *waiting in a queue*, or says *trash* rather than *rubbish*. Spelling differences are more apparent, but grammatical differences are much less so, although they are undeniably present in a variety of complex ways (Tottie, 2009). Some of the following differences that I have made a note of include (AmE variant first) playing *on/in* a team, *on/at* the weekend, I have not been there *in/for* ten years. In each case, the AmE version is heard more and more in just the past few years, if my observations and notes are to be trusted (it is probably too soon yet to have indisputable diachronic corpus evidence for these).

Perhaps more noticeable and attested is what I would refer to as 'the rise and rise of the phrasal verb', where I have the support of data submitted by the ever-vigilant members of the Language Observatory Group – a closed group of interested parties that I monitor on Facebook®. English phrasal and prepositional verbs (PV) occupy a mezzanine territory between grammar and lexis. As a result, they are a perfect example of *lexico-grammar*: their main verb properties are those of typical delexical verbs, while their particles have become grammaticised and welded to them in a variety of types of grammatical patterning (e.g. 'separable' versus 'inseparable'). They have a long history of change and evolution of form and function (Rodríguez-Puente, 2019). They also partake of an informal, conversational feel in contrast to the Graeco-Latin (near-)synonyms that can often be used instead. This fits with the notion of conversationalisation. Table 9.1 offers a selection of PVs recently attested in BrE with more formal equivalents, most of which my AmE correspondents and informants assure me are already well established in the North American lexicon.

TABLE 9.1 BrE recently observed PVs (adapted from McCarthy, 2019)

verb	recent phrasal uses / meanings
Listen up!	typically used as a command. Used to be just *Listen*!
check sth out	In my day, we used to just check things
dial down	reduce: e.g. *dial down the rhetoric*
put oneself out	*put oneself out there* – increase one's public profile, socialise more; used to mean 'inconvenience oneself'
Wait up!	typically used as a command. Used to be just *Wait*!
double down on	reinforce/reassert one's stance/position
call out	challenge, condemn, expose wrongdoing
push back	reject, react negatively against something
reach out (to)	contact (e.g. email somebody)
roll out	extend or distribute over a wider area or over a period of time
roll back	reduce to an earlier level (e.g. shop prices)
shout out	publicly acknowledge/praise someone on social media

One indicative example of a shift in meaning is: 'I just want to shout out to my amazing friend, [name] who is so talented, kind, loving, funny, ...' (social media post, 2018). The noun form is attested in the OED from 1990 with a meaning of 'acknowledgement/mention', but for me 'to shout out' often had a slightly negative connotation. However, when it comes to faddish PVs and their substantive equivalents, the BBC Radio 4 *Today* programme is the gift that goes on giving. On 31 October 2019 we were treated to an announcement at the beginning of the programme that the discussion would be about 'how President Obama has called out the woke generation'. Then we had the American economist Diane Swonk discoursing on the US Federal Reserve rate cuts. No half-measures here: 'the pushback and the fatigue of cutting rates', 'a rollback in tariffs', 'the pullback in investment', 'a pullback in hiring', 'the consumer pulled back in the height of the holiday season', 'a pullback in spending', 'consumers pulled back on discretionary spending' – all within the space of a short interview of no more than a couple of minutes. But the real corker came later in the programme, when presenter Nick Robinson apologised for ending an interview as it ran out of time by saying to the interviewee 'I'm so sorry to have to wind you up'. I wonder in how many senses he meant it.

I realise that the word 'faddish' can come over as prescriptive. Prescriptive I am not. As with all fashions, one can simply observe with a degree of wonder how quickly they catch on and how equally quickly they can fade away. Most of the items in Table 9.1 inhabit the world of social media, journalism and broadcasting, and, so far, I rarely if ever hear them outside of those environments. However, the rise and rise of the PV is an unstoppable part of the conversationalisation process and a shift towards a preference for non-classical words. For this we owe much to the global influence of AmE, which, if nothing else, is creative, flexible and dynamic. Such dynamism means that we can expect linguistic fashions to change at a fast pace. Furthermore, it could be a healthy sign that, at last, the voices of ordinary people have a wider public forum than ever before, thanks to social media, and if the fashionable uses of PVs spread to a wider public which accepts them, then that is a sign that the organism is in good shape and that linguistic creativity and adaptation are alive and well.

9.4 Grammar and moral panic

Occasionally, debates over grammar spill into the public domain and simmer till they boil over into moral panic. This was so elegantly and humorously emphasised by Ron Carter in commenting upon the way that public authorities often equate what they perceive as a lack of attention to grammar with a decline in standards of behaviour and social discipline:

> 'There is a clear connection made in such thinking between grammatical order and the social order where it is only a small step from splitting infinitives to splitting heads open on football terraces'.

(Carter 1997: 21)

Carter had to deal with government and media criticism in the early 1990s in relation to his work on the English Language National Curriculum in the United Kingdom. In the latter part of the 20th century there were heated debates in Britain about what was perceived to be a neglect of grammar teaching in the nation's schools. There was probably some truth in this in that formal, traditional, Latin-based grammar, as taught in the 'grammar' schools (selective secondary schools) was found to be unsuited to the new, comprehensive (non-selective) schools in the 1960s. But when research was undertaken to restore the balance of English language study, and recommendations were made, the government at the time did not like the outcome. The Language in the National Curriculum project, in which Carter was a leading figure, saw its teaching materials officially banned from use in schools. The materials were based on a socially embedded view of language and inspired by Halliday's grammar (see the discussion in Goodwyn, 2014). At the time, there was tabloid media outrage at the idea that William Shakespeare's plays might be replaced by pop song lyrics in the nation's schools. Carter never advocated such an extreme position, but I recall a certain news source in the early 1990s nicknaming him 'Red Ron', as though he were some subversive, fifth-column communist. Things settled over time, and the place of grammar in the National Curriculum for the English language is now established; it does require formal knowledge, as we saw on p. 128, even from primary school pupils, but it is by no means a return to the old days of sentence parsing, which I experienced in the grammar school that I attended and greatly enjoyed as an intellectual challenge. With its notions of word classes, subjects and predicates taught to me by a brilliant schoolmaster, traditional English grammar also helped me to understand the grammars of Latin, Welsh, French and Spanish – the other school languages that I studied, although that was undoubtedly because those languages were studied through grammar and translation during my schooling. Nobody had thought of communicative language teaching when I was a boy.

After the turbulent 1990s in the United Kingdom, which might be described as a modern version of 'grammar wars' (see section 4.4), the moral-grammatical landscape was punctuated again by controversy in 2013. The British Secretary of State for Education at the time, Michael Gove, endorsed a very conservative grammar primer, *Gwynne's Grammar* (Gwynne, 2013) and urged his own ministerial and civil service staff to use it and to get their grammatical act together, so frustrated was he by what he regarded as their poor and incorrect usage.

Gwynne's grammar modestly describes itself as 'The *ultimate* introduction to the writing of good English' (title page: italics as in the original). Its approach and content would not be out of place in the earlier sections of chapter 4 of this book. Gwynne firmly holds that creativity and style cannot be developed in writing English unless the basis of the grammatical system is first mastered, as he argues in his Preface. He also argues that English grammar has changed only negligibly since the late mediaeval period and that it can be modelled now as it was then. Latin grammar terms abound in his book, including 'gerund' and 'gerundive' (terms for which I have yet to find a practical need in describing English), and the approach is prescriptive. The book achieved great popularity during 2013–15, thanks to its official endorsement, but it was not without its vehement critics, epitomised by Oliver Kamm's searing demolition of Gwynne's position in the *The Spectator* magazine. Kamm does not pull his punches, describing Gwynne as 'an ignoramus who bungles basic grammatical concepts while insisting that certain weird peeves of his are the only "correct" way to write' (Kamm, 2015).

Gwynne's fame in the media might have been brief (at the time of writing, his star seems to have faded), but he was influential in the so-called 'bad grammar' awards – an annual event designed to show up 'incorrect' usage in the written documents produced by well-known figures, academics and institutions such as the BBC or the United Kingdom's National Health Service, and the public is invited to make submissions to it for consideration. What the Gove-Gwynne controversy has shown is the enduring power of traditional, static views of grammar, and the feeling that if standards were changing, that must mean that they were declining, and if they were declining, then someone was to blame (in Gwynne's case, that included academics and experts in child psychology in teacher training colleges, as he argues in an interview in *The Telegraph* newspaper; see Grice, 2013). Gove's grammatical fire did not go out so quickly: again in 2015, when Secretary of State at the Ministry of Justice, he issued a diktat to his staff banning the use of a range of what he considered to be grammatical howlers (Glaze, 2015).

9.5 Conclusion: re-wilding the grammatical environment

As we come to the end of this book, I think it fit to go back to the beginning and remind ourselves that grammar belongs to everyone and that it is incumbent upon applied linguists to understand the perspectives and concerns of the lay population, but above all, to try to grasp the part played by its ordinary users in shaping it and changing it. The story of grammar in the hands of grammarians has been an attempt over two-millennia to cage it and tame it. Yet it seems constantly to escape from its cage and always to be one step ahead of those trying to (re)capture it. We would all like to think that there must be some set of rules somewhere, some system behind it all which we can rely on and lean upon in our social compact of communication and in teaching and learning it in our own language and in the pursuit of others. The evidence is, however, that such constancy and uniformity is but a mirage.

One of the cages in which grammar is trapped is the idea of a standard language. In the case of English, we have no government-sponsored national academy to advise on rules and correctness. Instead we have a catalogue of historical forces which led to a particular way of using the language becoming the variety associated with success, power and prestige. That variety spread its tentacles around the world in the form of the colonial standard. But where it took root, its offspring grew to maturity to claim their title as new standards, with new varieties 'de-standardising' the old one. These new, 'de-homogenized' varieties (Parakrama, 1995) themselves possess internal variety, just as the old imperial national language always did, and so will it always go on. Writing on 'standard English', Peterson (2020) questions the term *standard*, and prefers *standardised*, which avoids reification of the concept of a standard language. Grammatical change has been well documented in many of the places around the world where English established itself (see the papers in Collins,

2015), and the fluidity of English in the world has led Pennycook (2007) to question the reality of what we call English as an international language.

Who leads the changes in grammar, and how? There are individuals and groups who push things forward. Creative writers have long experimented with grammar and embraced variety and variation. Shakespeare's works exhibit a good smattering of non-standard forms. Norman Blake suggests that the distinction between standard and non-standard in Shakespeare's day was more fluid anyway. In the case of phrasal verbs, for example, Shakespeare could have both borrowed from non-standard varieties and invented new ones himself (Blake, 2006: 3). Hope (2003) has also emphasised the great variation in grammar in Shakespeare's works, suggesting a fluid era of grammatical change in the late 16th to early 17th century in England. And yet to suggest that Shakespeare's grammar is anything but perfectly in compliance with the unchanging and unchangeable 'rules' is received by some as tantamount to heresy. More than 20 double comparatives such as *more hotter, more kinder, more rawer* and others that are now considered non-standard but heard widely in the day-to-day speech of English users around the world are to be found in Shakespeare's works. In the Renaissance era when Shakespeare wrote, double comparatives were not stigmatised (González Díaz, 2003; Hope, 2003: 53), but by the 18th century they were. Greenwood (1711/1753: 116) branded them as not 'good' English, and Lowth dismissed them as 'improper' (Lowth, 1762/1799: 27). Shakespeare is rightly held in respect for the beauty of his language, but this translates into a belief that it represents perfection and occupies a high moral ground from which grammar has been slipping and sliding ever since. We might not agree with that view as applied linguists, but we cannot deny its existence and its hold on the popular imagination, as I know from experience in the Q&A sessions at talks that I give to local societies, and we should at the very least understand its historical and cultural roots.

Another feature of Shakespeare's time was a great variation in punctuation, including the use of the *'s* apostrophe (Hope, 2003: 33–41). The *'s* apostrophe has become the theatre of another grammar war – one that is fought among the general public in the United Kingdom. The so-called *greengrocer's apostrophe* (the use of apostrophes to mark plural nouns) and their non-use to denote the possessive, together with the confusion of *its* and *it's*, *you're* and *your*, *there's* and *theirs*, *were* and *we're*, has filled many a blog, online forum and social media platform. The department store Marks and Spencer (M&S) attracted the headline 'M&S IN GRAMMAR BLUNDER' in 2006 on the UK *Mirror* newspaper website when it confused *ones* (pronoun) and *one's* (possessive determiner).[1] The same website in 2015 reported praise for a nine-year-old girl who spotted 15 apostrophe 'howlers' in a stroll around her hometown in the north of England,[2] including non-standard plurals such as *pie's, pasty's* and *sandwich's*. Britain even boasts its own mysterious character who calls himself a 'grammar vigilante' and goes around correcting non-standard use of apostrophes under cover of darkness.[3] Mind you, English is not alone in this: a similar grammatical vigilantism for Spanish exists in Ecuador.[4] Until 2019 the United Kingdom had its own Apostrophe Protection Society, which has since closed, its founder admitting to having lost the battle because of people's laziness and ignorance.[5] It is the people – the ordinary folk of every day – who lead the changes in apostrophe use and in many other aspects of grammar; we pay homage to the William Shakespeares of this world because they are on permanent record, revered in the literary canon and publicly mythologised to a position of unassailability.

Grammar in the media and in the streets and squares of our towns is always on the move. The linguistic landscape is the living, uncaged grammar reference book. Advertising plays with grammar. 'Give Merry. Give Kiehl's' appeared on a sign in a London skincare and hair care shop recently. The unusual *give* + adjective syntax catches the eye; then we are taken to *give* + possessive noun. Most people would have no trouble in interpreting the message: giving gifts from this shop will bring joy to the recipient. O'Sullivan (2020) has shown how features of Irish English are exploited in radio advertising in Ireland. English is a global advertising language (Simões Lucas Freitas, 2014), and unusual (to the standard BrE speaker) grammar often appears in the strangest of places. I recall on my first visit to Japan being struck by the number of English slogans on tee-shirts that defied conventional syntax. What mattered was not the syntax of the slogans; what mattered was that they were in English.

Yet that global spread of English brings with it a set of different issues. The journeys of refugees and economic migrants, from war-torn and economically troubled parts of the world often towards Europe has found a new role for English grammar: the syntax of the poor and despairing who often barely have enough English to communicate basic needs and who struggle to assimilate in an alien environment of reception centres and ghettoised accommodation. In a corpus-based ethnographic study of the closed community of a refugee reception centre in Ireland, Harrington shows how the residents communicate with a survival level of grammar to express temporal meanings (Harrington, 2018: 94–109). No standardly inflected regular past tense verb appears in the top 250 tokens in his data, and among irregular past forms, only *was* appears in the top 150 tokens. The speakers substitute present continuous forms for standard past continuous and present simple forms for standard past simple ones. This is the grammar of necessity – forms uncaged from their standardised meanings and corralled for survival, which is a far cry from the elegant English as a lingua franca grammar of academic and professional international communication.

The influence of public media (broadcasting, advertising, social media) is significant in prompting and promoting grammatical change. In contrast to the exceptional geniuses of the creative industries are the ordinary folk who make meaning; theirs is the creativity of the everyday, the 'art of common talk' (Carter, 2004b). And the grammar of common talk is spontaneous. Is grammar therefore a completely wild organism which only the purists want to preserve in aspic, where the new, cosmopolitan young will rejoice in the grammar of the mobile phone and happily mutilate the apostrophe in text messages and social media, where *for* becomes *4*, where *you* becomes *u*, *about* becomes *abt*, *because* becomes *cos* or *b/c*, and where standard syntax, punctuation and spelling are defenestrated in a frenzy of jabbing thumbs? Generally speaking, the answer is yes, although a recent study in the Netherlands found that people seeking love on dating apps were less likely to succeed if their grammar, spelling and punctuation were perceived as poor or careless[6], and one in the USA found that singletons who were questioned about the qualities of potential partners considered 'grammar important, ahead of confidence and good teeth' (Blakely, 2019). More directly useful, a data firm specialising in the analysis of disinformation planted online by foreign powers in British political elections homed in on suspects partly on the basis of repeated grammatical errors (Ben Nimmo of the Graphika company, BBC Radio 4, *Today* programme, 1 December 2019). I admit to applying the 'weird grammar' test to spam and phishing emails claiming to be from my bank or internet service provider: any basic grammar errors and into the bin they go, straight away.

Conventional grammatical standards are far from dead, and they are a concern among the population; we should not just dismiss them as fuddy-duddy and pedantic. However, grammar will go on changing regardless. Today's e-communications could well help to speed up the changes, with grammar residing in a wilder, ungoverned, more fluid environment. In taking grammar out of its cage of reference books and textbooks and the worlds of professional communicators, e-communication helps to re-wild the language in a largely ungoverned environment, facilitating an accelerated evolution where random mutations create new forms that are well adapted to their environments and where the voice of the ordinary, everyday population has a greater chance to be heard.

We have come a long way since the grammarians of antiquity set about their task, and I hope that we have learnt something. Practicality and good governance demand that we offer to everyone the opportunities to be enjoyed through knowledge of standardised grammatical conventions, but a good grammatical education, whether in a first or second language, must surely include an awareness of what grammar is, what it is not, how it works, and how to make it work for you. I have dwelt on English in this book for reasons outlined from the start, but I suspect that human beings are the same the world over, and that what can be said about English grammar will find echoes in the grammars of other languages, once we see a way through the intellectual labyrinths. For me, the approaches to grammar that I have particularly advocated in this book – neo-Firthian, emergent, corpus-based, with socioculturally embedded language education and process or 'grammaring' oriented learning – work well together. They represent mutually supportive innovations, but ones that do not deprive us of enough challenges to keep us busy for many years to come.

Notes

1 www.mirror.co.uk/news/uk-news/ms-in-grammar-blunder-654467
2 www.mirror.co.uk/news/uk-news/nine-year-old-spotted-15-6713651
3 www.theguardian.com/education/2017/apr/03/banksy-of-punctuation-puts-full-stop-bad-grammar-bristol
4 www.theguardian.com/world/2015/mar/05/ecuador-graffiti-accion-ortografica-quito-grammar
5 www.bbc.co.uk/news/world-us-canada-50692797
6 *The Times* newspaper, 19 November 2019: 3

REFERENCES

A. G. K. 1928. 'Review', *American Speech*, 3(4): 334–339.
Aarts, B. 2012. 'The subjunctive conundrum in English', *Folia Linguistica*, 46(1): 1–20.
Aarts, F. 1987. 'Dutch progress in English syntax: Zandvoort's Handbook of English Grammar and After'. In G. H. V. Bunt, E. S. Kooper, J. L. Mackenzie and D. R. M. Wilkinson (eds), *One Hundred Years of English Studies in Dutch Universities*. Amsterdam: Rodopi: 67–79.
Aarts, F. 1994. 'William Cobbett's 'Grammar of the English Language'', *Neuphilologische Mitteilungen*, 95(3): 319–332.
Aijmer, K. 2002. *English Discourse Particles*. Amsterdam: John Benjamins.
Aijmer, K. 2018. 'The Swedish modal auxiliary ska/skall seen through its English translations', *BELLS. Bergen Language and Linguistics Studies*, 9(1): 139–154.
Alexander, C. 1795. *A grammatical system of the English language: comprehending a plain and familiar scheme, of teaching young gentlemen and ladies the art of speaking and writing correctly their native tongue*. Third edition. Boston: I. Thomas and E. T. Andrews.
Alexander, L., Allen, W. S., Close, R. and O'Neill, R. 1975. *English Grammatical Structure*. London: Longman.
Aleksandrova, O., Mendzheritskaya, E. and Malakhova, V. 2017. 'Dynamic Changes in Modern English Discourse', *Training, Language and Culture*, 1(1):0160100–117.
Alford, H. 1864. *The Queen's English: Stray Notes on Speaking and Spelling*. London: Strahan and Co.
Allen, W.S. 1947/1974. *Living English Structure*. Fifth edition. London: Longman.
Amador Moreno, C. 2012. 'A corpus-based approach to contemporary Irish writing: Ross O'Carroll-Kelly's use of 'like' as a discourse marker', *International Journal of English Studies*, 12(2): 19–38.
Amador Moreno, C. 2019. *Orality in Written Texts*. London: Routledge.
Amador Moreno, C., McCarthy, M. J. and O'Keeffe, A. 2013. 'Can English provide a framework for Spanish response tokens?', *Yearbook of Corpus Linguistics and Pragmatics 2013*: 175–201.
Amsler, M. E. 1989. *Etymology and Grammatical Discourse in Late Antiquity and the Early Middle Ages*. Amsterdam: John Benjamins.

Andersen, R. 1991. 'Developmental sequences: The emergence of aspect marking in second language acquisition'. In T. Huebner and C. A. Ferguson (eds), *Crosscurrents in Second Language Acquisition and Linguistic Theories*. Amsterdam: John Benjamins: 305–324.

Andersen, G. 1998. 'The pragmatic marker like from a relevance-theoretic perspective'. In H. Jucker and Y. Ziv (eds), *Discourse Markers: Descriptions and Theory*. Amsterdam: John Benjamins: 147–170.

Anderwald, L. 2016. *Language between Description and Prescription: Verbs and Verb Categories in Nineteenth-Century Grammars of English*. Oxford: Oxford University Press.

Arsleff, H. 1970. 'The History of Linguistics and Professor Chomsky', *Language*, 46(3): 570–585.

Atherton, C. 1996. 'What Every Grammarian Knows?', *The Classical Quarterly*, 46(1): 239–260.

Auer, A. 2006. 'Precept and practice: The influence of prescriptivism on the English subjunctive'. In C. Dalton-Puffer, D. Kastovsky, N. Ritt and H. Schendl (eds), *Syntax, Style and Grammatical Norms: English from 1500–2000*. Bern: Peter Lang: 33–54.

Azar, B. S. and Hagen, S. A. 2009. *Understanding and Using English Grammar*. Fourth edition. White Plains, NY: Pearson Education.

Bailey, N., Madden, C., and Krashen, S. D. 1974. 'Is there a 'natural sequence' in adult second language learning?', *Language Learning*, 24(2): 235–243.

Baker, P. 2015. 'Does Britain need any more foreign doctors? Inter-analyst consistency and corpus-assisted critical discourse analysis'. In N. Groom, M. Charles and S. John (eds), *Corpora, Grammar and Discourse*. Amsterdam: John Benjamins: 283–300.

Bardovi-Harlig, K. 1992. 'The relationship of form and meaning: A cross-sectional study of tense and aspect in the interlanguage of learners of English as a second language', *Applied Psycholinguistics*, 13: 253–278.

Bardovi-Harlig, K. 2000. *Tense and Aspect in Second Language Acquisition: Form, Meaning, and Use*. Oxford: Blackwell.

Basbøll, H. and Jensen, V. B. 2015. 'Rask: A linguistic giant between the 18th and 20th century', *Historiographia Linguistica*, 42(1): 153–167.

Battistella, E. 1999. 'The persistence of traditional grammar'. In R. S. Wheeler (ed.), *Language Alive in the Classroom*. Westport, CT: Praeger: 13–22.

Beattie, J. 1788. *The Theory of Language, in Two Parts*. London: Printed for A. Strahan and T. Cadell in the Strand; and W. Creech, Edinburgh.

Bell, D. 2007. 'Sentence-initial *and* and *but* in academic writing', *Pragmatics*, 17(2): 183–201.

Berlitz 1966. *English First Book*. Paris: Societé Internationale des Écoles Berlitz.

Berry, H. M. 1975. *Introduction to Systemic Linguistics 1: Structures and Systems*. London: Batsford.

Berry, H. M. 1975. *Introduction to Systemic Linguistics 2: Levels and Links*. London: Batsford.

Besse, H. 2001. 'Comenius et sa "méthode d'enseignement graduée"', *Langue Française*, 131: 7–22.

Biber, D. 1988. *Variation across Speech and Writing*. Cambridge: Cambridge University Press.

Biber, D. 1995. *Dimensions of Register Variation. A Cross-linguistic Comparison*. Cambridge: Cambridge University Press.

Biber, D. 2006. *University Language: A Corpus-based Study of Spoken and Written Registers*. Amsterdam: John Benjamins.

Biber, D. 2009. 'A corpus-driven approach to formulaic language in English: Multi-word patterns in speech and writing', *International Journal of Corpus Linguistics*, 14(3): 275–311.

Biber, D. and Finegan, E. 1991. 'On the exploitation of computerised corpora in variation studies'. In K. Ajmer and B. Altenberg (eds), *English Corpus Linguistics. Studies in Honour of Jan Svartvik*. London: Longman: 204–220.

Biber, D., Conrad, S. and Reppen, R. 1994. 'Corpus-base approaches to issues in applied linguistics', *Applied Linguistics*, 15(2): 169–189.

Biber, D., Johansson, S., Leech, G., Conrad, S. and Finegan E. 1999. *Longman Grammar of Spoken and Written English*. London: Longman.

Biber, D. and Gray, B. 2018. 'Academic writing as a locus of grammatical change'. In R. J. Whitt (ed), *Diachronic Corpora, Genre, and Language Change*. Amsterdam: John Benjamins: 117–146.

Blake, N. 2006. *Shakespeare's Non-Standard English*. Third edition. London: Continuum.

Blakely, R. 2019. 'Bad grammar spells disaster for daters', *The Times*, 19 November 2019: 3.

Bloomfield, L. 1927. 'On Some Rules of Pāṇini', *Journal of the American Oriental Society*, 47: 61–70.

Bloomfield, L. 1933. *Language*. New York: Henry Holt.

Blyth, C. 1997. 'A constructivist approach to grammar: Teaching teachers to teach aspect', *The Modern Language Journal*, 81(1): 50–66.

BNC Consortium. 2007. British National Corpus, XML edition, Oxford Text Archive. Retrieved from: http://hdl.handle.net/20.500.12024/2554.

Bolden, G. B. 2009. 'Implementing incipient actions: The discourse marker 'so' in English conversation', *Journal of Pragmatics*, 41(5): 974–998.

Bowker, G. 2011. *James Joyce: A Biography*. London: Weidenfeld and Nicolson.

Brazil, D. 1995. *A Grammar of Speech*. Oxford: Oxford University Press.

Brazil, D. 1997. *The Communicative Value of Intonation in English*. Cambridge: Cambridge University Press.

Brightland, J. 1759. *The Grammar of the English Tongue: With the Arts of Logick, Rhetorick, Poetry &c*. London: Printed for James Rivington and James Fletcher.

Brown, G. 1823/1856. *The Institutes of English Grammar*. New York: Samuel S. and William Wood.

Bullokar, W. 1586. *Pamphlet for Grammar*. Imprinted at London: By Edmund Bollifant. Retrieved from: University of Oxford Text Archive records at http://ota.ox.ac.uk/desc/0025.

Burchfield, R. 1991. 'The Fowler brothers and the tradition of usage handbooks'. In G. Leitner (ed.), *English Traditional Grammars: An International Perspective*. Amsterdam: John Benjamins. 93–111.

Bursill-Hall, G. L. 1966. 'Notes on the semantics of linguistic description'. In C. E. Bazell, J. C. Catford, M. A. K. Halliday and R. H. Robins (eds), *In Memory of J. R. Firth*. London: Longman: 40–51.

Burton, G. 2018. 'Why do all coursebooks teach the same grammar?' Paper presented at the 52nd Annual IATEFL Conference, Brighton, UK.

Burton, G. 2019. 'The canon of pedagogical grammar for ELT: a mixed methods study of its evolution, development and comparison with evidence on learner output'. Unpublished PhD dissertation, University of Limerick, Ireland.

Buschmann-Göbels, A. 2008. 'Bellum Grammaticale 1712. A battle of books and a battle for the market'. In I. Tieken-Boon van Ostade (ed.), *Grammars, Grammarians and Grammar-Writing in Eighteenth-Century England*. The Hague: Mouton de Gruyter: 81–100.

Busse, B., Gather, K. and Kleiber, I. 2018. 'Assessing the Connections between English Grammarians of the Nineteenth Century – A Corpus-Based Network Analysis'. In E. Fuss, M. Konopka, B. Trawiński and U. H. Wassner (eds), *Grammar and Corpora 2016*. Heidelberg: Heidelberg University Publishing: 435–442.

Butterfield, J. (ed.) 2015. *Fowler's Dictionary of Modern English Usage*. Fourth Edition. Oxford: Oxford University Press.

Buttery, P., McCarthy, M. J. and Carter, R. 2015. 'Chatting in the academy: informality in spoken academic discourse'. In N. Groom, M. Charles and S. John (eds), *Corpora, Grammar and Discourse. In honour of Susan Hunston*. Amsterdam: John Benjamins: 183–210.

Bybee, J. 2003. 'Mechanisms of Change in Grammaticization: The Role of Frequency'. In B. D. Joseph and R. D. Janda (eds), *The Handbook of Historical Linguistics*. Oxford: Blackwell: 602–623.

Caines, A. and Buttery, P. 2010. '"You talking to me?" A predictive model for zero-auxiliary constructions', Proceedings of the 2010 Workshop on NLP and Linguistics: Finding the Common Ground, ACL-2010, Association for Computational Linguistics: 43–51.

Caines, A., McCarthy, M. J. and O'Keeffe, A. 2016. 'Spoken language corpora and pedagogical applications'. In F. Farr and L. Murray (eds), *The Routledge Handbook of Language Learning and Technology*. Abingdon: Routledge: 348–361.

Caines, A., Buttery, P. and McCarthy, M. J. 2018. '"You still talking to me?" The zero auxiliary progressive in spoken British English, twenty years on'. In V. Brezina, R. Love and K. Aijmer (eds), *Sociolinguistic Variation in Contemporary British English: Exploration of the Spoken BNC 2014*. London: Routledge: 209–234.

Cajka, K. 2003. 'The forgotten women grammarians of eighteenth-century England'. PhD dissertation, University of Connecticut. Retrieved fromhttps://opencommons.uconn.edu/dissertations/AAI3118940/.

Cameron, D. 1995. *Verbal Hygiene: The Politics of Language*. Abingdon: Routledge.

Carter, R. 1997. *Investigating English Discourse*. London: Routledge.

Carter, R. 1998. 'Orders of reality: CANCODE, communication, and culture', *ELT Journal*, 52(1): 43–56.

Carter, R. 2004a. 'Introduction'. In *Trust the Text. Language, Corpus and Discourse*. London: Routledge: 1–6.

Carter, R. 2004b. *Language and Creativity: The Art of Common Talk*, London: Routledge.

Carter, R., Hughes, R. and McCarthy, M. J. 2000. *Exploring Grammar in Context*. Cambridge: Cambridge University Press.

Carter, R. and McCarthy, M. J. 1995. 'Grammar and the spoken language', *Applied Linguistics*, 16(2): 141–158.

Carter, R. and McCarthy, M. J. 1997. *Exploring Spoken English*. Cambridge: Cambridge University Press.

Carter, R. and McCarthy, M. J. 1999. The English *get*-passive in spoken discourse: description and implications for an interpersonal grammar. *English Language and Linguistics* 3 (1): 41–58.

Carter, R. and McCarthy, M. J. 2006. *Cambridge Grammar of English*. Cambridge: Cambridge University Press.

Carter, R., McCarthy, M. J., Mark, G. and O'Keeffe, A. 2011. *English Grammar Today*. Cambridge: Cambridge University Press.

Carter, R. and McCarthy, M. J. 2017. 'Spoken grammar: Where are we and where are we going?', *Applied Linguistics*, 38(1): 1–21.

Channon, A., Foulkes, P. and Walker, T. 2018. 'But what is the reason why you know such things?' Question and response patterns in the LADO interview, *Journal of Pragmatics*, 129: 154–172.

Chodowroska-Pilch, M. 2008. 'Verás in Peninsular Spanish as a grammaticalized discourse marker invoking positive and negative politeness', *Journal of Pragmatics*, 40(8): 1357–1372.

Chomsky, N. 1957. *Syntactic Structures*. The Hague: Mouton.

Chomsky, N. 1959. 'Review of Verbal Behavior by B. F. Skinner', *Language*, 35(1): 26–58.

Chomsky, N. 1964. 'The Development of Grammar in Child Language: Discussion', *Monographs of the Society for Research in Child Development*, 29(1): 35–42.

Chomsky, N. 1965. *Aspects of the Theory of Syntax*. Cambridge, MA: MIT Press.

Chomsky, N. 1966. *Cartesian Linguistics*. New York: Harper and Row.

Clancy, B. 2010. 'Building a corpus to represent a variety of a language'. In A. O'Keeffe and M. McCarthy (eds), *The Routledge Handbook of Corpus Linguistics*. Abingdon: Routledge: 80–92.

Clancy, B. and McCarthy, M. J. 2014. 'Co-constructed turn taking'. In K. Aijmer and C. Ruehlemann (eds), *Corpus Pragmatics: A Handbook*. Cambridge: Cambridge University Press: 430–453.

Cobbett, W. 1818/1831. *A Grammar of the English Language, In a Series of Letters*. London: William Cobbett, 11 Bolt-Court, Fleet-Street..

COBUILD 1987. *Collins COBUILD English Language Dictionary*. London: Collins.

COBUILD 1990. *Collins COBUILD English Grammar*. London: HarperCollins Publishers.

Collins, P. 1996. 'Get-passives in English', *World Englishes*, 15(1): 43-56.

Collins, P. (ed.) 2015. *Grammatical Change in English World-Wide*. Amsterdam: John Benjamins.

Compton, J. (ed.) 1941. *Spoken English*, London: Methuen and Co Ltd.

Conrad, S. 2000. 'Will corpus revolutionize grammar teaching in the 21st century?', *TESOL Quarterly*, 34: 548–560.

Cook, G. 1998. 'The uses of reality: a reply to Ronald Carter', *ELT Journal*, 52(1): 57–63.

Corder, S. P. 1967. 'The significance of learners' errors', *IRAL*, V(4): 161–170.

Corder, S. P. 1975. 'The language of second-language learners: The broader issues', *The Modern Language Journal*, 59(8): 409–413.

Council of Europe, 2001. *Common European Framework of Reference for Languages: Learning, Teaching, Assessment*. Cambridge: Cambridge University Press.

Coupland, N. 1988. *Dialect in Use: Sociolinguistic Variation in Cardiff English*. Cardiff: University of Wales Press.

Crystal, D. 2008. *Txtng: The Gr8 Db8*. Oxford: Oxford University Press.

Crystal, D. 2011. *Internet Linguistics: A Student Guide*. Abingdon: Routledge.

Csomay, E. 2004. 'Linguistic variation within university classroom talk: A corpus-based perspective', *Linguistics and Education*, 15(3): 243–274.

Davidson, T. 1874. *The Grammar of Dionysios Thrax*. Translated by Thomas Davidson. St Louis, MO. Printed by R. P. Studley Co.

De Beaugrande, R. 1991. 'Language and the facilitation of authority: The discourse of Noam Chomsky', *Journal of Advanced Composition*, 11(2): 425–442.

Department for Education. 2013. *English programmes of study: key stages 1 and 2 National Curriculum in England*. Accessed 1 December 2019. Retrieved from: https://assets.publishing.service.gov.uk/government/uploads/system/uploads/attachment_data/file/335186/PRIMARY_national_curriculum_-_English_220714.pdf

De Saussure, F. 1881. *De l'emploi du génitif absolu en sanscrit*. Geneva: Printed by J. G. Fick.

Devis, E. 1797. *The Accidence; or First rudiments of English grammar. Designed for the Use of Young Ladies*. Ninth edition. London: Printed for B. Law and C. Law.

Devis, E. 1782. *Miscellaneous Lessons Designed for the Use of Young Ladies. On a New Plan*. London: Printed for the Author and Sold by John Fielding.

D'Hont, U. and Defour, T. 2012. 'At the crossroads of grammaticalization and pragmaticalization: A diachronic cross-linguistic case study on *vraiment* and *really*', *Neuphilologische Mitteilungen*, 113(2): 169–190.

Dobbie, E. V. 1949. 'Zandvoort's "Handbook of English Grammar"', *American Speech*, 24(4): 289–291.

Dobson, A. 2018. 'Towards "MFL for all" in England: a historical perspective', *The Language Learning Journal*, 46(1): 71–85.

Dons, U. 2004. *Descriptive Adequacy of Early Modern English Grammars*. Berlin: Mouton de Gruyter.

Downey, C. 1991. 'Trends that shaped the development of 19th century American grammar writing'. In G. Leitner (ed.), *English Traditional Grammars: An International Perspective*. Amsterdam: John Benjamins: 27–38.

Downing, A. 1996. 'The semantics of get-passives'. In R. Hasan, C. Cloran and D. G. Butt (eds), *Functional Descriptions: Theory in Practice*. Amsterdam: John Benjamins: 179–206.

Downing, A. and Locke, P. 2006. *English Grammar: A University Course*. Second edition. Abingdon: Routledge.

Drury Hall, A. 1977. 'Tudor prose style: English humanists and the problem of a standard', *English Literary Renaissance*, 7(3): 267–296.

Dulay, H. C. and Burt, M. K. 1973. 'Should we teach children syntax?', *Language Learning*, 23: 245.

Dulay, H. C. and Burt, M. K. 1974. Natural sequences in child second language acquisition. *Language Learning* 24: 37–53.

Dykema, K. W. 1961. 'Where our grammar came from', *College English*, 22(7): 455–465.

Eastwood, J. 1994. *Oxford Guide to English Grammar*. Oxford: Oxford University Press.

Ellis, N. and Ferreira-Junior, F. 2009. 'Constructions and their acquisition Islands and the distinctiveness of their occupancy', *Annual Review of Cognitive Linguistics*, 7: 187–220.

Emsley, B. 1933. 'James Buchanan and the eighteenth century regulation of English usage', *PMLA*, 48(4): 1154–1166.

Errington, J. 2001. 'Colonial Linguistics', *Annual Review of Anthropology*, 30: 19–39.

Fairclough, N. 1995. *Critical Discourse Analysis*. London: Longman.

Farr, F., Murphy, B. and O'Keeffe, A. 2004. 'The Limerick Corpus of Irish English: Design, description and application', *Teanga*, 21: 5–30.

Farrell, A. 2020. *Corpus Perspectives on the Spoken Models Used by EFL Teachers*. Abingdon: Routledge.

Ferrara, K. 1992. 'The interactive achievement of a sentence: Joint productions in therapeutic discourse', *Discourse Processes*, 15(2): 207–228.

Fillmore, C. J. 1982. 'Frame Semantics'. In D. Geeraerts, R. Dirren and J. R. Taylor (eds), *Cognitive Linguistics: Basic Readings*. Berlin: Mouton de Gruyter: 373–400.

Filppula, M. 1999. *The Grammar of Irish English: Language in Hibernian Style*. London: Routledge.

Firth, A. and Wagner, J. 1997. 'On discourse, communication, and some. fundamental concepts in SLA research', *The Modern Language Journal*, 81(3): 285–300.

Firth, J. R. 1930/1964. *The Tongues of Men and Speech*. London: Oxford University Press.

Firth, J.R. 1951/1957. *Papers in Linguistics*. Oxford: Oxford University Press: 190–215.

Formigari, L. 2004. *A History of Language Philosophies*. Amsterdam: John Benjamins.

Fowler, H. W. and Fowler, F. G. 1906/1922. *The King's English*. Oxford: Clarendon Press.

Fowler, H. W. 1926. *A Dictionary of Modern English Usage*. Oxford: Clarendon Press.

Fries, C. C. 1927. 'The Rules of Common School Grammars', *PMLA*, 42(1): 221–237.

Fries, C. C. 1945. *Teaching and Learning English as a Foreign Language*. Ann Arbor, MI: University of Michigan Press.

Fries, C. C. 1952. *The Structure of English*. New York: Harcourt, Brace and Company.

Fulcher, G. 1991. 'Conditionals Revisited', *ELT Journal*, 45(2): 164–168.

Geisler, C., Kaufer, D. and Steinberg, E. 1985. 'The unattended anaphoric "this"', *Written Communication*, 2(2): 129–155.

Gethin, A. 1999. *Language and Thought: A Rational Enquiry into their Nature and Relationship*. Exeter: Intellect.

Givón, T. 1979. *On Understanding Grammar*. London: Academic Press.

Glaze, B. 2015. 'Michael Gove gives "patronising" grammar lessons to Ministry of Justice staff', *The Mirror*, 22 June 2015. Retrieved from: www.mirror.co.uk/news/uk-news/michael-gove-gives-patronising-grammar-5926858

González, M. 2005. 'Pragmatic markers and discourse coherence relations in English and Catalan oral narrative', *Discourse Studies*, 7(1): 53–86.

González, M. 2015. 'From truth-attesting to intensification: The grammaticalization of Spanish *la verdad* and Catalan *la veritat*', *Discourse Studies*, 17(2): 162–181.

González Díaz, V. 2003. 'Adjective comparison in Renaissance English', *SEDERI Yearbook of the Spanish and Portuguese Society for English Renaissance Studies*, 13: 87–100.

Goodwyn, A. 2014. 'English and literacy in education: national policies'. In C. Leung and B. V. Street (eds), *The Routledge Companion to English Studies*. Abingdon: Routledge: 16–32.

Goody, J. 1987. *The Interface Between the Written and the Oral*. Cambridge: Cambridge University Press.

Gottfried, R. 1979. 'Berlitz Schools Joyce', *James Joyce Quarterly*, 16(3): 223–238.

Green, J. R. 1965. 'Language laboratory research: A critique', *The Modern Language Journal*, 49(6): 367–369.

Greenbaum, S. 1996. *The Oxford English Grammar*. Oxford: Oxford University Press.

Greenbaum, S. (ed.) 1996. *Comparing English Worldwide: The International Corpus of English*. Oxford: Clarendon Press.

Greenbaum, S. and Nelson, G. 1999. 'Elliptical clauses in spoken and written English'. In P. Collins and D. Lee (eds), *The Clause in English. In Honour of Rodney Huddleston*. Amsterdam: John Benjamins: 111–125.

Greenwood, J. 1711/1753. *An Essay Towards a Practical English Grammar. Describing the Genius and Nature of the English tongue*. Fifth Edition, London, 1753.

Greenwood, J. 1737. *The Royal English Grammar*. London: Printed for J. Nourse.

Grice, E. 2013. 'The glamour of grammar: an object lesson', *The Telegraph*, 13 April 2013. Retrieved from: www.telegraph.co.uk/education/9987974/The-glamour-ofgrammar-an-object-lesson.html

Gwosdek, H. 2013. *Lily's Grammar of Latin in English. Edited and Introduced by Hedwig Gwosdek*. Oxford: Oxford University Press.

Gwynne, N. M. 2013. *Gwynne's Grammar*. London: Ebury Press.

Haas, F. 2018. 'You can't control a thing like that': Genres and changes in Modern English human impersonal pronouns'. In R. J. Whitt (ed.), *Diachronic Corpora, Genre, and Language Change*. Amsterdam: John Benjamins: 171–194.

Hakuta, K. 1976. 'A case study of a Japanese child learning English as a second language', *Language Learning*, 26: 321–351.

Hall, R. A. 1977. 'Some critiques of Chomskyan theory', *Neuphilologische Mitteilungen*, 78(1): 86–95.

Halliday, M. A. K. 1961. 'Categories of the theory of grammar', *Word*, 17(2): 241–292.

Halliday, M. A. K. 1966. 'Lexis as a linguistic level'. In C. E. Bazell, J. C. Catford, M. A. K. Halliday and R. H. Robins (eds) *In Memory of J. R. Firth*. London: Longmans: 148–162.

Halliday, M. A. K. 1967a. 'Notes on Transitivity and Theme in English: Part 1', *Journal of Linguistics*, 3(1): 37–81.

Halliday, M. A. K. 1967b. 'Notes on Transitivity and Theme in English: Part 2', *Journal of Linguistics*, 3(2): 199–244.

Halliday, M. A. K. 1967c. 'Notes on Transitivity and Theme in English: Part 3' *Journal of Linguistics*, 4(2): 179–215.

Halliday, M. A. K. 1975. *Learning How to Mean: Explorations in the Development of Language*. London: Edward Arnold.

Halliday, M. A. K. 1978. *Language as Social Semiotic: The Social Interpretation of Language and Meaning*. London: Edward Arnold.
Halliday, M. A. K. 1985. *An Introduction to Functional Grammar*. London: Edward Arnold.
Halliday, M. A. K. 1991a. 'Towards probabilistic interpretations'. In E. Ventola (ed.), *Functional and Systemic Linguistics: Approaches and Uses*. Berlin: Mouton de Gruyter: 39–62.
Halliday, M. A. K. 1991b. 'Corpus studies and probabilistic grammar'. In K. Ajmer and B. Altenberg (eds), *English Corpus Linguistics. Studies in Honour of Jan Svartvik*. London: Longman: 30–43.
Halliday, M. A. K. 1996. 'On grammar and grammatics'. In R. Hasan, C. Cloran and D. G. Butt (eds), *Functional Descriptions: Theory in Practice*. Amsterdam: John Benjamins 1–38.
Halliday, M. A. K. 2005. *Computational and Quantitative Studies. Volume 6 in the Collected Works of M. A. K. Halliday*. Edited by J. J. Webster. London: Continuum.
Halliday, M. A. K. 2007. *Language and Education. Volume 9 in the Collected Works of M. A. K. Halliday*. Edited by J. J. Webster. London: Continuum.
Halliday. M. A. K. and Hasan, R. 1976. *Cohesion in English*. London: Longman.
Halliday. M. A. K. and Hasan, R. 1989. *Language, Context, and Text: Aspects of Language in a Social-semiotic Perspective*. Oxford: Oxford University Press.
Halliday, M. A. K. and Matthiessen, C. 2004. *An Introduction to Functional Grammar*. Third edition. Revised by Christian M. I. M. Matthiessen. E-book published 2013. Abingdon: Routledge.
Handford, M. 2010. *The Language of Business Meetings*. Cambridge: Cambridge University Press.
Harmer, L. C. and Norton, F. J. 1935. *A Manual of Modern Spanish*, London: University Tutorial Press.
Harrington, K. 2018. *The Role of Corpus Linguistics in the Ethnography of a Closed Community*. Abingdon: Routledge.
Harris, T. 2001–02. 'Linguistics in applied linguistics: A historical overview', *Journal of English Studies*, 3: 99–114.
Harris, Z. 1952a. 'Discourse Analysis', *Language*, 28(1): 1–30.
Harris, Z. 1952b. 'Discourse Analysis: A Sample Text', *Language*, 28(4): 474–494.
Hata, K. 2016. 'Contrast-terminal: The sequential placement of trailoff *but* in extensive courses of action', *Journal of Pragmatics*, 101: 138–154.
Hawking, S. 1988. *A Brief History of Time*. London: Bantam Books.
Hawking, S. 2001. *The Universe in a Nutshell*. London: Bantam Books.
Hawkins, J. A. 1987. 'Implicational universals as predictors of language acquisition', *Linguistics*, 25: 453–473.
Hawkins, J. A. and Buttery, P. 2010. 'Criterial features in learner corpora: Theory and illustrations', *English Profile Journal* 1. Retrieved from: http://journals.cambridge.org/action/displayJournal?jid=EPJ.
Hayes, D. 2009. 'Non-native English-speaking teachers, context and English language teaching', *System*, 37: 1–11.
Heine, B. 2003. 'Grammaticalization'. In B. D. Joseph and R. D. Janda (eds), *The Handbook of Historical Linguistics*. Oxford: Blackwell: 575–601.
Helasvuo, M.-L. 2004. 'Shared syntax: The grammar of co-constructions', *Journal of Pragmatics*, 36: 1315–1336.
Heritage, J. and Sorjonen, M.-L. 2018. *Between Turn and Sequence: Turn-initial Particles across Languages*. Amsterdam: John Benjamins.
Hewings, M. 1999. *Advanced Grammar in Use*. Cambridge: Cambridge University Press.
Higdon, D. L. and Bender, T. K. 1983. *A Concordance to Conrad's Under Western Eyes*. New York: Garland Publishers.

Higdon, D. L. and Bender, T. K. 1985. *A Concordance to Conrad's The Rover*. New York: Garland Publishers.

Hinkel, E. 2016. 'Prioritizing grammar to teach or not to teach: A Research perspective'. In E. Hinkel (ed.), *Handbook of Research in Second Language Teaching and Learning*. 3. Abingdon: Routledge, 369–383.

Hoey, M. 2005. *Lexical Priming: A New Theory of Words and Language*. London: Routledge.

Hoey, M. and O'Donnell, M. B. 2015. 'Examining associations between lexis and textual position in hard news stories, or according to a study by …'. In N. Groom, M. Charles and S. John (eds), *Corpora, Grammar and Discourse*. Amsterdam: John Benjamins: 117–143.

Holmes, J. 1983. 'Speaking English with the appropriate degree of conviction.' In C. J. Brumfit (ed.), *Learning and Teaching of Languages for Communication*. London: Centre for Information on Language Teaching: 100–113.

Hope, J. 2003. *Shakespeare's Grammar*. London: The Arden Shakespeare.

Hopkins, G. M. 1985. *Gerard Manley Hopkins: Poems and Prose*. London: Penguin.

Hopper, P. 1987. 'Emergent grammar', *Proceedings of the Thirteenth Annual Meeting of the Berkeley Linguistics Society 1987*: 139–157.

Hopper, P. 1988. 'Discourse Analysis: Grammar and Critical Theory in the 1980s', *Profession*: 18–24.

Hopper, P. 1996. 'Some recent trends in grammaticalization', *Annual Review of Anthropology*, 25: 217–236.

Hooper, P. 1998. 'The paradigm at the end of the universe'. In A. G. Ramat and P. J. Hopper (eds), *The Limits of Grammaticalization*. Amsterdam: John Benjamins: 147–158.

Hopper, P. 2011. 'Emergent grammar and temporality in interactional linguistics'. In P. Auer and S. Pfänder (eds), *Constructions: Emerging and Emergent*. Berlin: Walter de Gruyter: 22–44.

Hopper, P. and S. A. Thompson 1993. 'Language universals, discourse pragmatics, and semantics', *Language Sciences*, 15(4): 357–376.

Hornby, A. S. 1954. *A Guide to Patterns and Usage in English*. London: Oxford University Press.

Howatt, A. P. R. 2014. *A History of English Language Teaching*. Second Edition, with H. G. Widdowson. Oxford: Oxford University Press.

Hu, G. 2003. 'English language teaching in China: Regional differences and contributing factors', *Journal of Multilingual and Multicultural Development*, 24(4): 290–318.

Huddleston, R. and Pullum, G. K. 2002. *The Cambridge Grammar of the English Language*. Cambridge: Cambridge University Press.

Hunston, S. 2001. 'Colligation, lexis, pattern and text'. In M. Scott and G. Thompson (eds) *Patterns of Text, in Honour of Michael Hoey*. Amsterdam: John Benjamins: 13–33.

Hunston, S. and Francis, G. 2000. *Pattern Grammar: A Corpus-driven Approach to the Lexical Grammar of English*. Amsterdam: John Benjamins.

Hyland, K. 2002. 'Directives: Argument and engagement in academic writing', *Applied Linguistics*, 23(2): 215–239.

Hyland, K. 2008. 'As can be seen: Lexical bundles and disciplinary variation', *English for Specific Purposes*, 27(1): 4–21.

Hyland, K. 2009. *Academic Discourse: English In A Global Context*. London: Continuum.

Itkonen, E. 1991. *Universal History of Linguistics: India, China, Arabia, Europe*. Amsterdam and Philadelphia, PA: John Benjamins.

Jespersen, O. 1905. *Growth and Structure of the English Language*. Leipzig: B. G. Teubner.

Jespersen, O. 1909–40. *A Modern English Grammar on Historical Principles*. Volumes I–VII. Heidelberg: C. Winter.

Jespersen, O. 1924. *The Philosophy of Grammar*. London: George Allen and Unwin.

Johansson, S. and Norheim, E. H. 1988. 'The subjunctive in British and American English', *ICAME Journal*, 12: 27–36.

Johns, T. 1991. 'From printout to handout: Grammar and vocabulary teaching in the context of data-driven learning', *CALL Austria*, 10: 14–34.

Johnson, S. 1755. *A Dictionary of the English Language*. Digital edition available online with facsimile pages at: https://johnsonsdictionaryonline.com.

Jones, C. and Waller, D. 2010. 'If only it were true: the problem with the four conditionals', *ELT Journal*, 65(1): 24–32.

Jonson, B. 1640/1909. *The English Grammar*. Edited with an introduction and notes by A. V. Waite. New York: Sturgis and Walton Company.

Kachru, B. B. 1985. 'Standards, codification and sociolinguistic realism: the English language in the outer circle'. In R. Quirk and H. G. Widdowson (eds), *English in the World: Teaching and Learning the Language and Literatures*. Cambridge: Cambridge University Press: 11–30.

Kamm, O. 2015. 'Ignore the 'good grammar' crowd and your prose will be better for it', *The Spectator*, 25 June 2015. Retrieved from: https://blogs.spectator.co.uk/2015/06/ignore-the-good-grammar-crowd-and-your-prose-will-be-better-for-it/

Kaplan, R. B. and Grabe, W. 2002. 'A modern history of written discourse analysis', *Journal of Second Language Writing*, 11: 191–223.

Kelly, L. G. 2002. *The Mirror of Grammar: Theology, Philosophy and the Modistae*. Amsterdam: John Benjamins.

Kelly Hall, J. 1997. 'A consideration of SLA as a theory of practice: A response to Firth and Wagner', *The Modern Language Journal*, 81(3): 301–306.

Kern, J. 2014. '*Como* in commute: The travels of a discourse marker across languages', *Studies in Hispanic and Lusophone Linguistics* 7 (2): 275–298.

Kiparsky P.. 2009. 'On the Architecture of Pāṇini's Grammar'. In G. Huet, A. Kulkarni and P. Scharf (eds), *Sanskrit Computational Linguistics*. ISCLS 2007, ISCLS 2008. Lecture Notes in Computer Science, Vol. 5402. Berlin, Heidelberg: Springer-Verlag: 33–94.

Kirch, M. S. 1963. 'The role of the language laboratory', *The Modern Language Journal*, 47(6): 256–260.

Kitigawa, C. and Lehrer, A. 1990. 'Impersonal uses of personal pronouns', *Journal of Pragmatics*, 14(5): 739–759.

Kjellmer, G. 2009. 'The revived subjunctive'. In G. Rohdenburg and J. Schlüter (eds), *One Language, Two Grammars?: Differences between British and American English*. Cambridge: Cambridge University Press: 246–256.

Knappe, G. 1999. 'The Rhetorical Aspect of Grammar Teaching in Anglo-Saxon England', *Rhetorica: A Journal of the History of Rhetoric*, 17(1): 1–34.

Koerner, E. F. K. 1970. 'Bloomfieldian linguistics and the problem of 'meaning': A chapter in the history of the theory and study of language', *Jahrbuch für Amerikastudien*, 15: 162–183.

Koops, C. and Lohmann, A. 2015. 'A quantitative approach to the grammaticalization of discourse markers. Evidence from their sequencing behaviour', *International Journal of Corpus Linguistics*, 20(2): 232–259.

Kortmann, B. and Luckenheimer, K. (eds). 2012. *The Mouton World Atlas of Variation in English*. Berlin: de Gruyter.

Kruisinga, E. 1911/1932. *A Handbook of Present-Day English*. Fifth edition. Groningen: P. Noordhoff.

Lakoff, R. 1974. 'Remarks on this and that', *Papers from the Regional Meeting: Chicago Linguistic Society*, 10: 345–356.

Langendoen, D. T. 1966. 'A Note on the Linguistic Theory of M. Terentius Varro', *Foundations of Language*, 2(1): 33–36.

Lantolf, J. P. and Appel, G. 1994. *Vygotskyan Approaches to Second Language Research*. Norwood, NJ: Ablex.

Larsen-Freeman, D. 1997. 'Chaos/complexity science and second language acquisition', *Applied Linguistics*, 18(2): 141–165.
Larsen-Freeman, D. 2003. *Teaching Language: From Grammar to Grammaring*. Boston, MA: Heinle.
Larsen-Freeman, D. 2010. 'Not so Fast: A Discussion of L2 Morpheme Processing and Acquisition', *Language Learning*, 60(1): 221–230.
Lebedeva, S. and Orlova, S. N. 2019. 'Semantics and pragmatics of the double modal "might could"', *Training, Language and Culture*, 3(2): 71–84.
Lee-Goldman, R. 2011. '"No" as a discourse marker', *Journal of Pragmatics*, 43: 2627–2649.
Leech, G. 1991. 'The state of the art in corpus linguistics'. In K. Aijmer and B. Altenberg (eds), *English Corpus Linguistics. Studies in Honour of Jan Svartvik*. New York: Longman: 8–29.
Leech, G., Hundt, M., Mair, C. and Smith, N. 2009. *Change in Contemporary English*. Cambridge: Cambridge University Press.
Leech, G. and Svartvik, J. 1994. *A Communicative Grammar of English*. Second edition. London: Longman.
Lemieux, C. P. 1964. 'Harold E. Palmer's Contribution to the Oral Method of Teaching Foreign Languages', *The Slavic and East European Journal*, 8(3): 320–326.
Lerner, G. H. 1991. 'On the syntax of sentences in progress', *Language in Society*, 20(3): 441–458.
Lerner, G. H. 1996. 'On the 'semi-permeable' character of grammatical units in conversation: Conditional entry into the turn space of another speaker'. In E. Ochs, E. Schegloff and S. Thompson (eds), *Interaction and Grammar*. Cambridge: Cambridge University Press: 238–276.
Levine, G. S. 2014. 'Principles for code choice in the foreign language classroom: A focus on grammaring', *Language Teaching*, 47(3): 332–348.
Lightbown, P. M., and Spada, N. 2006. *How Languages are Learned*. Oxford: Oxford University Press.
Lily, W. 1534/1680. *A Short Introduction of Grammar. Compiled and set forth for the bringing up of all those that intend to attain to the knowledge of the Latin tongue*. 1680 edition, London: Printed by Roger Norton.
Littlewood, W. 2011. 'Communicative language teaching: An expanding concept for a changing world'. In E. Hinkel (ed.), *Handbook of Research in Second Language Teaching and Learning*. Abingdon: Routledge: 541–557.
Long, M. 1996. 'The role of the linguistic environment in second language acquisition', In W. Ritchie and T. Bhatia (eds), *Handbook of Second Language Acquisition*. San Diego, CA: Academic Press: 413–468.
Love, R., Dembry, C., Hardie, A., Brezina, V. and McEnery, T. 2017. 'The Spoken BNC2014: designing and building a spoken corpus of everyday conversations', *International Journal of Corpus Linguistics*, 22(3): 319–344.
Lowth, R. 1762/1799. *A Short Introduction to English Grammar*. Philadelphia, PA: Printed by R. Aitken.
Maat, J. 2010. 'The Artes Sermocinales in Times of Adversity. How Grammar, Logic and Rhetoric Survived the Seventeenth Century'. In R. Bod, J. Maat and T. Weststeijn (eds), *The Making of the Humanities. Volume 1 –Early Modern Europe*. Amsterdam: Amsterdam University Press: 283–295.
Macht, K. 1991. 'Karl and Max Deutschbein's English Grammar Manuals'. In G. Leitner (ed.), *English Traditional Grammars: An International Perspective*. Amsterdam: John Benjamins: 257–276.
Mair, V. H. 1997. 'Ma Jianzhong and the invention of Chinese grammar', *Journal of Chinese Linguistics Monograph Series*, No. 10, Studies on the History of Chinese Syntax: 5–26.

References

Malinowski, B. 1923. 'The Problem of Meaning in Primitive Languages'. In C. K. Ogden and I. A. Richards (eds), *The Meaning of Meaning*. London: Kegan Paul, Trench, Trubner: 296–336.

Marckwardt, A. H. 1968. 'Charles C. Fries', *Language*, 44(1): 205–210.

Markee, N. and Kasper, G. 2004. 'Classroom talks: An introduction', *The Modern Language Journal*, 88(4): 491–500.

Maule, D. 1988. '"Sorry, but if he comes, I go": Teaching conditionals', *ELT Journal*, 42(2): 117–123.

McCarthy, M. J. 1984. 'A new look at vocabulary in EFL', *Applied Linguistics*, 5: 12–22.

McCarthy, M. J. 1994. 'It, this and that'. In M. Coulthard (ed.), *Advances in Written Text*. London: Routledge: 266–275.

McCarthy, M. J. 1998. *Spoken Language and Applied Linguistics*. Cambridge: Cambridge University Press.

McCarthy, M. J. 2002. 'Good listenership made plain: British and American non-minimal response tokens in everyday conversation'. In R. Reppen, S. Fitzmaurice and D. Biber (eds), *Using Corpora to Explore Linguistic Variation*. Amsterdam: John Benjamins: 49–71.

McCarthy, M. J. 2003. 'Talking back: 'small' interactional response tokens in everyday conversation', *Research on Language in Social Interaction*, 36(1): 33–63.

McCarthy, M. J. 2010. 'Spoken fluency revisited', *English Profile Journal*, 1. Retrieved from: http://journals.cambridge.org/action/displayJournal?jid=EPJ

McCarthy, M. J. 2013. 'Corpora and the advanced level: problems and prospects', *English Australia Journal*, 29(1): 39–49.

McCarthy, M. J. (ed.) 2016. *The Cambridge Guide to Blended Learning for Language Teaching*. Cambridge: Cambridge University Press.

McCarthy, M. J. 2017. 'Changes in English grammar – The tortoise, not the hare', *EMC Emagazine*, 78: 50–52.

McCarthy, M. J. 2019. *Grammar and Usage: Your Questions Answered*. Cambridge: Prolinguam Publishing.

McCarthy, M. J. and Carter, R. 1997. 'Grammar, tails and affect: constructing expressive choices in discourse', *Text*, 17(3): 405–429.

McCarthy, M. J. and Carter, R. 2002. '*This that and the other*: Multi-word clusters in spoken English as visible patterns of interaction', *TEANGA, the Journal of the Irish Association for Applied Linguistics*, 21: 30–52.

McCarthy, M. J., McCarten, J., Clark, D. and Clark, R. 2009. *Grammar for Business*. Cambridge: Cambridge University Press.

McCarthy, M. J., McCarten, J. and Sandiford, H. 2005. *Touchstone. Student's Book. Level 1*. Cambridge: Cambridge University Press.

McCarthy, M. J., McCarten, J. and Sandiford, H. 2012. *Viewpoint. Student's Book 1*. Cambridge: Cambridge University Press.

McCarthy, M. J., McCarten, J. and Sandiford, H. 2014. *Viewpoint. Student's Book 2*. Cambridge: Cambridge University Press.

McIntosh, A. 1961. 'Patterns and Ranges', *Language*, 37(3): 325–337.

McNelis, C. 2010. 'Grammarians and rhetoricians'. In W. Dominik and J. Hall (eds), *A Companion to Roman Rhetoric*. Oxford: Wiley-Blackwell: 285–296.

Michael, I. 1970. *English Grammatical Categories and the Tradition to 1800*. Cambridge: Cambridge University Press.

Michael, I. 1991. 'More than enough English grammars'. In G. Leitner (ed.), *English Traditional Grammars: An International Perspective*. Amsterdam: John Benjamins: 11–26.

Migge, B. and Ní Chiosáin, M. (eds) 2012. *New Perspectives on Irish English*. Amsterdam: John Benjamins.

Milroy, J. and Milroy L. 1991. *Authority in Language: Investigating Standard English*. Second edition. London: Routledge.

Mitchell, L. C. 2001. *Grammar Wars: Language as Cultural Battlefield in 17th and 18th Century England*. Aldershot: Ashgate Publishers.

Mitchell, T. F 1957. 'The language of buying and selling in Cyrenaica: a situational statement', *Hespéris*, XLIV: 31–71.

Mitchell, T. F. 1966. 'Some English phrasal types'. In C. E. Bazell, J. C. Catford, M. A. K. Halliday and R. H. Robins (eds), *In Memory of J. R. Firth*. London: Longman: 335–358.

Mitchell, T. F. 1971. 'Linguistic "goings-on": collocations and other lexical matters arising on the linguistic record', *Archivum Linguisticum*, 2: 35–69.

Mondada, L. and Pekarek Doehler, S. 2004. 'Second language acquisition as situated practice: Task accomplishment in the French second language classroom', *The Modern Language Journal*, 88(4): 501–518.

Mugglestone, L. C. 1997. 'Cobbett's Grammar: William, James Paul, and the Politics of Prescriptivism', *The Review of English Studies*, 48(192): 471–488.

Mulroy, Z. 2019. 'Spelling and grammar test from 1984 has people getting just half the answers ', *Mirror Online*. Retrieved from: www.mirror.co.uk/news/weird-news/spelling-grammar-test-1984-people-14193609

Murphy, J. J. 1974. *Rhetoric in the Middle Ages: A History of Rhetorical Theory from Saint Augustine to the Renaissance*. Berkeley, CA: University of California Press.

Murphy, R. 2004. *English Grammar in Use*. Third edition. Cambridge: Cambridge University Press.

Murray, L. 1822/1996. *English Grammar Adapted to the Different Classes of Learners*. Reprint of the 1822 edition. With a new introduction by D. Reibel. London: Routledge/Thoemmes Press.

Myers, G. and Lampropoulu, S. 2012. 'Impersonal *you* and stance-taking in social research interviews', *Journal of Pragmatics*, 44(10): 1206–1218.

Nesfield, J. C. 1898/1908. *Manual of English Grammar and Composition*. London: Macmillan and Co.

Norrick, N. R. 2009. 'Conjunctions in final position in everyday talk'. In B. Fraser and K. Turner (eds), *Language in Life and a Life in Language: Jacob Mey–a Festschrift*. Bingley: Emerald Group Publishing: 319–328.

Norrish, J. 1983. *Language Learners and their Errors*. Oxford: Macmillan.

Nunan, D. 1988. *Syllabus Design*. Oxford: Oxford University Press.

Oberhelman, H. D. 1960. 'The foreign language laboratory in secondary schools', *Hispania*, 43(1): 145–148.

O'Keeffe, A. 2006. *Investigating Media Discourse*. London: Routledge.

O'Keeffe, A. 2011. 'Teaching and Irish English: Irish English is widely understood as a robust native variety by Irish English language teachers', *English Today*, 27(2): 58–64.

O'Keeffe, A. and Amador Moreno, C. P. 2009. 'The pragmatics of the be + after + V-ing construction in Irish English', *Intercultural Pragmatics*, 6(4): 517–534.

O'Keeffe, A. and Mark, G. 2017. 'The English Grammar Profile of learner competence: Methodology and key findings', *International Journal of Corpus Linguistics*, 22(4): 457–489.

O'Keeffe, A. and Mark, G. 2018. 'The grammars of English'. In P. Seargeant and A. Hewings (eds), *The Routledge Handbook of English Studies*. London: Routledge: 136–149.

Oxford English Dictionary. 2018. '*Grammar, n.*' *OED Online*. Oxford: Oxford University Press.

O'Neill, R. 1973. *Kernel Lessons Plus*. Harlow: Longman.

O'Neill, R. 1978. *Kernel One*. Harlow: Longman.

Osborne, J. W. 1964. 'William Cobbett and English Education in the Early Nineteenth Century', *History of Education Quarterly*, 4(1): 3–16.

Ostler, N. 2005. *Empires of the World: A Language History of the World*. New York: HarperCollins.

O'Sullivan, J. 2020. *Corpus Linguistics and the Analysis of Sociolinguistic Change: Language Variety and Ideology in Advertising*. Abingdon: Routledge.

Pagani, L. 2011. 'Pioneers of Grammar. Hellenistic Scholarship and the Study of Language'. In F. Montanari and L. Pagani (eds), *From Scholars to Scholia: Chapters in the History of Ancient Greek Scholarship*. Berlin: De Gruyter: 17–64.

Palander-Collin, M. 1998. 'Grammaticalization of 'I think' and 'methinks' in late Middle and Early Modern English: A sociolinguistic perspective', *Neuphilologische Mitteilungen*, 99 (4): 419–442.

Palmer, F. R. 1968. *Selected Papers of J. R. Firth 1952–59*. London: Longmans, Green and Co.

Palmer, H. E. 1916. *Colloquial English. Part I. Substitution Tables*. Cambridge: W. Heffer and Sons.

Palmer, H. E. 1917. *The Scientific Study and Teaching of Languages*. London: George. G. Harrap and Company.

Palmer, H. E. 1922. *The Oral Method of Teaching Languages*. Cambridge: W. Heffer and Sons.

Palmer, H. E. 1924. *A Grammar of Spoken English on a Strictly Phonetic Basis*. Cambridge: W. Heffer and Sons.

Parakrama, A. 1995. *De-hegemonizing Language Standards: Learning from Post-Colonial Englishes about 'English'*. Basingstoke: Macmillan.

Pekarek Doehler, S. 2011. '"CA for SLA": Analyse conversationnelle et recherche sur l'acquisition des langues', *Revue Française de Linguistique Appliquée*, xi(2): 123–137.

Pekarek Doehler, S. 2011. 'Emergent grammar for all practical purposes: the on-line formatting of left and right dislocations in French conversation'. In P. Auer and S. Pfänder (eds), *Constructions: Emerging and Emergent*. Berlin: Walter de Gruyter: 45–87.

Penhallurick, R. 2010. 'Welsh English'. In B. Kortmann and K. Luckenheimer (eds), *The Mouton World Atlas of Variation in English*. Berlin: de Gruyter: 58–69.

Pennycook, A. 1996. 'Language Policy as Cultural Politics: The Double-Edged Sword of Language Education in Colonial Malaya and Hong Kong', *Discourse: Studies in the Cultural Politics of Education*, 17(2): 133–152.

Pennycook, A. 1998. *English and the Discourses of Colonialism*. London: Routledge.

Pennycook, A. 2007. 'The myth of English as an international language'. In S. Makoni and A. Pennycook (eds), *Disinventing and Reconstituting Languages*. Clevedon: Multilingual Matters: 90–115.

Pennycook, A. 2012. 'Lessons from Colonial Language Policies'. In R. D. González and I. Melis (eds), *Language Ideologies: Critical Perspectives on the Official English Movement*. Abingdon: Routledge: 195–220.

Percy, C. 2010. 'Women's grammars'. In R. Hickey (ed.), *Eighteenth-Century English: Ideology and Change*. Cambridge: Cambridge University Press: 38–58.

Peterson, E. 2020. *Making Sense of 'Bad English': An Introduction to Language Attitudes and Ideologies*. Abingdon: Routledge.

Peverelli, P. 2015. *The History of Modern Chinese Grammar Studies*. Berlin: Springer-Verlag.

Phillipson, R. 1992. *Linguistic Imperialism*. Oxford: Oxford University Press.

Phillipson, R. 2001. 'English for globalisation or for the world's people?', *International Review of Education*, 47(3–4): 185–200.

Pimsleur, P. 1959. 'The functions of the language laboratory', *The Modern Language Journal*, 43(1): 11–15.

Poole, S. 2010. 'Et cetera', *The Guardian*, 4 December 2010. Retrieved from: www.theguardian.com/books/2010/dec/04/fred-halliday-pj-orourke-reviews

Poutsma, H. 1904–26. *A Grammar of Late Modern English: For the Use of Continental, Especially Dutch, Students.* 4 vols. Second, revised edition of volume 1, 1928. Groningen: P. Noordhoff.
Prakken, D. W. 1964. 'The use of the language laboratory', *The Classical World*, 57(7): 301–303.
Probyn, C. T. 1978. 'James Harris, and the Logic of Happiness', *The Modern Language Review*, 73(2): 256–266.
Quintilian 1910. *Institutes of Oratory*, translated by Rev. John Selby Watson. London: George Bell and Sons.
Quirk, R. 1958. 'Review of A Handbook of English Grammar by R. W. Zandvoort', *The Review of English Studies*, 9(36): 448–450.
Quirk, R., Greenbaum, S., Leech, G. and Svartvik, J. 1985. *A Comprehensive Grammar of the English Language.* Harlow: Longman.
Rask, R. 1832. *Engelsk Formlære, udarbejdet efter en ny Plan.* Copenhagen: Gyldendalske Boghandlings Forlag.
Richards, J. C. and Rodgers, T. S. 2014. *Approaches and Methods in Language Teaching.* Third edition. Cambridge: Cambridge University Press.
Robins, R. H. 1966. 'The Development of the Word Class System of the European Grammatical Tradition', *Foundations of Language*, 2(1): 3–19.
Robins, R. H. 1996. 'The initial section of the tékhnē; grammatikē'. In P. Swiggers and A. Wouters (eds), *Ancient Grammar: Content and Context.* Leuven: Peeters: 3–15.
Rodríguez-Puente, P. 2019. *The English Phrasal Verb 1650-Present.* Cambridge: Cambridge University Press.
Rogers, D. E. 1987. 'The Influence of Panini on Leonard Bloomfield', *Historiographia Linguistica*, 14(1): 89–138.
Romaine, S. and Lange, D. 1991. 'The Use of *like* as a Marker of Reported Speech and Thought: A Case of Grammaticalization in Progress' *American Speech*, 66(3): 227–279.
Rühlemann, C. 2007. *Conversation in Context: A Corpus-driven Approach.* London: Continuum.
Sadler, J. E. 1970. 'Comenius as an international citizen'. In C. H. Dobinson (ed.), *Comenius and Contemporary Education.* Hamburg: UNESCO Institute for Education: 60–75.
Sadler, J. E. 2014. *J. A. Comenius and the Concept of Universal Education.* Second edition. Abingdon: Routledge.
Salaberry, M. R. 2000. *The Development of Past Tense Morphology in L2 Spanish.* Amsterdam: John Benjamins.
Saussure, F. de 1916/1971. *Cours de Linguistique Générale.* Published by Charles Bally and Albert Sechehaye. Paris: Editions Payot.
Schaafsma, H. M. 1968. 'Using the language laboratory in the university', in J. D. Turner (ed.), *Using the Language Laboratory.* London: University of London Press: 75–103.
Schegloff, E. A. 1987. 'Recycled Turn Beginnings'. In G. Button and J. R. E. Lee (eds), *Talk and Social Organization.* Clevedon: Multilingual Matters: 70–85.
Schegloff, E. A. 2001. 'Getting serious: Joke → serious "no"', *Journal of Pragmatics*, 33(12): 1947–1955.
Scheppergrell, M. J. 1991. 'Paratactic *because*', *Journal of Pragmatics*, 16: 323–337.
Shirai, Y. and Andersen, R.W. 1995. 'The acquisition of tense-aspect morphology: A prototype account', *Language*, 71(4): 743–762.
Schlesinger, I. M. 1975. 'Grammatical development – the first steps'. In E. H. Lenneberg and E. Lenneberg (eds), *Foundations of Language Development: A Multidisciplinary Approach.* Volume 1. New York: Academic Press: 203–222.
Schweinberger, M. 2012. 'The discourse marker LIKE in Irish English'. In B. Migge and M. Ní Chiosáin (eds), *New Perspectives on Irish English.* Amsterdam: John Benjamins: 179–201.
Selinker, L. 1972. 'Interlanguage', *IRAL*, 10(3): 209–231.

Simões Lucas Freitas, E. 2014. 'Language of advertising'. In C. Leung and B. V. Street (eds), *The Routledge Companion to English Studies*. Abingdon: Routledge: 505–515.
Sinclair, H. 1975. 'The role of cognitive structures in language acquisition'. In E. H. Lennebergand E. Lenneberg (eds), *Foundations of Language Development: A Multidisciplinary Approach*. Volume 1. New York: Academic Press: 223–238.
Sinclair, J. M. 1966. 'Beginning the study of lexis'. In C. E. Bazell, J. C. Catford, M. A. K. Halliday and R. H. Robins (eds), *In Memory of J. R. Firth*. London: Longman: 410–430.
Sinclair, J. M. 1991. *Corpus, Concordance, Collocation*. Oxford: Oxford University Press.
Sinclair, J. M. 2004. *Trust the Text. Language, Corpus and Discourse*. Edited with Ron Carter. London: Routledge.
Sinclair, J. M. and Coulthard, R. M. 1975. *Towards an Analysis of Discourse*. Oxford: Oxford University Press.
Singh, F. 1987. 'Power and politics in the content of grammar books: the example of India', *World Englishes*, 6(3): 253–261.
Skinner, B. F. 1957. *Verbal Behavior*. London: Methuen & Co.
Smith, R. 2016. 'Building "Applied Linguistic Historiography": Rationale, Scope, and Methods', *Applied Linguistics*, 37(1): 71–87. Retrieved from: https://academic.oup.com/applij/article/37/1/71/1741459.
Smith, R. C. 1999. *The Writings of Harold E. Palmer*. Tokyo: Hon-no-Tomosha.
Smith, R. C. 2011. 'Harold E. Palmer's alternative 'applied linguistics', *Histoire Épistémologie Langage*, 33(1): 53–67.
Stack, E. M. 1960a. 'Pattern drills for the language laboratory', *The French Review*, 33(3): 272–280.
Stein, G. and Quirk, R. 1991. *On having a look in a corpus*. In K. Ajmer and B. Altenberg (eds) *English Corpus Linguistics. Studies in Honour of Jan Svartvik*. London: Longman, 197–203.
Stenström, A.-B. 1998. 'From sentence to discourse: *Cos because* in teenage talk'. In A. H. Jucker and Y. Ziv (eds), *Discourse Markers: Description and Theory*. Amsterdam: John Benjamins: 127–146.
Stern, H. H. 1983. *Fundamental Concepts of Language Teaching*. Oxford: Oxford University Press.
Stewart, D. C. 1979. 'The Legacy of Quintilian', *English Education*, 11(2): 103–117.
Stieglitz, G. J. 1955. 'The Berlitz Method', *The Modern Language Journal*, 39(6): 300–310.
Stirling, L. 1999. 'Isolate *if*-clauses in Australian English'. In P. Collins and D. Lee (eds), *The Clause in English. In Honour of Rodney Huddleston*. Amsterdam: John Benjamins: 273–294.
Stubbs, M. 1986. 'A matter of prolonged fieldwork: towards a modal grammar of English', *Applied Linguistics*, 7(1): 1–25.
Subbiondo, J. L. 1976. 'The Semantic Theory of James Harris: A Study of Hermes 1751', *Historiographia Linguistica*, 3(3): 275–291.
Sullivan, P. 2008. 'Playing the Lord: Tudor *Vulgaria* and the Rehearsal of Ambition', *ELH*, 75: 179–196.
Swan, M. 2005. *Practical English Usage*. Third Edition. Oxford: Oxford University Press.
Sweet, H. 1892/1989. *A New English Grammar: Logical and Historical*. Two volumes. Oxford: Clarendon Press.
Sweet, H. 1899. *The Practical Study of Languages: A Guide for Teachers and Learners*. London: J. M. Dent and Co.
Sweeting, A. and Vickers, E. 2007. 'Language and the History of Colonial Education: The Case of Hong Kong', *Modern Asian Studies*, 41(1): 1–40.
Switaj, E. K. 2013. 'The ambiguous status of native speakers and language learners in Ulysses', *Journal of Modern Literature*, 37(1): 143–157.
Talib, I. S. 2002. *The Language of Postcolonial Literatures: An Introduction*. London: Routledge.

Tao, H. 1999. 'The grammar of demonstratives in Mandarin conversational discourse: a case study', *Journal of Chinese Linguistics*, 27(1): 69–103.

Tao, H. 2003. 'Turn initiators in spoken English: A corpus-based approach to interaction and grammar', *Language and Computers*, 46: 187–207.

Tao, H. and McCarthy, M. J. 2001. 'Understanding non-restrictive *which*-clauses in spoken English, which is not an easy thing', *Language Sciences*, 23: 651–677.

Taylor, D. J. 1996. 'Style and Structure in Varro?' In P. Swiggers and A. Wouters (eds), *Ancient Grammar: Content and Context*. Leuven: Peeters: 91–103.

Thane, P. D. 2018. 'The present state of the Aspect Hypothesis: A critical perspective', *Eurasian Journal of Applied Linguistics*, 4(2): 261–273.

Thavenius, C. 1983. *Referential Pronouns in English Conversation*. Lund: Gleerup.

Thomas, A. L. 1987. 'The use and interpretation of verbally determinate verb group ellipsis in English', *IRAL*, XXV(1): 1–14.

Thomas, M. 2004. *Universal Grammar in Second Language Acquisition: A History*. London: Routledge.

Thornbury, S. 1998. 'Grammar, power and bottled water', IATEFL Newsletter: 19–20.

Thornbury, S. 2001. *Uncovering Grammar*. Oxford: Macmillan Heinemann English Language Teaching.

Tibbetts, A. M. 1966. 'Were Nineteenth-Century Textbooks Really Prescriptive?', *College English*, 27(4): 309–315.

Tieken-Boon van Ostade, I. 2008. 'Grammars, grammarians and grammar writing: an introduction'. In I. Tieken-Boon van Ostade (ed.) *Grammars, Grammarians and Grammar-Writing in Eighteenth-Century England*. Berlin: Mouton de Gruyter: 1–14.

Tieken-Boon van Ostade, I. 2010a. 'Lowth as an icon of prescriptivism'. In R. Hickey (ed.), *Eighteenth-Century English: Ideology and Change*. Cambridge: Cambridge University Press: 73–88.

Tieken-Boon van Ostade, I. 2010b. 'Eighteenth-century women and their norms of correctness'. In R. Hickey (ed.), *Eighteenth-Century English: Ideology and Change*. Cambridge: Cambridge University Press: 59–72.

Timmis, I. G. 2016. *Historical Spoken Language Research: the Bolton/Worktown Corpus*. Abingdon: Routledge.

Tottie, G. 2009. 'How different are American and British English grammar? And how are they different?' In G. Rohdenburg and J. Schlüter (eds), *One Language, Two Grammars?: Differences between British and American English*. Cambridge: Cambridge University Press: 341–363.

Traugott, E. C. 1982. 'From propositional to textual and expressive meanings; some semantic-pragmatic aspects of grammaticalization'. In W. P. Lehmann and Y. Malkiel (eds), *Perspectives on Historical Linguistics*. Amsterdam: John Benjamins: 245–271.

Traugott, E. C. 1995. 'Subjectification in grammaticalization'. In D. Stein and S. Wright (eds), *Subjectivity and Subjectivisation*. Cambridge: Cambridge University Press: 331–354.

Traugott, E. C. 2003. 'Constructions in Grammaticalization'. In B. D. Joseph and R. D. Janda (eds), *The Handbook of Historical Linguistics*. Oxford: Blackwell: 624–647.

Trueblood, T. 1933. 'Spoken English', *Quarterly Journal of Speech*, 19: 513.

Turner, J. (ed.) 1980. *The Works of William Bullokar. Volume II. Pamphlet for Grammar 1586*. Leeds: The University of Leeds School of English.

Turner, J. D. (ed.) 1968. *Using the Language Laboratory*. London: University of London Press.

Turner, J. F. 1980. 'The marked subjunctive in contemporary English', *Studia Neophilologica*, 52(2): 271–277.

Tyler, A. 1994. 'The role of syntactic structure in discourse structure: Signalling logical and prominence relations', *Applied Linguistics*, 15(3): 243–262.

Varro, M. T. 1938. *Varro: On the Latin Language, with an English translation by R. G. Kent*. Vol. 1, Books V–VII. London: William Heinemann.

Vasko, A.-L. 2010. *Cambridgeshire Dialect Grammar*. Helsinki: Research Unit for Variation, Contacts and Change in English VARIENG, University of Helsinki.

Vaughan, E., and Clancy, B. 2011. 'The pragmatics of Irish English: The use of English in Ireland shows specific features which contribute to its unique profile', *English Today*, 27(2): 47–52.

Véronique, D. 1992. 'Sweet et Palmer: des précurseurs de la linguistique appliquée à la didactique des langues?', *Cahiers Ferdinand de Saussure*, 46: 173–190.

von Fritz, K. 1949. 'Ancient Instruction in "Grammar" According to Quintilian', *The American Journal of Philology*, 70(4): 337–366.

Walsh, S. 2006. *Investigating Classroom Discourse*. Abingdon: Routledge.

Ward, J. 1995. 'Quintilian and the Rhetorical Revolution of the Middle Ages', *Rhetorica: A Journal of the History of Rhetoric*, 13(3): 231–284.

Warren, M. 2015. 'I mean I only really wanted to dry me towels because …'. In N. Groom, M. Charles and S. John (eds), *Corpora, Grammar and Discourse*. Amsterdam: John Benjamins: 145–160.

Watts, R. 1989. 'Taking the pitcher to the 'well': native speakers' perception of their use of discourse markers in conversation', *Journal of Pragmatics*, 13: 203–237.

Watts, R. 2008. 'Grammar writers in eighteenth-century Britain: A community of practice or a discourse community?' In I. Tieken-Boon van Ostade (ed.), *Grammars, Grammarians and Grammar-Writing in Eighteenth-Century England*. Berlin: Mouton de Gruyter: 37–56.

Weideman, A. 1999. 'Five generations of applied linguistics: Some framework issues', *Acta Academica*, 31(1): 77–98.

Weinert, R. 2012. 'Complement clauses in spoken German and English', *Folia Linguistica*, 46 (1): 233–265.

White, R. G. 1981/1882. *Words and their Uses, Past and Present. A Study of the English Language*. Boston, MA: Houghton, Mifflin and Company.

Whitney, W. D. 1893. 'On Recent Studies in Hindu Grammar', *The American Journal of Philology*, 14(2): 171–197.

Wikipedia. 2019. 'Grammar'. Retrieved from: https://simple.m.wikipedia.org/wiki/Grammar.

Wilkins, D. A. 1976. *Notional Syllabuses: A Taxonomy and its Relevance to Foreign Language Curriculum Development*. Oxford: Oxford University Press.

Wilkins, D. A. 1979. 'Grammatical, situational and notional syllabuses'. In C. J. Brumfit and K. Johnson (eds), *The Communicative Approach to Language Teaching*. Oxford: Oxford University Press: 82–90.

Wodak, R. and Meyer, M. (eds) 2009. *Methods of Critical Discourse Analysis*. Second edition. London: Sage Publications.

Woods, W. F. 1986. 'The Evolution of Nineteenth-Century Grammar Teaching', *Rhetoric Review*, 5(1): 4–20.

Yamaguchi, T. and Deterding, D. (eds) 2016. *English in Malaysia. Current Use and Status*. Leiden: Brill.

Yáñez-Bouza, N. 2008. 'Preposition stranding in the eighteenth century: Something to talk about'. In I. Tieken-Boon van Ostade (ed.), *Grammars, Grammarians and Grammar-Writing in Eighteenth-Century England*. Berlin: Mouton de Gruyter: 251–277.

Yu, L. 2001. 'Communicative language teaching in China: progress and resistance', *TESOL Quarterly*, 35(1): 194–198.

Zandvoort, R. W. 1945. *A Handbook of English Grammar*. Groningen: Wolters.

Zandvoort, R. W. 1969. *A Handbook of English Grammar*. Fifth edition. London: Longmans, Green and Co.

Zeevat, H. 2012. 'Objection marking and additivity', *Lingua*, 122(15): 1886–1898.

INDEX

Page numbers in *italics* and **bold** indicate Figures and Tables, respectively.

18th century grammar 26–32
19th century grammar 32–33, 39

academic domains 119–120
accidence 36
Accidence, The (Devis) 31–32
Age of Enlightenment 26–28
Alexander, L.G. 129
Alford, Henry 47
Allen, William Stannard 127
alternative framing 111
Amador Moreno, Carolina 99
American English (AmE) 140, 142–143
Amsler, M.E. 17
anacoluthon 118
ancient Greek grammarians 4
Apostrophe Protection Society 146–147
apostrophes 37, 146–147
appliable linguistics 83
applied linguistics 4–5, 46
Arabic grammar 18
Ars grammatica (Aelius Donatus) 17
aspect hypothesis 131–133
Aspects of the Theory of Syntax (Chomsky) 70
Atherton, C. 16
audiolingual language learning 64
audio technology 63–64

Bacon, Roger 19
be, negative forms of 88, **88**
Beattie, J. 31

Berlitz, Maximilian 61, 62
Berlitz method 54, 61–63
Biber, Douglas 104, 118, 119
Blake, Norman 146
blended learning 64
Bloomfield, Leonard 14, 59
blunders 48
Bopp, Franz 14
Brazil 107
Brightland, John 26
Brightland/Gildon grammar 26
British colonial education 38
British Education Act of 1870 45
British Empire 37–38
British English (BrE) 138–139, 142
British National Corpus 109
British Secretary of State for Education 144
Brown, Goold 35
Bullokar, William 20, 22
Bullokar's grammar 20–22
Burton, G. 127–130
by-agents 96–97
Bybee, J. 102

Cambridge Examinations 128
Cambridge Learner Corpus (CLC) 135
CANCODE corpus 119
Carter, Ron 104, 143–144
catenizing 55
cause-effect cohesive relation 111
Caxton, William 138

Index

chaos theory 134
Chinese grammar 18
Chomsky, Noam 14, 23, 58, 66–70, 93, 108, 130
chunking phenomena 56
clauses: functional elements of 79; *if*-clauses 111; theme 80; *then*-clauses 124; *which*-clauses 124–125; *see also* sentences
closed systems 77
Cobbett, William 34–35
COBUILD dictionary project 87, 91
collocation 10, 75–76
colloquialisms 37
colonialism 38
Comenius 23
common English 52
Common European Framework of Reference (CEFR) 11–12, 129
communicative-based teaching 7
communicative language teachings 144
complexity theory 134
concordances 87, 90–94, *91*
conditional sentences 8, 57, 71, 127–129
Confucius 18
conjunctions 110–112, 121
constructivism 133, 134
conversationalisation 138, 142, 143
conversation-analytical (CA) framework 111, 120
Cook, G. 105
Corder, S.P. 130
corpora 9–10, 12, 87
corpus analysis 9, 91
corpus linguistics 9–10, 85–86

data *see* grammar as data
data-driven learning 10
Davidson, T. 14–15
definite articles 31, 94, 122
De Lingua Latina (Varro) 15–16
derivation 16
de Saussure, Ferdinand 14
descriptive grammar 4, 32, 36
Deutschbein, Karl and Max 47
Devis, Ellin 31–32
Dictionary of Modern English Usage, A (Fowler) 48
Dictionary of the English Language, A (Johnson) 27
Dionysius Thrax 14–15
discourse analysis 8–9, 108–110, 118–119
Discourse Analysis (Harris) 108
discourse grammar 57, 108
Donatus, Aelius 17
double modals classification 124

e-grammar 12
electronic concordances 90–94
ellipsis 113–114
emergent grammar 102–103
English: common English 52; corpus-based explorations of 11; global spread of 147; standardisation 26, 33, 38, 63, 145
English as a foreign language (EFL) 6–7, 20–21, 38, 45, 52–54, 59, 86, 127–128
English demonstratives 81–82, *81*
English East Midland dialect 138
English grammar *see* grammar
English Grammar Profile (EGP) 130, 135
English Grammatical Structure (Alexander) 129
English Language National Curriculum 144
English-language teaching (ELT): communicative movement in 7; conditional sentences 129; data on 86; emergence of 51; evolution of 126–129; first language learners 128; form-meaning relationship 91; grammar for 53–58; grammatical canon 8; as invisible orthodoxy 126; second language acquisition (SLA) 7–8, 66, 71, 127, 133; uncritical acceptance of 127; *see also* language learning/teaching
English linguistic imperialism 38
English subjunctive 89–90
established usage, defined 3
etymology 27, 34 *see also* parts of speech
European non-native expert users 50–53
example sentences 37
existential paradigms 109–110

female grammarians 31–32
field 82
first-language acquisition 71
first language learners 128
Firth, J.R. 66, 74–76
flipped classrooms 64
fluidity of grammar 50–51
foreign language training 64
formal writing 104–105
formulas vs free expressions 51
Fowler, Henry 48–49, 141
Fowler brothers 46–48
free expressions vs formulas 51
frequency 87–90
Fries, Charles Carpenter 17, 35, 59–60
full words vs form-words 56

gender-neutral systems 77
Gethin, Amorey 69
get-passives 94–97
Givón, T. 73, 103

go 101
Google® Ngram Viewer 140–141
Gove, Michael 144
Gove-Gwynne controversy 144–145
grammar: for ancient Greek grammarians 4; Arabic grammar 18; Bullokar's grammar 20–22; Chinese grammar 18; data (*See* grammar as data); defined 25; definitions of 3–5; e-grammar 12; evolution of 39; Greek grammar 14–15; historical evolution of 5; interdisciplinary connections 8–9; Latin grammar 15–17, 19–22; Latin grammar influencing 19–20; lay perception of 5–6; oral transmission of 13; origins of 13–14; perceptions of 5–6; speaking vs writing 11–12; spoken (*See* spoken grammar); telegraphic grammar 12; universal (*See* universal grammar); written (*See* written grammar); *see also* English grammar
grammar as data: concordances 90–94; in corpora 87; frequency 87–90; meanings of grammatical forms 92–93; patterns 86–87, 90–91; probabilities 88–89; *see also* grammaticalisation
grammarians: 18th century 26–31; Aelius Donatus 17; of Age of Enlightenment 26–28; of antiquity 4, 15–18; Brightland, John 26; community of practice 26; Dionysius Thrax 14–15; female 31–32; Greenwood, James 27–28; Murray, Lindley 33–34; non-European 18; non-native expert-user 49; Quintilian 16–17; Varro 15–16; *see also* philosopher-grammarians
grammaring 134–135
Grammar-Land 39, *40*
grammar of discourse 60
Grammar of Spoken English (Palmer) 56
Grammar of the English Language, A (Cobbett) 34
grammar of the English Tongue, The (Brightland) 26
grammar publishing 63
grammar teaching 5–6; Berlitz method 61–63; language laboratories 64–65; on structuralist notions 59; structural-oral method 61; technologies 63–65; *see also* language learning/teaching
grammar-translation method 7
grammar usage manuals 46–49
grammar wars 26, 144
Grammar Wars (Mitchell) 53
grammatical adaptability 12
grammatical benchmark *138*

grammatical canon 8
grammatical howlers 145, 146
grammaticalisation: emergent grammar and 102–103; examples of 121–124; *go* 101; *know* 100; *like* 98–100; in other languages 101; resurgence of 103; significance of 100–102; *think* 100; *will* 101
grammatical rank scale 77–79, *78*
grammatical transformations 68–69
grammatical variations 137–139
graveyard categories 97
Greek grammar 14–15, *15*
greengrocer's apostrophe 146
Greenwood, James 27–28
Growth and Structure of the English Language (Jespersen) 50
Gwynne's Grammar (Gwynne) 144–145

Halliday, Michael: appliable linguistics 83; collocations 76; corpus analysis 93–94; on data 85–86; on grammar (as a term) 3–4; *Introduction to Functional Grammar* 83; *Language as a Social Semiotic* 82; lexicogrammar 10, 77
Halliday's grammar: categories of 77; clauses 79; grammatical rank scale 77–79; lexicogrammar 77; mood 80; prepositions 79; pronoun functioning 80; rankshift 79; situational categories of 82; as systemic grammar 81; theme 80
Handbook (Kruisinga) 52
Handbook of English Grammar, A (Zandvoort) 52–53
Harrington, Kieran 147
Harris, James 29–31
Harris, Zellig 108
Hawking, Stephen 86, 132
headers 115–116
helping verbs 27
Hermes (Harris) 29–31, *30*
Hopkins, Gerard Manley 72–73
Hopper, P. 103, 104, 107
Hornby, A.S. 128
howlers 145, 146
Hughes, Rebecca 104
Hyland, K. 120

idiom principle 51
if-clauses 111, 124
India 37–38
inflection 14
inflectional forms, defined 3
informal speaking 96–97, 103–104, 110–113, 124
information structure 81

inner circle 11
innovation in grammar 8–9, 11–12
Institutes of English Grammar, The (Brown) 35
Institutes of Oratory (Quintilian) 16–17
Institutiones Grammaticae (Priscian) 17
interactional linguistics 9
interdisciplinary connections 8–9
interlanguage 130
Introduction to Functional Grammar (Halliday) 83
Irish English 99, 137–138
I think 100
Itkonen, E. 23

Jakobson, Roman 14
Japan 54
Jespersen, Otto 50–51, 53
Johnson, Ben 22
Johnson, Samuel 27
Jones, Daniel 63
Joyce, James 61–62

Kamm, Oliver 144–145
Kernel Lessons Plus (O'Neill) 68
kernel sentences 68, 73
King's English, The (Fowler brothers) 47–48
Kruisinga, Etsko 52, 53
KWIC concordances 90

L2 learners 130–131
language: colonialism and 38; correctness in 16; in late Medieval period 24; purity in 16; rhetoric 16–17; standardisation 26, 33, 38, 63, 145
language acquisition 23, 71, 132–133, 135 *see also* second language acquisition (SLA)
Language as a Social Semiotic (Halliday) 82
Language Centres 65
Language in the National Curriculum project 144
language laboratories 64–65, 74
language learning/teaching: audiolingual 64; Berlitz method 61–63; corpora contributions to 105; as creative activity 130; general public and 5–6; Language Centres 65; listening and speaking in 55–56; oral method of 56; technologies 63–65; *see also* English-language teaching (ELT), grammar teaching
Language Observatory Group 142
language-teaching technologies 74
Larsen-Freeman, D. 134
late Medieval period 24
Latin grammar 15–17, 19–22, 26
learner performance 135

learners, grammatical profiling of 135–136
Learner's Dictionary of Current English, A (Hornby) 128
lexical collocations 76
lexicogrammar 10, 77, 142
lexis and grammar **76**
like 97–100
Lily, William 20
Lily's Latin grammar 20–22
linguistic grammar 4
linguistic imperialism 38
linguistics: becoming more scientific 35; corpus 9–10; interactional 9; modern theory 23
Living English Structure (Allen) 127
Lowth, Robert 28–29, 130

Maat, J. 17
Malinowski, Bronislaw 74
Manual of English Grammar and Composition (Nesfield) 37–38
Matthiessen, Christian 83
media, influence of 147
Miscellaneous Lessons Designed for the Use of Young Ladies (Devis) 31–32
Mitchell, Terence 75
modality 51–52
mode 82
modern linguistics theory 23
Modistae (Modists) 19
mood 80
moral panic, grammar and 143–145
morpheme acquisition studies 130–132
morphology 14
multi-dimensional features of text 118
Murray, Lindley 33
Murray's grammar 33–34

National Corpus of Contemporary Welsh project 11
National Curriculum for English 139
National Curriculum for the English language 144
neo-Firthian grammar 74–76, 83–84, 92–93, 107–108, 131, 134
Nesfield, J.C. 37
New English Grammar (Sweet) 36
Newitz, Annalee 77
non-European grammarians of antiquity 18
non-inner circle 11
non-native expert-users 50–53
notional-functional approach to teaching 7

open choice principle 51
orthography 27

ought, use of 141
out-of-context sentences 72
Oxford English Dictionary 3, 99, 138
Oxford University Press 48–49

Palmer, Harold E. 54–58, 63, 127
Pamphlet for Grammar (Bullokar) 20–22, *21*
Pāṇini 14, 59
Panini's grammar 14, 32
paradigmatic language 58–59
parse, defined 10
parts of speech 15, 17, 27, 34, 57 *see also* etymology
pattern grammar 10
pedagogical grammar 33
personal pronouns 115, 119
philosopher-grammarians 19
Philosophy of Grammar, The (Jespersen) 51
phonetics 36, 54, 57–60, 75
phonology 5, 14, 35–36, 79
phrase structure tree-diagram 67, *67*
poetry 72–73
Port-Royal grammar 23
Poutsma, Hendrik 51–52, 53
Practical Study of Languages, The (Sweet) 36
pragmaticalisation 101
pragmatic markers 97, 99–101, 121
pragmatics 9
prepositional verbs (PV) 142–143, **142**
prepositions 79
preposition stranding 29, 49
prescriptive grammar 4, 32, 35, 53
printing press 23, 138
Priscian 17
probabilities 88–89
professional domains 119
pronoun functioning 80
pronouns 82, 109, 115–117, 119
pronoun systems 77
prosody 27, 34
provincialisms 37
public media, influence of 147
punctuation 146–147

Queen's English, The (Alford) 47

ragbags 97
rankshift 79
Rask, Rasmus 32
regional pronunciations 34–35
Reibel, David 33
response token 124
rhetoric 16–17, 18, 29
Robins, R.H. 17

Robinson, Nick 143
Royal English Grammar, The (Greenwood) 27–28

's apostrophe 146–147
Saussure, Ferdinand de 56
Scandinavian influences on English 50
Schegloff, E.A. 121
School of Oriental and African Studies 75
Scientific Study and Teaching of Languages, The (Palmer) 55
second language acquisition (SLA) 7–8, 66, 71, 127, 133, 134 *see also* language acquisition
sentence grammar 57
sentences: conditional 8, 57, 71, 127–129; example 37; Hopper and 107; kernel sentences 68; kernel sentences 73; out-of-context 72; *see also* clauses
Shakespeare, William 25, 29, 50, 101, 146–147
Short Introduction to English Grammar, A (Lowth) 28–29
Sibawayh 18
Sinclair, H. 73
Sinclair, John 86
situational ellipsis 113–114
Skinner, B.F. 69
slot-and-filler substitution tables 54, *55*, 56
social media postings 6, 12, 140
sociocultural theory 133–134
special grammars 120
specialised discourses 119
Spoken British National Corpus 88, **88**, 90, 96–97, 119
spoken grammar 58, 94, 104–105, 111, 118–119 *see also* informal speaking, written grammar
spoken language: Palmer and 56; primary status of 51
standardisation 26, 33, 38, 63, 145
standard language culture 138–140
stranded prepositions 29, 49
structuralism 58–61
Structure of English, The (Fries) 60
subjectification 101
subjunctive 62, 87–90, 129
substitution tables 54, *55*, 56
Sweet, Henry 36, 53, 54
Swonk, Diane 143
syntactic accomplishment 111
Syntactic Structures (Chomsky) 66, 68
syntagmatic language 58–59
syntax: Cobbett's grammar 34; computational 87; defined 3, 14;

Greenwood's grammar 27; Johnson's grammar 27; kernel sentences 70; modified by conversational encounters 124; Sweet's grammar 36
systemic-functional grammar 81–82

tag, defined 10
tails 117
Teaching and Learning English as a Foreign Language (Fries) 59–60
technologies 12, 63–65, 74, 90–94 *see also* grammar as data
telegrams 12
telegraphic grammar 12
tenor 82
tense-aspect 91, 103–104, 114, 131–132
tenses 27
text messaging 6, 12
textual cohesion: conjunctions 110–112; discourse analysis and 108–110; ellipsis 113–114
textual ellipsis 114
the, definite article 94
theme 80
then-clauses 124
this vs *that* 109–110
Thomas, M. 19
Thrax, Dionysius 14–15
Threshold Level pan-European project 129
transformational-generative grammar 70
transformational grammar (TG) 68–69, 71–74
transitive verbs 100
transitivity 80
tree-diagram 67
turn-final conjunctions 111–112

turn-initial conjunctions 110–111
turn-taking 120–124
two-word utterances 71

units, defined 77
universal grammar 19, 23; Chomsky and 66–67; defined 29–31; Jespersen's grammar and 51; language learning and 130; rhetoric and 29
usage, defined 48
utterances 60, 71, 74, 118

Varro 15–16
Verbal Behavior (Skinner) 69
verbally indeterminate ellipsis 114
verbs: helping 27; transitive 100; *see also* prepositional verbs (PV)
vernacular languages 24
vulgarisms 37

Welsh English 137
which-clauses 124–125
White, Richard 47
who vs. *whom* 140–141
will 101
word classes 19, 20, 35, 97
word-formation 14
World Atlas of Variation in English (Kortmann and Lunkenheimer) 137
written grammar 13, 94, 104–105, 118–119, 124 *see also* spoken grammar

yes/yeah and *no* 121–122
You know 100

Zandvoort, Reinard 52–53